To Tracey and Murat Yurtbilir who made this book possible and Tracey's mother Eileen who made happiness possible

First published in 2017 by Barrallier Books Pty Ltd,
trading as Echo Books

Registered Office: 35-37 Gordon Avenue, West Geelong, Victoria 3220, Australia.

www.echobooks.com.au

Copyright ©

National Library of Australia Cataloguing-in-Publication entry.

Creator: Gibbs, Wylie (Wylie Talbot), 1922– author.

Title: Compassionate steel : the memoirs of Wylie Gibbs, surgeon, grazier and federal
politician/Wylie Gibbs.

ISBN: 9780648074571 (paperback)

Subjects: Gibbs, Wylie (Wylie Talbot), 1922-,
Gibbs, Wylie (Wylie Talbot), 1922---Travel.
Surgeons--Australia--Biography. Politicians--Australia--Biography

Book layout and design by Peter Gamble, Canberra.
Set in Garamond Premier Pro Display, 12/17 and Minerva Small Caps.

www.echobooks.com.au

Compassionate Steel

Steel

Wylie Gibbs

CONTENTS

INTRODUCTION

When in 1951 I was presented to the late King George VI, I was honoured but perplexed and bothered. I was working at the Royal Postgraduate Medical School at the time and my wards contained many people with lung cancer. When presented, his Majesty asked what I did. I replied:

> 'I'm a trainee surgeon, Your Majesty. I think it something worthwhile.'

The King nodded and then, with a slight curl to the lip said:

> 'Especially if you know what you're doing.'

On driving away from Buckingham Palace I said:

> 'The King's got lung cancer!'

This was doubly strange. I hadn't heard that he had that horrible disease and yet my workplace was always abuzz with the medical problems of the good and great. No rumour had escaped. Did the king know something was wrong but hadn't been told? We all knew of his other smoking-related problems such as serious circulatory problems with his legs, treated with sympathectomy.

He didn't die for nearly twelve months later of the disease, but it surely would have been detected by XRay.

The point of this was that I didn't need an X Ray: I knew it from his appearance.

I claim no pre-eminence here. Any good doctor, surrounded with such cases would recognise another.

The point of all this? Too much reliance is placed today on the result of tests and clinical acumen is in the dust bin of old-style medicine. This is a huge mistake. In this book I mention two cases where this was necessary for diagnosis; one, sadly too late: my dear friend Jimmy Johnson died of a heart attack two days after a normal electrocardiogram purported to show a normal heart.

We're learning much, much more about the underlying processes of life and how this may be used to help allay suffering. Despite this, there are countless volumes yet to be learned and sweeping aside all older ideas is a mistake.

'Be not the first by whom the new is tried
Nor yet the last to lay the old aside.'

I hope you will enjoy some of the experiences, mostly surgical, that I had during a life spent loving the privilege of participating in the so-called healing art.

Death of a Prime Minister

'The PM would like to see you in his office.'

The Government Whip raised his eyebrows quizzically as he poked his head into my office. I'd gone to Canberra on a Monday night to do some research. At a previous summons the PM had asked me to accompany him to Viet Nam.

'Thanks Bill.' I said and with a look of wild surmise I clattered down the stairs in the Whip's wake.

Harold's face was drawn: he was obviously in pain. The problem, he said, was with his Left shoulder, any movement was excruciating. As he stripped to the waist, he mentioned that he'd had trouble with his other shoulder some time previously but it was now pain-free.

I examined him. He was slightly stooped. There were signs of wear and tear in his Right shoulder, but its movements were full and pain-free. Not so his Left. All movements were severely restricted and extremely painful: the features of a frozen shoulder.

Pain in the Left shoulder can be a sign of coronary artery disease, so I carefully listened in to his chest. There were no ominous moist sounds at the lung bases. Reassured, I manipulated the painful entity a la John Jefferies, about whom more anon. I reassured him, but wrote a note for him to have an electrocardiogram on the following morning. This proved to be normal and his pain next day, though still present, had improved considerably. By Friday morning he was much better, but moving his shoulder still caused some pain and its movements were still limited. He was his normal cheery self.

Forty-eight hours later he was dead.

There's always a background in such events, of course, the most significant one quite possibly, no, very probably, being a phone call on the fateful Sunday morning from that execrable example of all that's rotten in politics, Billy McMahon. Billy later denied it, no doubt to escape opprobrium, but he was a well-known liar and Harold's housekeeper made the definite affirmation that it was indeed he who'd called. His voice: high pitched and slightly squeaky, was absolutely unmistakeable.

Positively lusting after his job, this deformed character, waging a skilful campaign against Harold, had already won over many unworthy MPs by promises of preferment if he recruited the necessary numbers. Dudley Irwin, another Government Whip, who'd sent a memo to Harold advising him of an allegedly rising swell against him proudly told me himself that, if/when Billy won the day he'd be given a ministry.

One of Billy's planks was Harold's performance at Question Time. He did have a point: instead of concise, witty rejoinders, as in Bob Menzies' day, Harold would ramble on and on—and on. At least twice I'd pleaded with him to keep it sharp and brief and no doubt others had too, to no avail.

That phone call was probably Billy telling Harold that he had the numbers at last. The latter, knowing the former only too well, would probably have assumed that he was lying, but it wouldn't exactly have made his day.

He was also having serious problems with Black Jack MacEwen a tough operator to say the least, leader of the Country Party coalition with Harold's Liberals.

Last but not least, his wife, Zara, for all her qualities an unlikely life's partner for one so clean cut as Harold, was having an affair with Jeff Bate, Member for Tilba Tilba Cheese, a likeable if slightly raffish character.

Harold himself had, understandably, developed a friendship with a lady, the nature and extent of which nobody, the lady herself excepted, can possibly know. She was present with a small party on Portsea beach when he arrived to take his final, fatal steps into extremely turbulent water.

There are only three credible possibilities. Ridiculous speculation about submarines and the like are, of course, unworthy of any consideration.

1. He deliberately committed suicide.

When I attended him on the Friday morning I saw no signs of depression. I was sensitive to his moods and, after all, I was dealing with the Prime Minister. Moreover, he wasn't a coward.

Most suicides like to communicate finally in some way—usually by means of a letter.

Had he decided to do away with himself, surely he would at least have given some hints—perhaps a farewell sign of some kind—to his lady friend, actually on the beach?

But he had a frozen shoulder! Any movement would have been painful and restricted in amplitude, a combination that must at the very least have hampered his battle against that treacherous, raging sea.

It's very important to realise in this context that Harold loved pitting himself against the elements, taking pride in the risks he took in the water, perhaps to bolster his *amour propre*. A good, honest but insufficiently strong Prime Minister, he was strong, resolute and resourceful in literally troubled waters. Not strong enough either, perhaps, in those of a domestic kind.

2. My view, for what it's worth, is that, upset—to say the least—by Billy's phone call, together with all of his political and domestic problems: the possibility of a broken marriage, whoever was responsible, would inevitably have had profound consequences: more so then than now. He assessed that perilous flood and decided to give it a go, his strong subconscious, mentioned later, telling him that it didn't matter too much if he didn't make it.

3. There's a third possibility. I had a very dear friend whom I'd visited during a Parliamentary break. Giving me a classical history of coronary heart disease, I urged him to have an ECG at once. This showed no abnormality at all. Relief! All clear! Excepting that he was found dead under a favourite tree a few days later. ECGs aren't totally reliable. Could this have been Harold's problem? A normal ECG with an underlying, fatal cardiac problem? He wasn't wearing a wet suit. One imagines that a sudden chill could cause spasm of a diseased Coronary artery with consequent clotting of blood within it.

Who knows? He certainly had no chest signs of a coronary occlusion when I examined him. I strongly favour the second alternative. However that may be, poor Harold visited the bottom of the monstrous world to the detriment of Australia and, incidentally, unimportantly, my political future. Unimportantly? Well, not very importantly, from every point of view. Hardly chuffed at the time, I was infinitely better off out of the dirty game that's politics. I can't guarantee that my conscience would have remained clear had I not lost my seat. That loss took me back to my profession full-time, after an interval which allowed me to recover myself after working hard in a busy, rambling electorate and at the same time practising my profession whenever I had any spare moments. Call it hubris; call it presumption, I'd always, naively, thought that I'd do more good if I were able to apply whatever knowledge and skills I might have on a wider field.

One evening Harold asked me if I'd like to accompany him to Viet Nam as his medical advisor, but the main reason for my presence would, I realised, be to try to pick up the pieces if the Viet Cong expressed disapproval of his presence in a practical way.

I was at his side throughout our entire time there, excepting for one occasion when he had discussions with General Westmoreland. That name resonated. There's no doubt that, like Henry V's cousin he'd have liked more men to expend on the battlefield. The end result of the General's enterprise was decidedly less successful than Henry's at Agincourt.

Unlike *Pooh Bahs* of today, we flew to Singapore on a regular scheduled flight, though Harold, his secretary, General Wilton and two off-siders, three bureaucrats, the Head of the Commonwealth Police and I were screened off from the madding crowd. The policeman, there to stave off any assassination attempt on Harold, confided that this was an impossible task if the VC really meant business.

From Singapore we flew to Saigon in an RAAF Viscount. Ton Son Nut Airport was an experience, littered with the detritus of crashed and generally shot up planes. We often flew hither and thither from here across Viet Nam in American helicopters, witnessing signs of the fighting: artillery duels in particular. It gave one a strange feeling when the gunners unshipped their weapons after take-off. The only casualty there was Harold's secretary, who collapsed on the tarmac, whether from fright or heat couldn't be established.

A planeload of journalists had followed us, but we only saw them occasionally. Once or twice I had drinks with them at the Hotel Caravelle. We went up on to the roof one evening to witness a napalm attack.

Before we left Oz I'd prepared a couple of pages of health advice for everybody, press included.

Naturally I met the local panjandra, including General Cao Ky, whom I liked very much. He was a quiet, thoughtful, brave man who flew missions in his prop-driven fighter against enemy jets. At our first grand dinner it was pleasing to discover that birds' nest soup, despite its origins, was a true delicacy. As I sat, quietly eating, Harold suddenly called out, for all to hear:

'Just look at how Wylie's handling his chop sticks!'

With all eyes suddenly upon me, those implements went completely awry, food falling from my nerveless grasp!

Looking around to admire the magnificent venue, one couldn't help noticing that the cornice had been shattered by intense gunfire, the result, I was told, of the CIA's assassination of Emperor Bao Dai who didn't fit in with the US' scheme of things. How many others were murdered at the same time?

It was quite exciting travelling to these events, hurtling along in a convoy, hemmed in by motorcycle police, sirens wailing! We always drove with windows almost closed. The VC had a nasty habit of lobbing grenades through open car windows. There can't have been any air-conditioned cars in Viet Nam at that time as the interiors were always hot.

When Harold (I always called him sir) was having his conference with Westmoreland it was arranged for me to inspect Saigon's leading hospital.

Naturally I immediately made my way up to the operating theatres. There I found a recently graduated doctor grappling with a chest wound, courtesy the VC. These were common because the VC had the nasty habit of throwing grenades into restaurants. This youngster had the chest well and truly open and was dealing quite well, if very slowly, with the bleeding. A badly damaged lung awaited his attention. Naturally I wasn't at all pleased that a senior surgeon hadn't got off his fundament to try to save a life, but was assured that that was the practice there, inherited from French precedent. True or false? I don't know.

I was also taken—this time with Harold—to an American hospital and saw how wonderful was the treatment. One man had had his femoral artery severed by a VC bullet: a rapidly fatal event as one can well imagine. He'd instantly been picked up by medics in their helicopter who staunched the bleeding, transfused and resuscitated him and had him in the operating theatre twelve minutes after his wounding.

The medics who performed these humanitarian tasks were the truly magnificent heroes of that war. Completely dauntless, they'd land in the midst of most intense fire, coolly resuscitating victims whilst all hell let loose at them.

Throughout this expedition I dosed everyone with the drug Enterovioform, supposed to ward off food infections, to keep everyone on deck. It did appear to do so, as the only case of Delhi belly was a major, the General's ADC, who declined with thanks—well, he did decline. The only trifling problem here is that this drug was subsequently shown to cause SMON, subacute myelo-optic atrophy, AKA blindness. Sending the PM blind would indeed have been an achievement!

There were many memorable experiences: seeing vast rubber plantations shattered by gunfire; lush, rolling countryside seen from the air; the grand Mekong river; several patients, nursed and fed by relatives and forced to share a bed in a rural hospital and the looks of dire hatred on the faces of the poor deluded inhabitants of a Communist village I'd trundled through in a little two-man tank, in the middle of Soekano's rabid attempt to take the whole of Borneo by force. I noted with displeasure that the Australian-made corrugated so-called galvanised iron used to buttress the trenches was already quite rusty. Few experiences were medical. Another was staying in the house the King of Siam had built for Anna.

Oh, yes: a bureaucrat did cut his head by hitting it on a tank stand at the Australian Army cantonment. Harold, too, cut himself shaving before some function in Thailand. I hadn't come prepared for that and had to settle for toilet paper as a haemostatic agent.

He and I were now on friendly terms. Once, later, in Australia, when dining together, he ordered a Martini as a pre-luncheon drink. I regard that beverage as a poison, but what can one do when dining with the PM? I had the same. Because the attendant, like time's winged chariot, was hurrying near, Harold ordered another but I drew the line. As we conversed, he had his glass in his hand, occasionally gesturing with it to make a point. Suddenly his hand shook so much that he spilled much of his drink.

'There you are, you see, Wylie' he said, 'I have a very powerful subconscious. Something said to me: Harold, you shouldn't be having that second Martini! I'm sure that's why it happened'. This just possibly provides a clue to his regrettable end.

As an aside, for some obscure reason, Martinis are supposed to be the jolly old thing. I had the pleasure of dining at the lodge with Bob Menzies on a couple of occasions. Each time we had to drink the wretched things which Bob insisted on mixing personally, in imitation, I've been told, of Winston Churchill. Folly, thy name is Man!

My career ended when the contest for leadership between jolly Jack Gorton and Paul Hasluck took place. During the campaign I was constantly plagued by urgings, in one case pleading, from many of Gorton's supporters, Malcolm Fraser included, but my answer was always the same: Paul Hasluck is the better man. My wife tells me that I was an idiot: I should have agreed to support Gorton but vote for Hasluck. I'm glad I didn't. Earth's dregs control politics. That's why it's in such a dreadful state.

Cutting a longish story short, when a redistribution of electoral boundaries took place prior to the subsequent elections, I found myself landed with the Labour voting sections of my two adjacent Tory colleagues. They received my choicest parts. I was kindly allocated their Labour rumps. They'd ostentatiously supported Gorton.

Some years previously, before the Viet Nam War, shocked by the atrocities the Communists committed as they began their putsch South and poor little Laos, in the line of advance, having terribly few medical amenities, I—quite stupidly—thought that surgical help there might bolster the country a little against the forces of night; at the worst, provide some humanitarian aid. I sought help from the Federal Australian Government, Paul Hasluck, then Foreign Minister to wit. His refusal was a kindly one. The contact begat thoughts that I should enter Federal politics.

For my sins, I'd been a member of the State Executive of the Tory party for some years and, though far from impressed by most of the characters I'd met, a move to Canberra seemed logical.

I applied for the Brisbane bay-side electorate of Bowman, with neither time nor inclination to lobby anyone: Party head-quarters, local branches or individuals. I quite simply hate and despise lobbying to the nth degree. Decisions of this, or, indeed, of any significant kind, should be made solely on factual data, entirely objectively. Emotionalism is at odds with reason.

My feelings sprang partly from natural diffidence (the hate part) and partly because, as a member of selection committees, I'd receive visits to my professional rooms from candidates about to appear before my committee who'd suddenly developed symptoms demanding my urgent attention. One of these later became a judge of the Supreme Court of Queensland. A few others, including that judge, succeeded in becoming members of parliament. I never attended selection meetings when one of those creeps consulted me (that's the despising bit).

Came my selection night, a speech had to be made before the committee. In the very middle of my spiel there was an urgent phone call, relayed to the room, the only time in my experience that such a meeting had been interrupted by a phone call. It was for me. There'd been an affray: two people, knifed in the abdomen were in shock and bleeding internally. I gave the registrar who'd phoned instructions for treatment, pending my arrival, audience wide eyed as my instructions were technical: better entertainment than E.R!

Speech unfinished, I raced up the road to Ipswich. One of the victims needed splenectomy, that organ having almost been severed by a knife-thrust.

That was the second case: the blood transfusion was keeping up with the bleeding.

The other had copiously bleeding incised wounds of the liver. Suturing this isn't easy and demands the utmost care: it's very friable and sutures readily cut out. The trick is to insert interlocking sutures parallel to the wound and then—with the utmost care—suture the wound together across the parallel sutures, easier said than done, especially with blood gushing copiously everywhere. A strong will to self-control is vital: don't panic!

I couldn't have been the favoured candidate: nobody phoned. Surprised, I read about my success in the paper the following morning. How Beelzebub must have laughed!

You see, there'd been a curious incident whilst organizing my campaign. I was deeply depressed, just having lost a most dearly loved one, incidentally on a Friday evening. Next morning, I had to perform three major operations: removal of stones from a patient's common bile duct; a gastrectomy and a mastectomy for cancer, all of which required strictest attention to detail. To say I didn't much feel like working on that day puts it mildly. However, the operations went smoothly and the intense concentration probably had some therapeutic value.

Soon afterward, at night—the only time available to me—I was irrigating some Lucerne (alfalfa) on my farm, Queensland, as usual being in drought. I pumped from a waterhole adjacent to a road along which high tension electricity power lines had recently been strung. The aluminium pipes were long and as I manoeuvred one of them, I felt a metallic scraping.

Ah! I thought I must have hit the power line...Strange! I'm still alive!!

But was it the power line?

Indifferent as to whether or not I died, I tried it again. It was indeed the power line. The only reason, in my view, why I was still extant, apart from a miracle, was that I was wearing wellies and the ground was very dry.

Was it a sign that I'd make a mark in politics? Of course it wasn't. Always very agnostic about such things, at the time I nevertheless thought that such an odd deliverance might have been of significance.

When campaigning, I reluctantly forced myself to knock on doors. On the other hand, I didn't mind spruiking on street corners. Helpers came forward; time-servers too, looking for an opportunity to gain a toehold on the greasy pole, I met some fine people who, like me, suffered from the delusion that we lived in a democracy and that their work was for the betterment of their country. I had that airy-fairy notion progressively crushed out of me, but this tale isn't about politics.

With two girls at an expensive boarding school and other children to be educated, I had to continue practicing my profession. In those days a Federal Australian parliamentary salary wasn't sufficient to keep the financial nose above water, especially as I had to relinquish my consultant post. After my electoral success, my brother, later Chief Justice of Australia's High Court, phoned not only to congratulate me, but also to remind me that I now had to resign from what was laughingly called an office of profit under the crown. Four half days away from my practice, one unpaid and what pay there was pretty abysmal! Profit?

I entered Canberra in style. Sir Robert Menzies was giving out the prizes at my girls' school and offered me a lift in his aircraft: not the huge, expensive behemoths present-day pollies swan around in but a twin piston-engined Convair.

Having resigned my Ipswich post and with the private practice there sold, the Wickham Terrace enterprise had to provide the necessary supplementary funds. Parliamentary sessions lasted from Tuesday afternoon to Friday morning, leaving Mondays, weekends—when there wasn't a football match or budgerigar society meeting in the electorate—and Friday afternoons free—and of course there were many Parliamentary recesses. Postoperative care, especially with less serious cases, could mostly be left with the referring doctor if I trusted him. For really major surgery the Whip was always cooperative, allowing me whatever leave was necessary. Enough work rolled in to keep the finances just afloat.

A practice—free, of course, because the patients, remember, were either politicians or their hangers-on—rapidly grew in Parliament House, to the extent that I was allocated a consulting room in the building, the old one, nearer to Lake Burleigh Griffin: an easy walk over pleasant lawns, before the move to more exalted accommodation had been made. It was quite busy, with a constant stream of ailments, real and imaginary, to care for. A few of these were noteworthy, the runner-up being a senior cabinet minister who, out of the blue, developed terminal cancer. I hadn't the heart to tell him outright, saying instead that he had a serious problem and should consult his doctor on his return to Perth, his home town.

A couple of patients who, influential and still around the ridges must be nameless, were neurotic to a degree.

Many politicians proved to be as thick as two planks. For instance, KL, a patient and the senator chosen to chair a committee to decide whether or not Oz should be metricated was nice enough but wouldn't have known the difference between Christmas and New Year's Day. Well chosen! Apart from neurotic aches and pains, probably the most common ailment was middle ear infection, the result of flying when the individual had a cold. Oft times I was simply being exploited but I didn't mind, any more than I've ever worried about so-called kerbside consultations. That's what I'm here for! Incidentally, though the more moderate Labour members consulted me, I never had the pleasure of treating the more rabid left wingers. Matters eased in my second term when the Labour Party also returned a doctor.

One of my great pleasures was a happy acquaintanceship with dear old Arthur Caldwell, Leader of the Opposition, one of the very few totally honest politicians; a good and kind man. There were tales when Whitlam was bullying his way to the top that Arthur would go to Bob Menzies to pour out his heart. We met because we often took the same car home at night. Unlike most in his position, he never made a questionable shilling out of it and wasn't at all well off after he'd retired (parliamentary pensions hadn't become so outrageously inflated). It was my pleasure, when later associated with the drug companies, to obtain some expensive medicines for Mrs. Caldwell. You're in Heaven, Arthur, happy that few if any of your colleagues are there too.

Bob Menzies retired at the end of my first term at Canberra. I was very sorry to see him go. He was a politician through and through but managed to be a very nice man at the same time. Harold Holt was his successor and though I regretted the change, nobody ever being able to take Bob's place, I became very fond of him as I got to know him better. As the Treasurer, he'd asked me to analyse health schemes in other countries and make recommendations, resulting in my first overseas trip as an MP. I strongly doubt if any of my recommendations still see the light of day.

The Way Things Were

When I was born more than ninety years ago, the practice of medicine was primitive compared with its far greater sophistication today, not, of course, realised at the time. There was, indeed, a vast body of knowledge about how the body worked but nobody could do much about it.

Physicians have always regarded themselves as a breed superior to surgeons, but, in the period under discussion, surgeons had far more curative procedures at their disposal. Physicians in the early Twentieth Century had effective treatments for a mere handful of complaints: they could ease coughs; somewhat prolong the lives of sufferers from heart failure with digitalis, discovered almost three hundred years previously; could treat syphilis—common then—by injecting vast quantities of water containing an arsenical preparation and use sedatives and pain killers. There were also a few metals: gold for rheumatoid arthritis a very old treatment indeed, witness Chaucer's aside about the doctor on the Canterbury pilgrimage:

> 'For gold in physick is a cordiall, therefore he loved gold in speciall.'

Mercury (by injection) was another metal in therapeutic use. It was the forerunner of present-day fluid tablets. It was also once used in the treatment of syphilis, though, by our time, arsenic had taken its place.

John Hunter, father of modern surgery, purposely inoculated himself with syphilis and then tried various remedies, mercury in particular, in quest of a cure.

That was about it. They had a vast array of medical preparations largely derived from plants, but very few of these did anything but ease symptoms. Pneumonia could be diagnosed but not treated. Streptococcal septicaemia could be diagnosed but all the physician cold do was watch the patient die. Diabetics died, their lives extended by just a little.

About this time, however, the lives of sufferers from pernicious anaemia could be saved, could they bring themselves to eat vast quantities of raw liver. An injectable treatment was discovered when I was six years old, but I was twenty-six before the mechanism was understood.

Surgeons, with their knives could cure appendicitis; sometimes even cancer; hernias could be repaired and stomachs, gallbladders and enlarged prostates removed, but the brain was still the province of general surgeons, the death rate of neurosurgical patients very high. The chest couldn't be opened largely because anaesthetics, delivered by rag and bottle, didn't allow the lungs to be kept inflated so that they could keep the blood oxygenated. Lungs of course collapse when the chest is opened. Vascular surgery was in the future and it took the Second World War to put plastic surgery on its feet.

Fluid replacement was in its extreme infancy and many surgical patients died of dehydration. Infection carried off even more.

In the year of my birth a most dramatic break-through saw the introduction of insulin as a treatment for diabetes mellitus. Its discoverer was a surgeon, William Banting. Imagine him, with his student assistant Best, entering whole wards full of dying children and bringing them dramatically back to life!

He won the Nobel Prize, which he generously shared with Best. No ribbon to wear in his coat, but what a wonderful reward must be the thought of alleviating such suffering; saving innumerable young lives!

Poliomyelitis was still a scourge until I was about thirty. I remember schools being closed when an epidemic swept through my town. Limping, crutch-borne people were everywhere. For years at the rear entrance to my hospital a poor woman, totally paralysed, lay in an iron lung: a long oblong box which housed her and breathed for her. A small mirror allowed her to see comings and goings. That was her life.

There was no treatment for any of the infectious diseases, syphilis excepted.

As a child a couple of years into schooling I well remember the vicissitudes of a schoolmate, Max Haenke, who had contracted bronchopneumonia: his parents' maid was a close friend of our own. His battle with the grim reaper went on, seemingly for ages. Pus collected in his chest and was drained, but his course was inexorably downhill. Bronchopneumonia killed most of the millions who died in the influenza pandemic that swept through the world at the end of the first Great War.

This illness was quite distinct from lobar pneumonia: much more dramatic, for which, too, there was no treatment. This illness culminated in a crisis, when the temperature rose dramatically. Were the patient to live, it suddenly subsided, leaving a limp, sweat-soaked patient who gradually returned to health. Otherwise the temperature rose further and the patient soon died.

Imagine the feelings of family as the crisis arrived and they awaited its culmination. Medicine could do nothing.

I well remember the distress of my brother when a school mate, accidentally kicked on the shin at football died a few days later from staphylococcal septicaemia. Not long afterward a cousin who had pricked his finger on a rose thorn died of streptococcal septicaemia.

We were introduced to sulphanilamide in my clinical years, almost, it seemed, as an after-thought, when studying pharmacology. A fundamental break through, it was the first drug which could fairly be relied upon to cure certain infections. Prior to this, a patient's immune state and the luck of the draw determined the outcome of infectious diseases.

The discovery in 1932 of something that really worked was dramatic: Gerhardt Domagk had been working on synthetic dyes for the Bayer section of IG Farbenindustrie, specifically to find antibacterial drugs. He found that a beautiful red dye, Prontosil rubrum—I remember ampoules of it—cured streptococcal infections in mice. Its safety and efficacy in humans hadn't been established when his daughter developed the same affliction as my cousin, from a needle prick. She was obviously dying, but there was a serious ethical dilemma here: would the father merely hasten his daughter's death by administering this unproven dye? He did the only possible thin: administering his Prontosil and she was cured.

Greedy Bayer kept the discovery under wraps, hoping to cash in, but the secret leaked out and a French firm discovered that the active part of the dye was a white substance, sulphanilamide. Neither company made a killing. The drug had been synthesised first fifty years previously: they couldn't patent it.

Curiously—human behaviour really is curious—this life-saver only really became widely used after it saved the life of one of the Roosevelts. Joe Blow cured: who he? A Roosevelt cured? We must use this drug!!! My illness in 1936 was due to the Streptococcus organism, but despite Dr. Holmes à Court's eminence there was no suggestion that prontosil should be administered. My illness had occurred a short time before the Roosevelt episode. It was only the advent of World War II that saw its widespread use

People with toxic goitre usually died, iodine prolonging their lives but a little. Even when I was a resident medical officer the only treatment was the surgical removal of most of the thyroid gland, a most hazardous undertaking because of the effects of the toxicity upon the heart.

The most successful treatment, in Queensland at least, was in the hands of Charlie Lilley, doyen of an influential family. He called his approach 'stealing the thyroid'. The patient was kept in isolation in a separate ward where one whispered if speech was necessary and sudden sounds prohibited. The patient was sedated and given Lugol's Iodine. Charlie watched the patient: day and night, with meticulous care and, when he judged the time right, the heavily sedated patient was taken to the Theatre. And the operation carried out under local anaesthetic. The stress of rag-and-bottle anaesthetics would have been too much for the patient's heart.

What public hospital would allow of such treatment today?

In the absence of antibiotics and a very incomplete knowledge of fluid replacement, not to mention primitive anaesthesia, major surgery, limited in scope, was hazardous. My teacher George Brandis' demand for a closed-off side ward for his post-op. Abdomino-perineal patients— more of them anon—would only rarely be acceded to today, nor would one be needed.

Nowadays, just about everyone admitted to hospital has an intravenous needle stuck in the arm and fluid administered in that way. In 1945, junior resident medical officers, myself included, were called upon to cut open a vein at the ankle and tie in a cannula for the administration of blood or fluids, a reasonably time consuming process. In a hospital of more than two thousand patients, we were only required to do this occasionally, an indication of the rarity of intravenous therapy in those days less than sixty years ago.

One of the subjects in my first year of medicine was botany, which I loved. It was studied because plant extracts played such an important, if ineffective, part in medical treatment. In my fourth year, one of my most

important text books for the study of therapeutics was Hale White's
Materia Medica, which contained details of plant remedies almost
exclusively.

> We knew not but knew not that we knew not: but were by
> no means fools.

Prized more than anything else was clinical acumen: uncommon
then; vanishingly rare today, when diagnosis rests far too much on reams
and reams of tests which, because of the subtle differences between our
bodies and the way in which they react, give a diagnostic picture, but not
the whole one.

Early Influences

I awoke one February morning in 1936, feeling dreadful, with a strange spongy feeling in my scalp. A mirror reflected back an unbelievable sight: a horribly puffy, alien face with slit-like eyes. Really me?

It was. I was seriously ill—for almost a year.

This wasn't my first encounter with medicine and its practitioners.

A delightful friend, Vinnie Beirne, later slaughtered at the Battle of el Alamein, lived next door and we often got into scrapes together. One evening we got the bright idea of feeding newspaper into a lawnmower, then running with it, strewing the next-door backyard with paper shreds: someone else could pick them up. I fed the paper in, Vinnie ran with it, on one occasion too soon: the tip of my left middle finger flew off, severed by the spinning blades. I gazed in horror at a white circle of bone surrounded by flesh, soon hidden by a rush of blood. Again unlike today, our family doctor, Gilmore, anaesthetised me with chloroform in my mother's bed and stuck the bits together, a trifle crookedly. The finger is fully functional.

Each successive encounter strengthened my resolve. When I grew up I'd be a medico: not a family doctor but a surgeon.

I think I've always regarded myself as one, even before I had the faintest idea of what that calling's all about. Perhaps it was partly because my mother willed it and perhaps that in turn was due to the fact that her maternal grandfather had been the first doctor in the Australian town of Mudgee. My uncle Archie by marriage was also a prominent Sydney surgeon.

Gilmore, remembered for his laugh, as of a delirious donkey, said:

> You're going to be a doctor, aren't you, Wylie? Well, take a
> look at your urine down this microscope!

As I looked I he described the plethora of red cells and casts which met an astonished gaze—a picture still remembered.

> You have acute nephritis. It's hospital for you.

And it was so, in a sprawling single story bungalow type building. I was kindly given a strategic room with wide Georgian doors, whence I watched most of the comings and goings, the stories behind many of which were related by the compassionate nurses. Some of the local doctors would drop in for a kindly word or two, but none of this helped my condition, which failed to improve. I was eventually taken home and put under the care of a charming private nurse. Still no better, Gilmore did something I find difficult to forgive: he referred me to a urologist, a person who operates—on prostates, yes, and kidneys, too—but is not a nephrologist, the doctor more properly equipped to deal with my medical problem, not that anybody knew much of practical use about it. The unforgivable bit is his motivation: his daughter was going out with the surgeon's son, and I suspect he was helping the man's business.

This idiot now ordered an intravenous pyelogram, a totally inappropriate investigation and one not without risk in those early days of the procedure. A dye, opaque to x rays, is injected into a vein and a series of X ray pictures is taken as the kidneys excrete it. The poison in question, Uroselectan B, inevitably showed nothing abnormal, because my disease, especially in a relatively early phase, produces no gross effects upon kidney structure, only the microscopic architecture being affected.

Contributing nothing, it nearly killed me. For a couple of weeks, I was most dreadfully ill, with spine chilling, well remembered nightmares. My brother, well into his Arts/law degrees, fainted when his medical student fellow-collegians gave their prognosis.

My mother rang my Sydney uncle:

'Bring him down right away'

I couldn't have withstood a train or boat journey, so had to fly, with a no doubt reluctant mother. In those days, Brisbane airport was at Archerfield and as we waited to board I was excited to see what probably constituted the entire Australian Air Force on the tarmac: a flight of Hawker Demon biplanes, gleaming silver in the sun, on a propaganda flight right around the continent: not a good idea. Some of them actually did make it home!

Planes were still primitive. Ours, no exception, was a Stinson trimotor, which crashed into the mountains to the South of Brisbane not long afterwards. For me it was a great thrill to watch the squares of cultivation; the geometry of house roofs, usually with the adjacent green puff of a tree; the roads; the gleaming rivers as we chugged along at a few thousand feet.

Air travel in those days was quite an event and the names of passengers who'd taken this intrepid step were recorded in the Sydney Morning Herald.

My uncle met us at the airport and took me to my hospital. That night the matron, Sophie Durham, called in and took my pulse with an amazingly large 'pocket' watch.

'Wylie, this is the watch I used to take the pulse of your Uncle Wyle as he was dying on the Island of Lesbos.'

The first Light Horseman killed on Gallipoli. His brother Cecil followed him almost immediately at the unnecessary slaughter of the Nek.

My distinguished looking physician, Dr. Holmes à Court thought that my tonsils might be aggravating my condition. An ENT man concurred. I thoroughly disagreed but didn't have a vote, so my tonsils were promptly removed—using the old rag-and-bottle anaesthesia described more fully later.

It hadn't been established at that time, but acute nephritis is an abnormal immune response to a streptococcal infection which my tonsils had obviously harboured.

That evening my suspicion of nutritionists—shared, I recently discovered, by that charming writer about foods, Michael Pollan—was established when, almost immediately post operatively, I was offered crumbed brains for my dinner. Brains have never personally been regarded as a culinary delight, but covered in harsh bread crumbs, incredibly abrasive to a recently assaulted throat? No thank you!

As it happened, I was wrong; Dr. Holmes a'Court was right. I began to improve and after a few weeks flew back to Brisbane in the still extant Stinson.

At the time of my serious illness there was neither treatment for it nor a knowledge of its cause, so this was a good example of clinical acumen. Though the cause of the disease was then unknown, a careful history and examination revealed only one abnormality: my infected tonsils. This, then, was the most probable cause.

It took some months to regain strength and whilst this was happening I did something inexcusably stupid. In those days many young boys experimented with chemicals, making all kinds of exciting products: oxygen; hydrogen, rotten-smelling hydrogen-sulphide and so on. On one occasion I made chlorine gas and kept it in glass jars sealed with window glass. After some weeks, believing the gas would now be diluted, I thought

I'd see just how it smelled. The gas attacks of the First World War were still fresh in everybody's memories. I inhaled—and nearly asphyxiated. My mother heard my uncontrollable coughing and came out to see what was happening. I downplayed it:

'That'll kill the germs in my respiratory tract!' I gasped.

It probably did, but for years afterward I was racked with recurrent bronchitis. It had killed much of the lining of my respiratory system.

Whilst recuperating, another GP kindly took me on his rounds, explaining something of the patients whom he was visiting. Sometimes his senile mother came along. Her efforts to get out of the car in her son's absence, together with her anxious ramblings, drove me to distraction.

The same doctor invited me to view some minor surgery. I almost fainted when first I saw the sharp steel of his scalpel sever skin and make the tissues bleed. Fortunately, there was a chair handy.

Another youthful medical encounter, less dramatic, nevertheless was very disabling. I'd periodically—too often—been struck down by a mysterious respiratory complaint: I'd feel absolutely dreadful and, though bedridden, my temperature stubbornly refused to rise.

'Bronchial catarrh' opined Gilmore: wrong of course. it was severe hay fever. There were no antihistamines in those days and, indeed, one seldom if ever heard the term allergy.

In my infancy I was afflicted by croup: acute tracheitis or tracheobronchitis. For this, my mother lit a Vapocresoline lamp beside my bed: a rather ornate, gilded frame which held a little lamp with a white glass globe. Above this was a small circular dish into which the medicament was poured. I must say that I loved that lamp and found its operation most soothing. Tracheobronchitis can cause a very serious, even fatal obstruction to the airway. Mine fortunately didn't come into that category.

Mother also spread a heated grey paste on to a cloth and applied it to my chest. This was Antiphlogistine, aka Aunty Flo, a completely different substance from today's white analgesic rub of that name. The word is a quaint anachronism and, of course, means that it's an antagonist of phlogiston, a mythical substance, which when, supposedly combined with others under suitable circumstances, aided combustion. That theory was knocked on the head as long ago as 1774, when Joseph Priestley discovered oxygen. Strange ideas persist!

My nieces recently came up with a newspaper account of a fatal case of tracheobronchitis which, at the dawn of the Twentieth Century, involved my Grandfather who, in his seventies, was converted by Mary Baker Eddy and sailed to America, where he studied for a degree in Christian Science.

A man was on trial for the wilful manslaughter of his four-year-old son whom he took to my Grandfather for treatment. He'd been to a doctor who diagnosed diphtheria. In evidence he said that there were a few white spots on the tonsils, so he misdiagnosed the case. Diphtheria, as we'll learn later, causes a prolific greyish membrane over the fauces.

The doctor prescribed diphtheria 'antitoxin' taken orally and thus a completely ineffective nostrum. The Christian Scientist father didn't administer it, going instead to my Grandfather, whose treatment consisted in an intensive regimen of prayer. After initial improvement, the child suddenly died, no doubt of asphyxia from the undiagnosed tracheobronchitis. My Grandfather escaped with some rigorous questioning, unlike the poor father who was convicted of wilful manslaughter. At no time was the efficacy of the 'antitoxin' queried; nor was the misdiagnosis.

Up to my clinical years at University I was plagued by frequent colds and respiratory problems; rotten earache, too, until my mother said:

'Wyle, why don't you try taking Pentavite?'

Health neurosis was not nearly so widespread in those days and this was one of only a few multivitamin preparations on the market. It worked wonders, but, as my weekly allowance was far from infinite, after a couple of bottles of that, I opted for the cheaper Vitamin C tablets. From enduring persistent earache and very frequent colds up until 1943, I've had few since. So-called nutritionists have been trying to discover all kinds of evils associated with this vitamin. At time of writing I've been taking it regularly for more than seventy years and am still here with no kidney stones (one of the alleged complications of taking it) despite having taken it daily in Hellishly torrid climes.

My first brush with Orthopaedics occurred some years after finger severance. I'd gone with fellow Cubs on a hike, supervised by two senior Scouts: bullies. Bivouacked by a stream they proceeded to torment us. When it was my turn to be a victim, Tubby Paton chased me and, as I ran down the inclined creek bank, I caught my foot in a tree root, pitching forward. Tubby caught my Right foot as it came up and twisted it cruelly as my head hit the ground. In the days following, the foot became increasingly painful until, only able to hobble about, I was sent to an Orthopod, a friend of my Sydney uncle, who diagnosed osteitis of the Calcaneum (heel bone). It was actually an avascular necrosis, caused by the blood supply to part of the bone having been avulsed. Modern treatments differ, but my lower leg was encased in plaster of Paris and I was forbidden to walk for six weeks.

Condemned to a sedentary state, I began to put on so much weight that I was diagnosed as Froelich's syndrome. Certainly I believe that when my head hit the ground on that excursion the blood supply to my Pituitary gland was also affected. However, that may be, I was as fat as a pig for some years. Towards the end of my Matriculation year, I suddenly began to feel unusually warm—but well—and the fat just melted away.

With the British Empire at war, my definitive studies now began.

STUDENT LIFE

First year was a bit of a doddle: physics and chemistry, already studied for matric and biology, including botany, as already mentioned. There were many aspects to that Biology course, including absolutely fascinating Embryology. One was and still is totally amazed at the progress of a single cell as it continuously replicates and creates forms that trace evolutionary history, from the most primitive organism, through a resemblance to a shark, on through successive stages in which the organs and other structures of the individual progressively form.

Ontogeny recapitulates phylogeny!

Boomed our lecturer, Ernie Goddard, meaning just what's been said. He was a dyed in the wool Darwinist—there's more to that process than simple Darwinism—and he continued booming. Unfortunately, his lectures were always after lunch and his method of emphasis proved to be powerfully soporific, especially as the lights were always out, the projector on. One afternoon there was a startling scuffling sound. The lights immediately went up, revealing a student lying in the aisle jactitating and frothing at the mouth. Lab. Assistant: another Ernie rushed to put a peg in his mouth to protect tongue and lips from being chewed: the first epileptic fit I'd seen.

Early in December, 1940, strolling from the tram stop to College, after discovering at the University that I'd passed First Year, I'd just reached the College entrance when I suddenly went completely blind;

'O dark, dark, dark, amid the blaze of noon,
Irrecoverably dark, total eclipse
Without all hope of day!'

Irrevocably dark? I wondered so.

A sudden end to a promising career, I told myself, stunned, but not unduly upset. I felt my way upstairs to my well-remembered room, then sat for some time at my desk. Wondering if splashing cold water on my face would help; touching the wall until the door was reached, my halting way was made to the lavatory wash basins. Blackness gradually turned to dun and before long, dim outlines slowly strengthened until eyesight fully returned. I packed and hauled a huge suitcase downhill to Roma Street station and the train home to Ipswich. As I sat down in the carriage, a violently intense headache struck, lasting until well after I'd struggled through the back gate of my home. I discovered in clinical years that I'd suffered a migraine. I've never had such a bad attack since: plenty of milder ones. Nowadays fortification spectra with little or no headache occasionally appear.

Second year: physiology and anatomy. The latter meant the dissecting room; the dissecting room meant bodies, but also Buckley's Canadiol Mixture. The cooling weather aggravated my cough so, forcing down a breath-taking sip of white sludge from a bottle in my locker, I'd don a white coat and enter the dissecting room

The cough dated back to my experiment with chlorine gas. That's where Buckley's came in. It tasted horrible and it's doubtful if it did any good, despite its claims: In blizzardly cold Canada where lives ... I once asked the doctor who'd taken me on his rounds what he thought of Buckley's. He quoted Banjo Patterson's snake bite cure poem:

'Half a teaspoon killed an emu; half a tumbler killed a goat;
All the snakes on earth were harmless with that powerful
antidote.'

I still took it.

Death now confronted us for the first time. For the next two years
we would be dissecting dead bodies, fortunate in that only four students
were allocated to each body, two to each side, a far more favourable ratio
than in most, if not all, other medical schools. It gave us a marvellous
opportunity to be familiarised with what goes where and does what in
our bodies.

Thorough anatomical knowledge is an absolute essential to good
practice, in every branch of medicine. Politics, scourge of mankind, has so
interfered in the teaching of medicine that in Britain today the teaching
of anatomy has almost been marginalised. Many British surgeons of the
future will, literally, be groping in the dark when they are forced to stray
beyond their normal remit or encounter some anatomical abnormality.
Diagnostic skills will also be seriously impaired.

As I write, the current issue of the *Royal College of Surgeons Bulletin* has
damning articles on this stupidity, quoting a survey which indicated that,
in Australia, the amount of litigation for malpraxis parallels the decline in
anatomical teaching: this idiocy is also affecting medical standards in Oz.

The other two basic studies underpinning any true knowledge of
the human body in health and disease, Physiology and Pathology are also
being dumbed down, giving way to such crap as communication skills. As
one senior member of the Profession remarked:

'What's the use of communication skills if there's nothing to
communicate?'

Wilkie, our anatomy professor, was actually a neuroanatomist, thus
not exactly full bottle on more mundane gross anatomy. I can still hear
the derisory cries when he once spoke of the eighth cervical vertebra—

there are eight cervical nerves but only seven cervical vertebrae. He did, however, know enough comparative anatomy to be able to tell us that he'd just dined in a reputable café. Ordering chicken, he was brought rabbit. He signalled the waitress:

'This is not chicken.'

'It is so!'

He prodded the preferred food with his fork:

'I am Professor of Anatomy at the University of Queensland. This is the gastrocnemius muscle of a rabbit.'

He won!

Of course close association with death resulted in various strategies to minimise the inevitable trauma. One of these—courtesy John, from Toowoomba—was a game of chance.

Summers here were very hot and the high ceilings of the dissecting room—formerly a Masonic temple—were littered with fans. The room was marked off into numbers which one selected, placing one's bets. All placed, a fair-sized portion of intestine was flung on to the whirling blades whence it—usually—flew off on to one or other number. Needless to say, this game was only played in the absence of teaching staff. On one hair-raising occasion the gut adhered to a fan blade and stubbornly refused to detach itself, despite a desperate turning on and off of the fan. Tensions rose when a lookout reported the impending arrival of a lecturer. It was only the quick witted help of an attendant (he and colleagues of course participated) who, like lightning, switched off the fans, produced a ladder and saved us from an unknown fate. When the panjandrum arrived, we were busily at work with scalpels and forceps.

Third year was much the same but more advanced.

Our building, on the corner of Albert and Alice Streets looked across Alice Street to the Botanic Gardens. In a yard at its rear, separated from lower Albert Street by a corrugated iron fence, a decrepit hut acted

as a common room. Seated on decaying chairs, many of us engaged
in a long running poker game, rather taking us away from dissection.
Possibly because the All High's awareness of this, we were suddenly told
that our dissection of the leg, to be completed by the end of that day,
would be marked, the results counting in the year's results. Fear struck
like a thunderbolt! For some forgotten reason I was, at that time, the
sole dissector of my side of the body. Nose alternately in Cunningham's
Anatomy and the leg, I strove with all my might, but at five pm the
dissection was at best half finished. Skulking around until six, when the
attendants were about to close the place, I hurtled down to the 'common
room' where my leg, securely wrapped but smelling strongly of formalin,
was secreted, threw it over the fence and then, at the speed of light, raced
through the main building and into Albert Street. It was still there! There
were usually few if any people about there at that time of day. Now came a
long walk to the corner of Edward and Adelaide streets, where the leg and
I caught the little matchbox tram to college.

The tram, so named from its shape and diminutive size, rattled
and growled from where I caught it up a steep hill to its terminus at the
Western end of Wickham Terrace. The faces of my fellow passengers were
black with suspicion. Students were never flavour of the month.

Once in my room, I dissected furiously for more than half the night
and, finally victorious, lugged the completed leg all the way back to the
so-called Anatomy School, not daring to brave the tram again in case
someone insisted that a suspicious-looking bundle be unwrapped. A
quick heave and it was over the fence and in its place by nine am, when
proceedings began. I passed!

During second and third years, virtually all of our time was spent
in the Anatomy and Physiology schools and walking between them.
This necessitated passing the Belle Vue Hotel, a lovely old building
since demolished by the Philistines of Government. Our favourite

barmaid was Flora. I still often felt ill in those days. Flora prescribed brandy lime and tonic and I must say that it did, at the very least, raise the spirits! Once, during biochemistry practicum. My partner and I, weighed down by indescribable boredom, repaired to the Belle Vue for inspiration. We took our seats in the private bar and ordered a couple of whiskies. As I raised my glass, I happened to glance at the occupant of the next door chair. It was Johnny Hines, our lecturer, obviously feeling the same way!

He had the habit of twitching his nose in the manner of a supercilious rabbit. His nose twitched now and thereafter we failed to recognise each other, but our drinks were downed rather hurriedly.

Fourth year meant promotion to the Medical School adjacent to the Royal Brisbane Hospital, our theory beginning to find its application: we'd entered clinical years. The theoretical subjects were pathology, medicine, tropical medicine, surgery, bacteriology, pharmacology and obstetrics and gynaecology, also a short course on pharmacy: learning to compound ointments and concoct mixtures in tribute to a dying art. I wonder how many chemists today know how to prepare mist senega et ammon carb or ung. BOZ?

At this moment we meet Jimmy Duhig, Professor of Pathology. An active round little ball of a man, he was a confirmed Communist—his uncle was the local Catholic Archbishop—but only occasionally subjected us to a political harangue.

A good, dedicated teacher, unfortunately for him and the teaching of Pathology in that university, he held altogether too busy an appointment at the hospital where he was expected to diagnose all of the pathology slides issuing from an institution of more than two thousand beds, unassisted and perform all of the post mortem examinations. He taught us at the same time—very well too—and conducted a private Pathology practice!

A most kindly man, he invited us all to participate in his post-mortem examinations. I never missed an opportunity, almost daily squeezing into his lovely Packard with umpteen others on the short journey to the post mortem room: a tremendous learning experience.

One day was most memorable. Jimmy had brought a hospital chart into the room:

'What do you think of this?'

It was a case of staphylococcal septicaemia, then inevitably fatal.

'Look at the temperature chart.'

It displayed the usual hectic character of that disease, but, instead of ending with a high spike and death, it subsided to normal in a day or two. Unbelievable! The reason? Jimmy had read of the development of a new wonder drug, penicillin and had prepared his own brew from the mould on an orange. Since that time over—and inappropriate—prescribing of the drug has bred the deadly MRSA which delightedly thrives on any and all of the penicillins.

Jimmy had a sad end. Because of his overwork—nobody could hope to cope with such a work load indefinitely—he misdiagnosed some pathology slides and, instead of being duly honoured for his magnificent achievements, was sacked from both posts. I understand that the successor in his Chair was totally hopeless.

Sic transit Gloria mundi!

Bacteriology was fascinating: growing cultures of many different bacteria, learning their nutritional and environmental preferences and, making slides of them, studying them under the microscope.

This discipline carried a bonus in alcohol-deprived wartime days. Sitting in the lab was a large demijohn of absolute alcohol in tenth normal hydrochloric acid. When a revel was projected, I'd siphon off some of this mixture, titrate off the acid and turn it into two beverages: pseudo Advocaat and ersatz cherry brandy. Mixing the two with ginger

ale made for a most pleasant if potent draught: ruptured rooster. No
hangovers!

Most at those alcoholic affairs were lovers of classical music and
records were played throughout the evening.

Early forties gramophone technology: one side of twelve inch
records, the largest, played on a simple acoustic gramophone at seventy-
eight revolutions a minute lasted about three and three quarters minutes.
Most people used steel needles but, to prolong the relatively expensive
records' lives we used cane needles which had to be sharpened after each
use. Indeed, if the work being played had notable tuttis the needle would
often pack it in before that side came to an end. Sharpening a needle with
a special little gadget which used a fine emery wheel rotated by hand, and
winding the gramophone furiously just before the end of a side was a full-
time occupation. When the vinyl LP records arrived, long movements as
in the *Eroica*, for instance, took on an entirely different character.

The two senior teaching physicians were as different as chalk is from
cheese: Professor Alex Murphy, thin, dapper, precise, rather precious
and a little affected and Otto Hirschfeld who perhaps overdid occerness,
but whose overflowing humaneness couldn't be concealed. As fat as his
colleague was thin, he was a wizard at treating diabetes. He also taught us
Pharmacology: the science behind therapeutics. One day he said to us:

> 'Wuz at th' races last Satdee (he always was) an' I said ter me
> mate:
> 'jus take a look at that 'orse's pupils' 'He gestured
> extravagantly with his hands 'They were as big as saucers:
> doped, yer see. I said: 'put yer shirt on 'im!' I made a packet!
> See: it pays ter know yer Pharmacology!'

At my final vivas I went to Murphy first, then went over to Otto:

> 'Ow'd yer get on with JC?' He asked, concealing a smile.

He was actually something of a Patrician, far from the common clay
he aped. He died of a dissecting aneurysm of the thoracic aorta: not long

after being ejected from his heart into the aorta, blood had found a weak spot in that great artery, splitting its wall as it travelled along between its layers.

He instantly knew what it was. His problem was probably inoperable even today. Alex Murphy was called in:

'You'll be all right, Otto.'

'You know I won't, Alex.'

I was very fortunate during my clinical years as a student. I came from Ipswich, Queensland and had met the Medical Superintendent of the local hospital, Dr. Trumpy, a couple of times, so took it upon myself to ask him if I might be permitted to trail around the wards after him at weekends. Instead of this, he instructed me to admit all patients who weren't very seriously ill and prescribe their treatment. Of course one of the resident doctors would study my case histories and treatment and sign them before any action was taken, but this was a wonderful piece of luck which helped boost my confidence—and clinical knowledge—to the nth degree.

On one noteworthy occasion he allowed me, himself assisting, to remove an appendix. He was incredibly self-restrained, probably because he didn't want to destroy my confidence when performing an operation at that early stage of my career. To his junior medical staff, he was something else again. The patient is anaesthetised.

'Ready?' to the anaesthetist.

'Yes, sir.'

The doctor makes an incision, failing to sever the skin completely.

'Cut it, son, cut it! Come on, cut it. For Christ's sake cut it.'

This is done, with inevitable bleeding.

'Oh, Christ, oh, Jesus! She's bleeding to death. Quick, quick. Sister, give him those Spencer Wells (the standard artery forceps). Oh, Jesus'

And so on.

Tall, plump and with a head bald as a billiard ball, he was most kindly at heart. Patients were always his prime concern and he knew the details of every patient in the hospital. Every night, after a resident had performed his night round, he would phone him and ask penetrating questions of each and every problem patient.

Every Sunday at lunchtime the resident doctors were invited to dine with him and his statuesque wife.

His matron was as formidable as he, again solely concerned with patient welfare. I've studied in; worked in numerous hospitals in various parts of the world. Never was there another hospital which came anywhere near the level of patient care—and good results—as was enjoyed by the patients at Ipswich Hospital. Not coincidently, the senior sisters in the hospital were all cast in the same mould. For them, the patient's welfare was all that mattered. They knew and cared about all of them, each and every one. They were wonderful, loving, caring, even saintly in their own earthy way.

Kitty Evans, down to earth and like many, keen on the horses, knew as much as any doctor. If a patient could be saved, Kitty would do it.

Millie Thoms, senior Theatre sister, was feared by all excepting Trump. The compelling eyes over her mask said it all. Woe betide the resident doctor if they hadn't received the message!

Contrast this with some of the Yanks I had to deal with in Saudi Arabia. They did nothing but sit on their fat arses all day, telling each other about the patients in approved post-modern style but knowing precious little about them in reality. When I did my rounds—at one specific ward in particular—I didn't trouble them: it would have been such an effort for one of them to hoist herself clear of her seat, so, with my interpreter and all of the case histories I made my rounds and put my orders into the hospital computer without further ado.

When I, a green student, entered one of the wards of Ipswich Hospital, the sister—who knew fifty times as much as I—and the nurses would stand smartly to attention. Reprehensible, old time imperialist stuff? Absolutely not. Everyone knew that I was just a kid. It was all about discipline and it was discipline—and love—that made everything function so effectively: correct medicines administered in their prescribed dose and at the correct time; patients clean and comfortable; wards spotless; staff alert to any possible crises which might affect a particular patient.

When, later, I was senior surgical consultant there, that same matron dragged a tear-stained nurse into my outpatients' department one afternoon. She gave me the eye. I was to bawl the girl out. In theatrically shocked and incredulous tones Matron told me that the nurse had given a patient a sleeping tablet twice the prescribed dose. This was actually still well within the safety limits but that wasn't the point. Careless in checking the orders, she'd made a serious blunder. After my effort she was taken to doctor Trumpy, a past master of the art of verbally flaying people alive. I'd warrant she never made another mistake.

Contrast that with an experience about thirty years later when I was Orthopaedic Consultant at Port Augusta Hospital. Because the nursing staff had failed to carry out my instructions, a dangerously ill patient very nearly bled to death. When, with the intention of improving the abysmal standard of nursing there, I began to point out where things went wrong, my serious, detailed criticism was cut off in full flight. I was more or less told to shut up or else. I'll tell you more about that later.

As a student I was also very fortunate in that a senior surgeon at the Brisbane Hospital, George Brandis, kindly took me under his wing. He'd been a practitioner in Ipswich years before and my father had apparently done him a good turn which he now repaid by suggesting that I attend his outpatient clinics and operating sessions. His teaching was thorough, witty and forthright, like the man himself. His handwriting was ghastly, somewhat resembling a seismograph reading during a grade nine earthquake on the *Richter* scale. For some inexplicable reason I could read it and sometimes, when it was beyond the capabilities of the hospital office, they'd seek me out for a translation. He was a big thing in my student life, his teaching quite phenomenally good. I never missed an opportunity to be with him.

From this time onward, for about fifty years, acquiring a knowledge of disease, the response of the human body to it and the surgical implications of that in particular dominated.

The doyen of the surgeons at Brisbane hospital at that time was Charlie Lilley, of a wealthy, oldish family, the most notable having been a Premier of Queensland. An unkind newspaper cartoon of the latter's time had as its caption:

'Consider the Lillies of the field, how they grow: they toil not, neither do they spin.'

Charlie did toil. A first class general surgeon, his forte, stealing the thyroid, has been mentioned.

An operation is seldom needed for this condition, thyrotoxicosis, nowadays. There are satisfactory medical treatments.

Charlie had a fiery temper. In those days there were no throwaway scalpel blades and each knife had to be sharpened after every operation and sometimes this task wasn't performed to perfection, to say the least. One day when I was watching, he was given one scalpel after another, none meeting with his approval. He finally flung one with considerable force across the room.

'Scalpel, sister. You know I need a scalpel. Where's the scalpel?'

'Sticking in the door, sir!'

And it was.

Temper seems to have been a family failing. My mother taught with his sister at the Ipswich Girls' Grammar School. Miss Lilley's temper tantrums were legendary and when they were turned on, the whole school fell silent listening, rapt, to the performance.

Charlie drove a large car and, when he did, affected a dustcoat. He was by no means young and this habit was no doubt acquired in the days of open tourer cars. It amused us to see E.T, an aspiring young surgeon wear one as soon as he was appointed to the consultant staff. More of him later.

The standard of surgery was very high, techniques and knowledge right up to the minute. Our Professor, Nipper Sutton, was another fine teacher, but when teaching on his ward rounds, couldn't be accused of brevity. I well remember trying everything I knew to ease the aching of my knees as I stood interminably around successive beds. A first class surgeon, he even performed some chest surgery—highly hazardous at that time— using dangerous high spinal anaesthesia.

Patient sitting, anaesthetic of a lighter specific gravity than cerebrospinal fluid is injected. Ensuing numbness is carefully monitored until the necessary level is reached. The patient is then upended until the tissues 'fix' the anaesthetic: numbness moved no further. Its ascent to too high a level would be fatal. To my knowledge he always cheated death. Such operations were usually limited to permanently collapsing tuberculous lungs.

All of my teachers were firm believers in clinical acumen. One took a full history, inspected and examined the patient thoroughly, irrespective of the time this might take. With adequate thought, an accurate diagnosis can then usually be made.

On one occasion, the new Professor of Medicine called Nipper in consultation. He offered all manner of tests and diagnostic gismos. Nipper merely shook his head and held up his hands:

'No thank you, I have these.'

The other senior surgeon was 'Nelly' Lee, so called because of his gentle, girlish voice. This far from matched his character. I thought that he was sometimes very brutal. Once, when I watched him operate, he looked up at the anaesthetist: in matter of fact, quavering girlish diction:

'Oh, doctor: the patient's dead up this end. What's he like up yours?'

The war obviously clouded student days. Though, full of youthful exuberance, we had our moments, these were muted and in many ways restrained. At the end of my first year I volunteered for the 7th Field Ambulance, obviously non-combatant: I strongly disapprove of killing, whether it be in war or any other time. I was paraded before Colonel Scholes:

'Finish your course, boy and then volunteer.'

I was lucky. That unit found itself in the way of advancing Japanese. On another volunteering occasion fortune smiled again. The war wasn't going well and the fact that mine was a reserved occupation was overlooked. I was accepted, subject to a medical examination. The examining doctor knew of my old medical history and rejected me. The unit spent the remainder of the war meandering around the Western Australian desert.

We did have our fun, but the war cast a shadow over our youth, especially when, one by one, our friends were killed.

Rotating Internship

The graduation ceremony was memorable for one reason only: the State Premier, Forgan Smith, self-appointed Chancellor of the University chaired the ceremony. Tired and emotional, his mortar board was on wrong way round and when we tipped ours at him, he fumbled in vain to be able to raise his in return.

Allocated a post at Brisbane General Hospital, I inevitably was given a place in George's team (George Brandis). He strictly insisted upon very high, standards, the patient's interests his prime concern.

His ideas and disciplines were inherited from his mentor, Ernest Miles who in turn sat at the feet of the great Hilton, author of the seminal 'Rest and Pain'.

George was primarily a proctologist, which means that his forte was surgery of the lower bowel and for this reason, of course, he operated upon piles aplenty. He did this with great skill at a time when surgeons were wont to make a hash of this. He did, of course, do a great deal of general surgery as well. He insisted upon keeping his hernia patients in bed for three weeks post operatively: unnecessary and totally impossible today where hospital beds are at a premium.

His *magnum opus* was abdomino-perineal resection of the rectum for cancer. This is a major undertaking even today, with its greater knowledge of blood, fluid and electrolyte replacement and the availability of broad spectrum antibiotics. At that time, the mortality rate of this operation was high: not with George. Even in this public hospital he insisted that patients undergoing the operation be nursed in a small, private side ward. All windows had to be kept closed:

'There's nothing in stuffy air that isn't in fresh air excepting the seeds of pneumonia!'

This in a curious high-pitched voice, a cross between a squeak and a rasp. For most of the time he looked out of eyes that were full of sardonic good humour—but his standards couldn't be breached.

On one occasion, as a student, I'd turned up as usual at his outpatient department, feeling proud at having built an electronic amplifier to replace my acoustic gramophone. The soldering had stained my hands and he spotted this immediately:

'What's on your hands?'

'They're stained from soldering sir. I've been making an amplifier for my records.'

'Engineering and surgery don't mix.'

He was right, but only at that time. For instance, the great Charnley, inventor of what's probably still the best hip replacement, called in an engineer when his early hip operations began to squeak.

One evening he wasn't happy about an unusually difficult piles operation. Feeling that she might possibly bleed in the night. He told his registrar:

'Watch her very carefully. If she does bleed, insert a large bore rubber tube.'

Not the best of registrars, when the patient duly bled, he didn't look carefully for a large tube, inserting two smaller ones instead. Next morning, George, examining the patient, turned to the registrar with a look of wild surmise:

'What's this?' (His usual question, in intimidating intonation, when he disapproved.)

'I couldn't find a large tube, sir, so inserted two smaller ones.'

'Very artistic' this in an admiring tone, 'just like the figure eight.' His voice changed dramatically. 'But why didn't you insert three tubes and make it look like the bloody ace of clubs?'

The war having ended, army personnel were trickling back to civilian life. One such was the new sister in charge of one of his wards. She was an ogre who continuously obstructed George's progress in a teaching round. At its end, he looked sadly round at his students, the sister still hovering near:

> 'In-ther-good-old-days, they called bitches witches and
> burned the bastards.'

Sound homespun philosophy there, I thought.

He was committee member of a turf club, so, when the usual course surgeon couldn't attend, I took his place. He gave me this advice:

> 'If a jockey falls hitting his head, don't worry. There'll be nothing in there to be injured!'

On my becoming engaged to be married, he wrote a congratulatory note:

> 'The testicle is mightier than the cerebrum.'

I did have some say as to which teams I'd be allocated, so these were predominantly surgical and I was spared the dread Obstetrics. However, my next, unsought, job was in anaesthetics, in those days, rag-and-bottle style.

Reams of gauze were wrapped around an oval, domed metal framework

(Schimmelbusch mask) and placed over the patient's face. Ethyl chloride was sprayed. When the patient, strapped to the trolley, ceased to count, the mask was flooded with ether, then dripped on at a variable rate. The patient underwent a stage of excitation, strong men requiring the combined strength of wardsman, anaesthetist and attendant nurse—occasionally others as well—to keep the struggling patient on the trolley.

The depth of anaesthesia of course depended upon the rate at which the ether was dripped. This was judged by the size of the patient's pupils and the respirations' depth and nature. For an abdominal operation, the surgeon required muscles to be as relaxed as possible, in other words, for the patient to be at death's door. Some surgeons were worse than others in their insistent demands that the patient be relaxed ever further. A struggle of wills, not without heat, between surgeon and anaesthetist not seldom resulted.

The end result was that patients usually vomited when recovering, sometimes so severely that suture lines were badly stressed, wounds sometimes even rupturing.

To avoid this, a gynaecologist I'd been allocated demanded chloroform anaesthesia: highly dangerous and much overrated. Its only virtue was that patients seldom vomited postoperatively.

A different, much more open mask was used. Administering it was a waking nightmare, putting it mildly. Death's common, due to ventricular fibrillation of the heart, whose musculature quivers instead of beating, with rapidly fatal results. Fibrillation is preceded by a halving and doubling of the heart rate, but the patient isn't properly anaesthetised until this occurs, so the unhappy anaesthetist sits, finger on the carotid artery, hoping for the best but assuredly fearing the worst, as the pulse duly halves and doubles. Nightmare? What an understatement! Imagine the relief when that was all over!

The anaesthetist, of course, inhaled the vapours., something I really enjoyed!

Next was the Children's Hospital, where one served for twice as long a time as in the other teams.

Diphtheria was still not uncommon and there was an epidemic of a dangerous parenteral diarrhoea amongst infants, not due to bowel infection, but, to 'mastoiditis'. Inverted commas were used because in young infants the mastoid process—behind the ear—is rudimentary.

There were so many cases that we, relatively raw, residents, were instructed in the art of chiselling away the bone until the upper part of the mastoid was exposed and the sticky, purulent exudate removed.

Penicillin wasn't yet in general use. Introduced at about the end of my term at the Children's, it had to be administered by painful injection, through needles which must have seemed to the quailing, struggling little patients to have the calibre of a twelve gauge shotgun. Doctors had to give it and it was harrowing. The poor kids howled with the pain afterward. The standard dose then was 15000 units injected every three hours—as compared with a million or more today. A special, rather crude long-acting version had been prepared for children to spare them a three hourly ordeal- hence the enormous needle.

Diphtheria could present as an emergency. The membrane formed by it sometimes spreads downwards from the throat until it blocks the airway, necessitating immediate tracheotomy. We were shown how to perform that operation. The patient was watched with utmost vigilance and when the sister saw that a tracheotomy was necessary she rang the tracheotomy bell, sounding all over the hospital. We all rushed for the ward, the winner performing the deed. You may be sure that this race was always to the swift, all breaking our necks to be there first.

Anaesthesia's out: the patient blue, chest convulsing desperately in an effort to draw in life-giving air. The throat rapidly cut; strap muscles of the throat separated: time absolutely of the essence and a cut made in the cartilaginous rings of the trachea. A towel is held over the wound whilst special forceps are inserted into the windpipe; blades then separated.

A tremendous spasm of coughing and spluttering follows, diptheritic membrane coughed all over the place—hence the towel. Some escapes, occasionally hitting the surrounding staff, but that ah, so precious air is drawn into the lungs, blueness giving way to a healthy pink. An articulated metal tube is quickly inserted and strapped into place.

The Children's received difficult cases from all over Queensland, mostly congenital abnormalities, some of which we'll see later.

I was attached to the surgical service which included Orthopaedics. My Orthopod, an overtly timid little man had a quiet voice, but a heart of steel, horrid. He was hopeless at dealing with club foot, though admittedly the best methods hadn't yet been devised.

I was appalled by his treatment of 'bandy' legs. A degree of bandyness is normal in young children, usually correcting itself with growth. This idiot, using a kind of padded pivot; would put the poor kid's leg on it, pressing hard until it broke, giving a funny little laugh. He'd then plaster it until it healed. He offered me the job. I refused.

All junior doctors there took it in turn at barbaric tonsillectomy sessions. A special hut was set aside for this slaughter. The little victims, premedicated and in white hospital gowns, would sit dejectedly on a bench running around the anteroom. They were firstly inspected for rotten teeth: there were always lots of them. This was an essential step: a diseased tooth, dislodged or broken during the operation and subsequently inhaled into the lungs would be disastrous.

There were two in the team, taking it in turn to operate or give the anaesthetic. There were no nurses to help. The victim anaesthetised, all bad teeth rapidly removed, was hurriedly carried into the theatre. During the dental extraction no anaesthetic (rag and bottle) could be given: time was of the essence. The child's placed on the operating table, a mouth gag inserted holds down the tongue, giving a view of the tonsils, illuminated by the operator's headlamp. A spring hanging from the ceiling, attached to the gag's handle holds the kid's head in the right position, to the bababababababa of the little pump blowing air through ether; through a hole in the tongue depressor into the patient's lungs. Tonsillectomy completed and serious bleeding staunched, the adenoids are scraped out with a special instrument. The gag's removed and the limp little body laid on one side in the recovery position on another bench out of view of the victims-to-be, blood exuding from mouth and nose We had to be quick and the system did work, God help us!

The hours we worked were very long in every team. Sometimes exhausted, no one complained: we were learning in a vast, complicated field. Now politics' intrusion is doing untold harm, as ever. In England, always following the letter of the law—even if stupid or unjust—the European Working Time Regulations are slavishly followed, limiting trainee doctors' working time to forty-eight hours a week, not nearly enough for a proper learning experience. Patients in the next generation will suffer.

Our most sleep-deprived job was in Casualty—more commonly called E.R. The hospital was huge by any standards, so one was called out many times at all hours of the night. Drug overdosing was virtually non-existent, a couple of regular paraldehyde addicts excepted. Drunken injuries, accidents and acute medical and surgical emergencies were the grist to our midnight mill.

During the day most of our work was to do with lacerations, abscesses, simpler fractures and coughs and colds. More serious problems were routed directly into the hospital wards or specialist clinics, the necessary decision being made by a registrar.

Registrars sometimes allowed us to set the simpler wrist fractures. For these and minor procedures needing anaesthesia—usually the opening of abscesses—there was a machine called the Heidelberg, dated 1897. People nowadays would be gaoled for using such a monstrosity but we had no option. It delivered a mixture of nitrous oxide and oxygen and, for longer cases, ether could be added. So awful was the machine that, before the patient became unconscious, they would go various shades of blue, often so dark that it was almost black. This encouraged great speed. Many patients smiled on beginning to recover. I'd often say:

'Silly, isn't it?'

They'd chuckle and agree. Nitrous oxide is laughing gas.

A series of hooks hung from the rafters in one section of Cas, a relic of the recent time when 606, arsphenamine, Ehrlich's magic bullet, was used to treat Syphilis. This drug required a large volume of fluid for its safe administration. Bullet? More like a howitzer shell! We were sometimes called upon to administer its successor, neoarsphenamine, for this condition. It came in ampoules marked with the eagle grasping a swastika: obviously war booty. For Syphilis affecting the Central Nervous system we used Tryparsemide: toxic, but something is better than nothing for such a destructive disease. Penicillin hadn't as yet been accepted as the treatment of choice and wasn't used for some little time afterwards.

My brother was in the army at the time. Before he was sent overseas he told me that he'd had, the previous night over dinner, an extraordinary conversation with a fellow officer.

'He was making the most fantastic claims, especially about his own capabilities. I thought of him as a mine of misinformation.'

'Have him take a Wassermann test. It sounds like GPI to me.'

(General Paresis of the Insane, after the spirochaete's depredations upon the brain). It transpired that he was WR++++, thus disappearing from my brother's ken.

After Cas, as we called it, I did a stint with Otto Hirschfeld, the very sage physician already mentioned. His forte was diabetes, but all kinds of medical ailments were admitted to his wards: long, rectangular rooms with beds ranged around their periphery, the sister's desk being at the end, nearest to the entrance. There was a balcony along one side, crammed with beds, a pleasant enough place in summertime; much the reverse in winter.

Most people there were Tuberculosis sufferers: the disease being much more common then, though, thanks to AIDS, numbers are increasing significantly again. I remember a couple of patients in particular who were suffering badly. Their larynxes had been affected, making both speech and swallowing difficult.

Streptomycin had just been discovered but was tightly restricted. I prayed that it might be given to these poor women who were suffering badly. I'd moved on before decisions had been made. Streptomycin is toxic to the nerve of hearing, many patients becoming deaf as a result of this treatment. Like most antibiotics, bacterial resistance has developed. A number of other, less toxic and more effective drugs have been developed, but new strains of the causative bacillus now resist just about everything. Bacterial resistance is becoming universal with the gravest of consequences.

My last hurrah at BGH, now Royal Brisbane, was with another surgical team: Mordo Sutton, brother of Nipper, blessed with a very different personality from his more earnest sibling; Konrad Hirschfeld, Otto's brother, very appropriately nicknamed King Kong and Graham (I think) Hogg, junior consultant Urologist.

Konrad was a nice man but came over as being slightly manic. He had a dearth of patients to cut up and told me to scour the wards in merely a hospital of more than two thousand beds in the care of decidedly territorial consultants, for candidates for his knife. I failed to carry out his instructions.

One reason for the dearth was both his enthusiasm and continual complaints about bizarre symptoms he claimed to suffer: colleagues thought him odd: until a clever clinician diagnosed chronic appendicitis. At operation the offending organ was found to be firmly adherent to his rectum: hence his weird symptoms. The operation was a great though temporary source of gossip. He was completely rehabilitated.

The difference between the two urologists was remarkable: the younger, more earnest; not yet quite on top of his game, especially when it came to transurethral prostatectomy, a relatively recent procedure which obviated the need to cut the patient's abdomen. A rigid tube (operating cystoscope) is passed up the patient's urethra into the bladder which, together with the prostate is inspected. Small pieces are then progressively cut from the enlarged prostate, each piece washed out by fluid run from a flask fastened overhead which constantly irrigates the bladder—and often the legs of the surgeon too. Blood stained in varying degrees, fluid flows out of an orifice in the cystoscope out through a drainage tube. Though surgeons wore plastic aprons, wet pants were common.

Initially a cold punch did the cutting, but as this often caused excessive bleeding, the hot wire was devised: a loop of metal which became red hot when the surgeon pressed a pedal. Rotating a small wheel caused the cutting wire to be drawn through the gland. I was lucky to see both methods. Mr. Hogg (Piggy, of course), the junior, wasn't nearly as adept as Mordo, a man eccentric to his eyebrows. An inveterate smoker, he smoked whilst scrubbing up, mask hanging loose. Scrubbing completed, he'd say:

'Now I'll kick a goal.'

Dropping the fag, he'd kick it with his foot, unerringly into a trash can.

'Raise my visor, Sister!'

And a sister would tie up his mask.

He nominated the size of each piece of prostate as he cut, according to the size of fish:

'This one's a mackerel. This one's only a whiting. Oh! This one's a shark! A whale!!'

Always the same: never put out, always joking; always utterly expert.

Sometimes a prostate required operating from above, retropubic prostatectomy being the preferable method. Technically more difficult than operations which required the bladder to be opened (suprapubic), the adenoma (the enlargement) was removed by cutting through the covering of the gland behind the pubic bone. The space here is very restricted; the chance of serious bleeding high. For this, Mordo had invented a special retractor which he called the Flying Saucer. This broadly described its shape. When he died, I bought it for old time's sake and used it a few times.

He kindly let me perform a great many operations, for which I have always been most grateful. In particular he taught me the art of cystoscopy and the means by which one could identify the ureteric orifices, through which urine from the kidneys enters the bladder. It's often necessary to pass fine catheters into the ureters, especially to perform retrograde pyelography: radio-opaque dye, injected via the catheter, outlines the kidney's collecting system, helping identify abnormalities.

His ward rounds could be hilarious. He loved joking with the patients, in a way only somebody absolutely on the top of his game can be. For instance: talking to a patient, the subject of meat pies came up, don't ask me how:

'There's only one way to eat them: you cut a small hole in the top and pour in Worcester sauce. Holding it to your ear whilst shaking it, you make sure it's mixed properly before you eat it.'

Patient: 'So you like meat pies then, do you sir?'

'Me?? Good Lord no. I hate the things!'

Apart from Mordo, some senior registrars thought that, nearing the end of my term, I could be trusted to do some of the easier abdominal operations such as appendicectomy and repairing ruptured peptic ulcers, not that either of them is necessarily easy!

Ruptured ulcer is easy to diagnose. The patient is stricken with sudden, agonising abdominal pain. When the abdomen is examined, its muscles are tightly contracted: 'board-like rigidity'. Despite this, bad clinicians do miss the diagnosis; after a time the rigidity disappears. The patient is now gravely ill.

When the abdomen is opened, fragments of food often meet one's gaze: I've not seldom seen green peas floating around.. One's search soon finds a hole in the stomach; sometimes the duodenum, the surrounding tissues being swollen and hard. All that's necessary is to clean up the peritoneum, stitch over the hole with omentum: a peritoneal fold, close up and insert a naso-gastric suction tube. Fluid replacement must, of course, be given, together with antibiotics.

George Brandis kindly kept in occasional touch throughout my time there, always stressing the need to go to England to study for my surgical fellowship. This needed money and I didn't wish to be a continuing drag upon my parents—and I'm a natural-born vagabond—so I applied for a position in the Northern Territory Medical Service: not only better paid; it promised adventure.

Whilst waiting, I spent a few months at dear old Ipswich General, no doubt working very hard. The clearest of my few memories of that time, however, is the bed in which I was supposed to sleep when on duty. The middle of it nearly touched the floor. My back never fully recovered.

I remember a comment made at that time by Dr. Trumpy. When outpatients department became very busy he'd help out in the clinics. One of the medical officers, Angus, was painfully slow. Trump turned up to take morning tea with us late one morning: we were civilized in those days. One couldn't say that he was entirely chuffed:

'I've seen more than sixty patients this morning. Angus has seen five and psychoanalysed the bloody lot!'

FLYING AND CUTTING IN THE NORTHERN TERRITORY

My appointment finally confirmed, I rang the Chief Medical Officer in Darwin. He told me that I'd been appointed to Katherine Hospital. I decided to drive there in the green Austin eight my parents had given me on my graduation. My mother saw us off on a late October afternoon, no doubt with misgivings.

A violent stormy front was passing. Wind and rain assaulted the car, shaking it and strewing the road with leaves and, more importantly, branches, which had to be dodged. We made it to Roma that night.

Next day, tarmac having run out, we churned, often crab-wise through sodden black soil. Why we weren't bogged's a mystery. The following day saw us into increasingly dryer country, but the gears became terribly stiff to shift until it was difficult to negotiate a hill. Calling in at a village large enough to sport a garage, I was told that my gearbox was bone dry. Humanity is frail. The route to Darwin had always been in doubt as road maps of the time didn't indicate that there was actually a road all of the way, with gaps and dotted lines interrupting the roads in central and North Western Queensland. However, I felt that there had to be some way of getting through. I nevertheless wanted the car to be at its best, so entrusted it to a relation's friend—and occasional drinking companion. He—or a minion—had drained, but neglected to fill—my gearbox.

One evening, travelling along a virtually unmade road, a storm developed over to our right and moved ever closer. If the road became wet, we would be bogged, so, one eye on the storm, I gave the little car all it had. Unfortunately my eyes became too preoccupied with the weather and I failed to take a cattle grid properly. This construction obviates obstructive gates and usually consists of a hole in the road with locomotive rails placed across it to prevent cattle crossing into someone else's paddock. This one was an economy one: there were short rails on either side. My right rear wheel missed the rails with a resounding thump! We came to a shuddering halt with the tire destroyed and the rear axle set obliquely across the car. This had caused all of the mechanical brakes to seize and we were miles from nowhere with an advancing storm.

When I'd jacked up the car to replace the tyre, I could just make out, amid the encircling gloom, the fractured centre bolt of the rear spring and the problem with the brake cables, which I released, allowing us to crawl, crab-wise, into the next town which, providentially, was Mount Isa, This allowed us a couple of days' respite after prolonged pummelling from bad and non-existent roads whilst the car was repaired. All would be tarmac from now on!

After Mount Isa, the road lay, with straight stretches many miles long, across a semi-arid landscape of red soil and straggling greyish green vegetation.

This had been and, indeed, apart from the present town, still was, a wilderness, places to sleep few and far between. Beggars couldn't be choosers and one became acquainted with pubs constructed entirely of corrugated iron sheeting, too cool during the night but absolute furnaces in the daytime. We'd entered the tropics.

The maps had been accurate and there'd been times when, far from anywhere, the 'road' would dissolve into numerous tracks leading to all points of the compass. No problem! Tracks lined with broken beer bottles invariably led us in the right direction.

When travelling across a plain towards the end of our severe shaking, we were enthralled to encounter a flock of brolgas: a variety of crane and their air-light, delicate dancing.

Mount Isa, an important mining town was embraced as some kind of Mecca. Thence there'd be no more navigating cavernous holes or jutting rocks; guessing which of several ill-defined tracks to follow.

When, later, I was consulting in Ipswich, a patient, tough and grizzled, told me that he'd ridden across this part of the country ages ago and was the first to exploit the mineralisation. I resisted the temptation to ask how rich he was. Mount Isa mines, now deep into the bowels of the earth, have produced fortunes in silver and lead.

Thence the tarmac, unremittingly straight, ended in a T junction. We turned left, to overnight in the gold mining town of Tennant Creek.

After a latish start: we'd watched Gene Kelly singin' in the rain at an open-air cinema, lunch was taken at 6a Bore: a single dwelling offering accommodation of sorts. The menu: goat or nothing, reminded me of a joke of my father: at a table in a similar establishment the guests were approached by the owner/waiter/chef:

'There's goat or galah. Goat's orf. What'll yers 'ave?'

We had surprisingly good goat.

Overnighted at Dunmarra station which put up PGs. on looking out of the window at dawn next morning an incredible sight gave one pause. Here was a large lagoon in semi-arid country. Gathered around it, each species within its own territory, were the entire wildlife of the area: kangaroo with kangaroo; wallaby with wallaby; each parrot type with its own; predators, too, taking no advantage of the situation. Each group in turn advanced to the lagoon to drink, the whole process conducted in an amazingly orderly fashion. Humans haven't the wit to be so civilized.

Our objective, Katherine cottage hospital, functioned under the watchful eyes of two nursing sisters, both late of Rev. Flynn's Australian Inland Mission, the hospital itself a rambling bungalow with a tiny cottage for the nurses next door.

The high-set doctor's residence was perhaps a hundred yards away. All were situated on the steep red banks of the Katherine River.

Not long previously, Flying Doctor Fenton had looked after the place. Eccentric, like so many there at that time, he'd owned a Tiger Moth aeroplane, using it to perpetrate many antics, such as flying low along the streets of Darwin and, bombing friends or acquaintances with bags of flour. The movie theatre in Darwin was unofficially segregated: the whites sat upstairs under cover in a two story tin shack to the rear, whilst the indigines sat in canvas chairs under the stars. Fenton, on occasion, would dive in front of the rear accommodation, fly low across the open space and then pull up just in time to miss the screen.

I conversed one day with one of his old drinking companions:

'We run outa beer one night. 'Let's go ter Broome'—on the Westralian coast, hundreds of miles South West—' 'n get a couple more cases.' 'e sez, So we did. I never saw th' place meself.'

Fenton decided to fly to China: quite a flight in such a plane. He was refused permission by the authorities, so, without a word, he built auxiliary tanks on to the plane—refuelling points were few and far between—and simply took off. An eyewitness told me that he saw the heavily laden plane only just skimming the waves until he was out of sight. He apparently said later that he couldn't gain any altitude for a long time and was a little worried in case he was caught by a larger than usual wave.

Early next morning, I wakened to a roar close over my head, followed by a disembodied screech: obviously the Last Trump. It was actually the daily DC3 flight to Adelaide. A strong up-draught from the river and the shortness of the airstrip, with a hill at its far end, obliged the pilot to skim the roof of the house, then bang the plane down at the proximal end of the strip. Katherine was one of several small towns visited en route,

Nobody had made the suggestion, but it seemed *comme il faut* to present myself to my Darwin bosses. Firstly, bringing some order to the chaotic dispensary. I was struck by the great quantity and variety of contraceptives—the pill hadn't as yet seen the light of day—and assumed in my innocence that a beneficent Territorial administration provided them free to people in outlying places.

We left for Darwin next morning, two hundred and twenty miles away, witnessing many whirlwinds: sudden circular agitations of leaves and charcoal briefly scuttling around before ascending:into dark columns of detritus busily revolving, high into the sky, then wandering across the terrain. The charcoal was from fires, lit by lightning or human, which burnt off vegetation desiccated by the fierce sun at the end of the previous wet season. The imminent next wet hadn't as yet arrived.

After about three hours, we were joined on our left by a black, serpentine pipeline: Darwin's water supply from the Manton dam, well to the West.

Arrived at the city in early afternoon, I presented myself to the Chief Medical Officer, learning that, though there were two chiefs, I'd be the only Indian. Obviously Darwin would be my main place of work, Katherine being handled in my spare time. I didn't meet the Medical Superintendent, until next day. He was always drunk by lunchtime. He rehabilitated himself when posted to more civilized surroundings.

It was in Darwin that I began learning about bureaucracy. My first lesson was that my two bosses were scions of senior medical bureaucrats who'd seen to it that their beloved offspring were strategically placed as the army left the Territory as the War was ending and civilians were allowed back. Both were then totally hopeless: one a drunk; the other a compulsive womaniser. I had sense of this when my chief turned pink about the ears when I innocently expressed surprise at the abundance of contraceptives at Katherine hospital. My mind ran riot thinking of the possibilities. Orgies at the hospital seemed more than likely. Who participated other than the CMO? Surely the Medical Superintendent wouldn't have been up to it. The softly spoken, seemingly demure, nurses behaved impeccably, and both came from a Presbyterian environment— but there was the evidence! Never underestimate the strength of the sex urge. The contraceptives had disappeared.by my next visit.

I soon realised that, in effect, other than Alice Springs, I ran the Northern Territory Medical Service. I allocated one day a week for Katherine, Darwin for the remainder of the week.

What was left of my first day was spent settling in, so, having been directed to our residence, no doubt arranged extemporaneously: I'd taken off for Darwin without notifying the brass.

A shower seemed a good idea, so I turned on the only tap—there was no hot water system—promptly scalding myself. That black pipeline didn't deploy itself across sun-baked soil for nothing. Early morning showers would be the order of the day.

For the first, but not the last, time the house offered by a kindly government was almost uninhabitable. An early mix of stone and fibro, it was host to an unimaginably high concentration of cockroaches. I complained and was given instead a pleasant house on stilts overlooking the bay.

Before it was ready I got to know a neighbour who, for want of a better word, existed behind that first house. He was a recent arrival, having been a prisoner of war of the Japs. A beneficent government, undoubtedly wanting to honour his sacrifice and ensure that he felt at home, dumped him in a facility-free gunya-like heap of rubbish that would have been in no way superior to his prison quarters.

On my second day, the CMO asked if I'd like to fly to Bathurst Island. Not an order, on reflection, I decided yes. Why not?

'Jack Slade's waiting outside in his car.'

Grabbing my stethoscope I sped to meet Jack, a well-built, hugely tall man of few words. His vehicle, like mine, was an International Utility truck. Why not a car? Ask the ineffably wise bureaucracy.

At the airport, Jack wheeled out our chariot of the skies: a De Havilland Dragon. The ends of the wings of this craft are square, unlike those of the better known, wing-tapered Dragon Rapide. A canvas-clad biplane, it had two Lycoming engines mounted on its lower wings. Reassuringly, the Darwinians informed me that it was held together by gum, tacks and Christ. Be that as it may, it weathered lots of stormy weather without falling apart!

Jack chocked the plane, briefly peered into the engines, turned on the petrol taps and rotated each prop twelve times anticlockwise, flipped them, each motor springing instantly alive, he removed the chocks, ushered me into the moving plane, hopped in himself and, after warming the motors, we were off, over the adjacent Arafura Sea. After perhaps half an hour, a dugout canoe with dun coloured sail was seen steering from Bathurst Island, East to the adjacent Melville Island.

We skimmed over a low, green cliff. To my horror, as we were landing swarms of children rushed out onto the strip, laughing happily, running all over the place full of the joys of life, circling the plane. I was sure they'd be cut to pieces: not those kids! Keen eyes and calculating minds kept them safe. They closed in, holding on to any handy projecting bit of the plane, dug in their heels and pulled us to a stop. They dragged the door open. Having descended, literally dozens of little hands grasped my arms, safari jacket, legs: anywhere, dragging me towards the presbytery—it was a

Catholic mission then. I've never experienced, at any other time or place, such an atmosphere of unalloyed happiness.

The priest strolled along the coconut palm-lined path to meet us. I felt slight discomfort. His jolliness was a little too forced, possibly because of his relative isolation:

'Sorry to have called you over ...'

Surprised, I'd had no idea that this was, in fact, a house call, so to speak.

'... but the Dengue's raging over here. First please look at the sisters. They won't tell you, but they're in worse condition than their patients.'

It was as he'd said. Dengue, aka Breakbone fever, a very nasty illness, will be discussed later. The poor nuns, though most delightful; as ever, most charmingly polite, didn't pause in their duties whilst I spoke, ignoring my advice to rest.

These Sisters of the Sacred Heart: wonderful, kindly and endlessly compassionate and others of the same organization to be mentioned later come as close to sainthood as any people I've ever met.

Chores completed, the verger exhibited his church, proudly demonstrating the dado and wooden screen, shattered with innumerable bullet holes. With amply justifiable pride he told me the story.

During the recent War he'd been an official observer, watching for enemy aircraft. He'd been given pictures of all relevant aeroplanes and he was in constant radio contact with the air force base across the water.

One morning, hearing unaccustomed noise, on looking up he saw a daunting enemy aerial flotilla, the combined roar of their engines shattering the morning calm. His urgent call to base was ignored:

'Silly old bugger: what would he know?'

This stupidity, by no means rare amongst military personnel, had the tiniest vindication. A small flight of Australian Wirraway planes was out on exercise. Nevertheless, this attacking force was far larger; the aircraft completely unlike Wirraways.

The result's history: few, if any Australian planes managed even to get off the ground: Darwin was devastated.

At the time of my visits the tails of a few aircraft still stuck out of the shallows adjoining the island. I doubt if any belonged to the enemy. On their way home, the invaders emptied their guns into the church.

As an aside, Darwinians at this debacle streamed South in any and every contrivance capable of locomotion. The hospital secretary rushed out, but the trundling sanitary wagon was the only vehicle in sight. When I arrived, he was still called Night Cart Nick.

Next trip to the island, I thought Jack and I would be joining the Wirraways. Taking off from the island was always as merry an event as our landing.

Before starting the engines, Jack allowed the kids to rotate each prop twelve times anti-clockwise. What would Health and Safety say today? Jack would be in gaol. The children happily taking it in turns to spin the prop, one to each revolution, counted in unison—and how they did count!!! A regular Rossini slow crescendo and when they shouted TWELVE!! The heavens almost cracked.

There'd been a shower of rain whilst in the little hospital and I'd wondered about the plane's exposure. After the children had done their stuff and both engines fired Jack and I climbed aboard. No hurry: weren't the kids holding back the plane? The engines having warmed, then revved for take-off, we trundled at increasing speed toward the cliff edge. Both engines suddenly conked, but we continued to roll—no brakes—coming to a halt at the very edge, affording a fine view of those wrecked planes.

The Dragon, returned to square one, courtesy of the children, Jack fiddled with the engines—for, in my view, an altogether too short a time—and then we were off again, this time successfully. I've had white knuckles on a number of occasions: none whiter than then!

Jack had a busy life, inspecting the health facilities in the outlying settlements and distributing needed medical supplies—often dumping them from the air in well-padded bundles. He also had a brief to inspect the numerous air strips left behind by the RAAF for signs of smuggling.

I decided to visit the Katherine once a week, often driving the 220 miles unless Jack had something to do in the vicinity. The plane only managed about eighty knots, so, after the first visit, it was rather tedious and more so when a detour was made to inspect various outlying airfields for signs of gold and other smuggling. Bouncing along at ten thousand feet all one saw was a sandstone range stippled with sparse grey-green covering trees The canvas chairs weren't excessively comfortable; less so when there was a bit of weather about. When that shook us too much we'd fly at eleven thousand feet or more. I'd swear I could feel up-draughts breezing through the floor. Occasionally I'd take the commercial flight with TAA, in a DC3, but this tied me down as to timing.

The other two doctors actually did some work on occasions, quarantining incoming overseas planes, not that there were a host of these at that time. Feeling even lazier than usual, they'd ask me. It was rather interesting: the Short flying boats were quite luxurious. Being a passenger must have been an enjoyable experience: only on a shorter journey. One hair-raising plane was the Lancastrian, a modified Lancaster bomber. As skipper of one of these my best childhood friend, Jack Scott, was shot down over Lille. The Lancastrian had had the fuselage cleared and divided lengthwise: half consisted of the petrol tank; half seated a handful of passengers, facing outward. The allegedly first class seats couldn't recline and one smoked at one's peril. One of these did disappear, presumably because some idiot did light up in more ways than one.

Cathay Pacific launched itself at about this time. Unlike their present high standard, their planes, DC4s, were in pretty poor condition, the loos in particular being primitive. I quarantined one in the middle of the aerodrome: its undercarriage collapsed as it landed.

There was more than enough work to keep me busy, not least surgical operations, which demand anaesthetics. But who was to give them? I certainly didn't trust either of the two lounging upstairs, even if they actually happened to be there. A problem? Not really.

The army had left behind an Oxford Vaporiser. Rather like a small black flying saucer, it used hot water to vaporise the anaesthetic ether and had a lever at its top to regulate its concentration. I'd induce the patients and, whilst operating, a sister saw to the airway. The breathing easily indicated depth of anaesthesia and I'd periodically examine the patient's pupils, kicking the lever one way or the other as necessary.

Before long, however, I heard of Percy, an Air Force doctor stationed some miles to the South at their base. He kindly agreed to give the anaesthetics.

The Outpatients' Department was also busy. The patients' cards had a box in the top right hand corner: length of residence in the N.T. This helped. If ten days or a fortnight was entered, one began writing out treatment for infected sand fly bites before the patient appeared. These biting midges were ferocious to say the least and it's not humanly possible to resist the urge to scratch their bites: hence the infection. We were grateful that our house was on stilts more than ten feet above ground: ten feet or so, I was told, is apparently the Darwin insect's ceiling.

Hotels provided a regular supply of minor casualties; otherwise there was nothing exceptional about the problems presenting. I remember, though, a first-born baby, howling uncontrollably, brought in by distraught parents. The mother was trying to calm the child without success.

'Don't hit the child so hard' I said.

The howling ceased. The ensuing look of wild surmise was quite memorable.

Much time was spent in the operating theatre, mostly run-of-the-mill procedures: appendicectomy, herniae and the like. On one occasion I was persuaded to perform a vaginal repair for uterine prolapse. The patient was worried by the condition and assured me that there was no possibility of going South for the operation. It went off well; the patient well satisfied. I believe that with a thorough knowledge of anatomy and having swotted up the operation, any excepting highly specialised operations may safely be performed by a person with good basic training. I knew a bush surgeon who proudly told me that, when performing an unfamiliar procedure he had a nurse hold a textbook open so the he could read what to do next!

One appendicectomy stands out. The patient was a newspaper reporter seconded to Darwin: the most apprehensive patient I've ever known. I don't blame him: here he was at the uttermost ends of the Earth at the mercy of two very young doctors. I chatted to him in an effort to calm him, learning that he especially loved Beethoven's sixth Symphony. As the anaesthetic mask was being laid over his face I began whistling its first dozen bars. It might at least have diverted his mind!

My surgical uncle in Sydney was friendly with another medical family, the Flynns. One of them, Frank, was a priest, member of the Order of the Sacred Heart. As he was here, I was anxious to meet him. During a postgraduate course in ophthalmology at London's Moorfield's Hospital he'd received the 'call'.

I soon had my wish. He was the most delightful man: friendly, always smiling: in public at least; ruddy complexioned with thinnish, faintly red, brushed back hair to match. His manner was dignified but not priestly. I never saw him without a cardigan under his khaki safari suit, a little surprising in the tropics, but he had a rheumatic condition which also made his eyes perpetually dry. He showed me the ingenious device he'd fitted to his glasses, which he always wore, to irrigate his eyes: a pair of fine tubes, each with a rubber reservoir fitted behind his ears.

At that time he was organising the building of Darwin's new cathedral, That didn't in any way interfere with his pastoral work: I'd frequently receive letters—with patient attached—from all over the Territory; spear wounds; acute surgical emergencies; lumps and bumps, you name it, all rattling up to the hospital in a battered ex-army bomb driven by Jim Kelleher, the pharmacist. Frank was a lovely, lovely man and it was always a pleasure to be in his company. I kept in touch with him for many years. The last time I saw him, in Port Moresby in 1972, still just a priest, he was teaching New Guinean women how to use the potting wheel. Highly intelligent and a great organiser, he should have been an archbishop at least. Too good a person, he wasn't ruthless, pushy and eager for power.

'No person he to fawn or seek for power
'With sermons fashioned to the passing hour.
'Likewise,
'The race is not always to the swift, nor the battle to the strong.
Never in any race, he was simply serving God.'

He phoned me one day, asking if I'd pop over to Bathurst Island to see a very sick little boy. Little Peter had swollen lymph glands everywhere. I presumed it to be leukaemia but hoped that it wasn't. I still remember the dignity of his mother, Camilla, as she flew back with us to Darwin, no doubt inwardly fearful, never having been in a plane before. Peter would be in hospital for some time, so Frank asked if we'd put up his parents—her husband's name was Matthew—keeping them as servants, so that they could visit their son. This we readily agreed to do. There wasn't much housework; the big plus was that I'd occasionally drive them along the coast, leaving them with lunch, then pick them up later with a huge sugar bag full of mangrove crabs, to be cooked in the copper boiler, stoked and ready to be lit, under the house. Absolutely scrumptious! Known more prosaically as mud crabs they're only second to coconut crabs as the most delectable of all crustaceans—yes, better than lobsters!

When Peter died, the alcohol-fuelled grief of this couple and their friends was frightening in its violence. As I write I can hear the shrieks as they banged around:

'Poor little Peter; poor little Peter!'

Our house wasn't called Gibber Gables for nothing. There was virtually no topsoil, so, on weekends, if work was slack, Matthew and I would drive into the rain forest and collect soil for the garden. Here he'd teach me some natural lore: for instance, what to do if pursued by a taipan, the most deadly of all snakes, silvery grey in colour, and growing to a length of six feet or more and moving more quickly than man can run. The answer: jump up on to the nearest tree stump. Taipans are territorial, becoming aggressive when their domain is invaded. Matthew also taught me such things as what plants were good or bad to eat. I occasionally proudly brought home a yam, identified by the heart-shaped leaves spiralling up a tree. He even taught me a few words of his language.

One of my trips South was especially eventful. I'd decided to travel further, take in the tiny village of Mataranka, then the copper field at Maranboy, where there were still a few miners.

A hundred and sixty miles along the road, in absolute wilderness, a man stepped out into my headlights, hand held up. A hold-up? Flashed through my head, but:

'Doctor Gibbs?'

I climbed out of the pick-up and nodded.

How on earth could he know who I am?

'A bloke's broken ees leg in th' Pine Creek Pub. 'dyer take a look at 'im please?'

'Of course, where's the pub?'

'Down this road 'ere. Foller me.'

He led me left, down a side road, past a huge water tank, to be mentioned later.

This must be on the railway line, I thought

It was indeed. About a hundred years ago, when the line was being pushed South, it was a seething, riotous, polyglot town of wild roistering well up to the standard of the Wild West.

The sizeable pub, of typical rambling outback design, soon loomed in the dark.

Bert lay on the floor in the public bar, left leg askew, drinkers goggling at him. I phoned Jack Slade:

'Get them to light a flare way. I'll bring a Thomas splint and anaesthetic gear.'

'OK blokes, come 'n help me with the flares.' Yelled the bartender/proprietor.

How often such emergencies had happened here in the past I don't know, but the bar emptied, everybody waiting beside the nearby airstrip until the plane was heard.

Forty four gallon drums half buried, filled with sand were already in situ:. The gang poured kerosene (paraffin) into each and lit them. They worked, but it can't have been much fun landing on a rough old strip in blackest night with only flares for illumination.

I thought I'd be giving the anaesthetic, Jack assisting. Wrong!

When the crowd had been shooed into another bar, Jack took a look at the patient, listened into his chest and proceeded to give the anaesthetic, superbly well. Marvelling, I said nothing. The fracture was easy to reduce, the leg, properly bandaged, then immobilised, in the splint. Traction was maintained by means of broad sticking plaster applied down both sides of the leg, then over a square piece of wood that kept the plaster separated to prevent it from pressing on his ankle.

Then a cord attached to the wood was pulled as firmly as possible and tied on to the end of the splint, named after its inventor, Welsh bone setter, Hugh Owen Thomas.

The man was on a stretcher when he awakened: very soon, thanks to an expertly given anaesthetic, then loaded on to the plane. This had no headlights and as it raced along that strip into the darkness I felt a wave of admiration for that brave pilot.

Unfortunately, that fracture had been a spontaneous one, due to bone weakened by secondary cancer infiltrating his femur. I sent him South for possible further treatment: radiotherapy sometimes encourages healing. I heard no more from the hospital to which he was sent: both slack and impolite, but his life expectancy must have been limited.

The additional seventy miles to the Katherine were uneventful. Next morning, when doing a round of the hospital, a woman suffering an abortion came in. Because she was bleeding profusely matters couldn't wait until I contacted Jack Slade—if indeed he wasn't off on a service trip to outlying mission stations. At best there'd be a delay of at least five hours, were one to operate in Darwin..

The anaesthetic ether, sitting in the hot pharmacy for goodness knows how long and probably so toxic that it would be criminal to administer it, there was only one alternative. I'd noticed a couple of vials of Pentothal, an intravenous anaesthetic, in the dispensary: a very recent introduction, so goodness knows how it had got there. It can't have been there for long because it was within the expiry date printed on its glass ampoule. I'd never given a Pentothal anaesthetic, but it was the least risky option. I read, re-read; read again the bumf always included with drugs, then ordered a start.

To perform a curette—the necessary procedure—the patient should be in lithotomy position: supine, legs up and well apart; knees bent; feet in stirrups. It's so called because it was the position traditionally used in pre-modern times to cut unfortunate patients for stone in the bladder.

Before continuing this story, a few words about cutting for stone might be of interest.

Bladder stone was common in pre-modern times, operations being performed without any anaesthetic other than a stiff dose of alcohol. There were two approaches by which the bladder was opened and stone extracted: the perineal approach requiring the 'lithotomy' position; the abdominal one's self-explanatory. There were catches to each: the perineal approach could result in incontinence: a permanent leak; the abdominal, requiring a cut just above the pubic bone could cause fatal peritonitis or a rupture. Both had high mortality rates and fear of stone was high. Witness the old prayer:

> 'Lord, when thou takest me, taketh me not through my
> water.'

Frere Jacques, immortalised in the song, was a lithotomist who cut via the abdominal wall. His results were remarkably good, his reputation spreading far and wide, so that, when the Marshall of France, a man of great power indeed, developed stone, he scoured the country until our hero was found and brought—no doubt trembling—to Paris.

The Marshall must have had a modern mind, as he used statistics before deciding to submit: he first watched Jacques operate upon a large number of sufferers. None died. Fantastic, so the Marshall underwent the operation.

That's the problem with statistics: they can't be relied upon where one individual item's concerned. They merely point out the odds. Though in favour of a successful outcome, that didn't happen. The patient died and Jacques made a quick, sharp exit.

But back to Katherine and the joint predicament: that patient and myself. Unfortunately, a thorough search managed to produce only one leg stirrup. A tottery drip stand was the sole substitute. Tottery it most certainly was. Despite everything, the leg repeatedly, when righted, almost immediately fell across to the other one. .

A terrible game of roundabouts began. The senior sister maintained the airway, especially important with Pentothal; the only other nurse assisted. Heart in mouth, I injected the anaesthetic, rushed round the head of the table to check the patient, round to insert the speculum, having straightened the constantly collapsing drip stand, back to assess the patient, straighten the drip stand and apply tenaculum forceps to the cervix uteri to bring it into view; across to administer more Pentothal when necessary; and so on and on, round and round and round, doing a little more of the operation on each revolution. The patient, thank God, recovered rapidly and at day's end was probably in better shape than I.

Next morning, the patient chipper and losing little or nothing, I continued on to Mataranka on the main North—South road, stopping off to visit a little family of three young girls, always ill, whom I'd often seen in Darwin, I'd brought along various medicaments, hoping to spare them a long journey. .

The father was paid by the Department of Aviation to keep the adjacent landing strip in good condition in case of emergency. Jack and I would often fly over it and it appeared to have been conscientiously looked after: fresh wheel tracks could always be seen zigzagging across the field.

On a subsequent occasion we had to land there with a plane-load of nursing sisters, en route, if I remember correctly, to Tennant Creek. Almost at touchdown, Jack suddenly shouted some unaccustomed impolite phrases and, forcefully juggling the controls, managed to slew the plane a little to the left, quite a feat at that late stage of landing. Shaken, to say the least, we disembarked. We'd just missed a great gully, literally by inches. That abysmal creature had been driving his truck in those zigzags to miss the washouts in a terribly eroded field. No more favours for that family.

There was another example of don't care negligence in the remote outback, in marked contrast with the usual mateship. A couple of pilots had called in to Darwin on their way to Alice Springs from Ireland, doubly interesting as they were flying another Dragon: a long trip at a very slow speed, bound for service with Conellan Airways in Alice Springs. After a couple of drinks one evening we bade them farewell, only to see them again on the following night in the hospital. All went well until they made a refuelling stop. Topped up, they warmed their engines; gave them a burst, then took off. Barely airborne, both motors cut out. The chief pilot told me that he tried to turn and land on the strip as he didn't savour the prospect of crashing into trees just ahead, but hadn't enough speed. They crashed, without enough force for it to be fatal. On hitting the ground, both pilots' feet went through the fabric: four fractured heels were on my hands. It obviously could have been much worse. Skill and luck had saved their lives.

The slob in charge of the fuel had left the petrol drums outside at night.

'Cheese it'd be a bugger ter have ter drag them forty four gallon drums inside ev'ry night!'

All very well, but the petrol expanded during the day's heat, contracting when the sun set, drawing dew into the drum. Water in the fuel caused the crash.

On to Maranboy. The bush telegraph had obviously been active as there was a fair turnout, despite the delayed consultation date, dotted around the periphery of a large clearing in the twisted trees.

A late arrival came as several complete surprises: the aged truck sported a bulging, obviously homemade cabin. The driver, when he emerged, was absolutely the hugest man I've ever seen, very tall and enormous in every way. Cramped in one recess of the cabin was his consort: without exaggeration the tiniest aboriginal woman one could imagine. Truly! The man was unique in another way: he'd survived the bite of the world's most venomous snake: the taipan. Until this time, there'd been no recorded survivors. He'd been bitten on the arm: but what an arm! It must have been twice the diameter of an athlete's thigh. That was probably his salvation. Less blood circulates through fatty tissue than most other parts of the body: one guesses that the venom leached so slowly that it wasn't lethal. However, he did have marked neurological problems. He understandably refused to come back to Darwin: men like that, living in isolation often hate to be brought into so-called civilization. This is particularly true of many aborigines. I found it difficult to keep them in hospital: they'd disappear if at all ambulant. Many, when sent to gaol even today, commit suicide.

I gave the man vitamin B tablets more in hope than anything else.

When the sisters back in the Katherine were told, they fell about laughing.

'Oh, that was Tiny Swanson. He's been here once or twice. Our great fear is that we'll have to admit him one day. How on earth will we nurse him?'

Some years later, on returning from England, and commencing practice in Ipswich, the following appeared in the local paper:

NURSING PROBLEM IN KATHERINE.

> A Mr. Swanson recently died in Katherine hospital in the Northern Territory. He weighed in excess of forty stone at the time of his death from heart trouble. Nursing proved to be a big problem. It was eventually solved by a local engineer who rigged up a gantry and tackle. This was the only way the patient could be lifted for bathing and treatment.

Not long after returning to Darwin from that expedition, the Pine Creek pub's proprietor paid a visit, his hernia needing repair.

'Had to see the two upstairs first. Y'know how it is: good customers 'n all. Had a yarn with C (the Medical Superintendent). Nick brought in a piece o' paper while we was talkin'. He whacked down a great stamp on it then signed it, looked up an' says: 'not bad for a day's work!'

No surprise there! But hardly pleasing to the physician/surgeon/anaesthetist/outpatient doctor—oh, and yes, temporary dentist.

The erstwhile occupant of that post had suddenly decided to down tools and seek pastures new. Previous experience in removing teeth at the Children's hospital was very much welcomed. No fillings were attempted: only extractions which, in adults, weren't always easy.

One poor bloke came in with severe toothache: right second lower molar. I anaesthetised the area, applied the tongs and pulled; rocked; rotated; did everything I could think of until I began to sweat nearly as much as the poor victim. More anaesthetic, more tugs. Suddenly, with a loud bang, out came the tooth—with at least a three quarter inch portion of the outer surface of the mandible attached. The tooth had obviously fused with it as the result of inflammation. Absolutely appalled, I showed it to him, rapidly checking the jaw which fortunately hadn't been broken. The patient didn't turn a hair, nor did he sue me. In fact, a few nights later he appeared on the doorstep with a bottle of scotch—not much today, perhaps, but more precious than gold at that time. He was the proprietor of a number of pubs, but his quota of that elixir was, he said apologetically, only two bottles a month. Next month he did the same, but sadly never again. The poor fellow wrapped himself around a tree when travelling at speed to visit one or other of his hostelries.

And speed is what everybody indulged in on that long, straight strip of quite well-made road, South to Alice Springs more than nine hundred miles away. Rarely at this time, but fairly regularly in the past, the two chiefs would hurtle down to the Katherine, see a couple of patients, then—I was reliably told—leave the others and sneak out through a back door to repair to a local hostelry. After drinking their fill there, they'd waste no time in making it to the Pine Creek pub, finally weaving their erratic way home. They both drove the latest model Chev—and there were vanishingly few of them in Oz at that early post war time.

One day the mechanic servicing our vehicles disgustedly showed me the amazingly distorted valves of the engine of one of them. The mechanic estimated that the car must have been driven over considerable distances at well over a hundred miles an hour. The Devil looks after his own!

The two weren't well regarded on the whole. It was common knowledge that they'd got their jobs through nepotism.

Towards the end of my Darwin days another victim of speed was flown back to Darwin: a young woman who'd turned off the highway at speed some four hundred miles South, turning over her vehicle and almost completely severing her right arm above the elbow. She'd leaned it on the window whilst racing down the tarmac. The only other working doctor by that time was a new, stroppy Sydney graduate and he gave the anaesthetic. I did my best to save the arm. The arteries were intact, if little else. However the Brachial Artery and its major branches were in severe spasm.

Repairing the nerves and muscles and reducing the fracture took ages, the task made no easier by the anaesthetist's continuing complaints. Completed in time for that early flight, I sent her down to Adelaide, knowing that the prognosis was poor, but hoping that the histamine released from the damaged muscles might possibly cause the arterial spasm to relax. I hoped that more could be done for her in Adelaide. It couldn't and that horrible spasm didn't relax. She lost her arm.

Speaking of anaesthetists, Percy from the air force announced one day, about a year prior to the latter episode that he was to be transferred. A dyed-in-the-wool urbanite, he'd seen remarkably little of the interesting surrounding countryside, so we took him on a farewell picnic to a pleasant remote beach overlooked by low cliffs fringed by Casuarina trees.

The tide, nearly at the end of an ebb, soon turned, the signal for countless thousands of soldier crabs to begin manoeuvres across the moist sand; so many that much of the beach itself appeared to move as the little round bluish-grey animals in close-packed columns marched to and fro. A fascinating sight: not for poor Percy. He was absolutely terrified; utterly petrified. The picnic was promptly transferred to our house—which at least looked out over a bay.

By this time, I'd begun studies for the first part of my surgical Fellowship exam. The house was on the edge of a cliff which flanked one side of a shallowish bay, Mindil Beach being at its base. In the dry season, it was reasonably safe to swim. Swimming during the Wet incurred a serious risk of being stung by the lethal box jellyfish, *Chironex Fleckeri*. There were no fatal incidents during my time—the people were savvy— but a couple of children, lucky enough to have encountered perhaps two tentacles (from the appearance of the wounds) or a very small creature, had suffered the most dreadful, deep spiral gouges in their legs that took ages to heal.

The cliffs, mottled with shades of reddish brown, yellow and white were quite picturesque. The great plus for me was the cool updraught of air at the very edge, where I sat during many lunchtimes, away from the mind-numbing heat, wrestling with Wood Jones' esoteric monograph on The Foot, watching hawks, wings outspread, motionless in the updraught, when attention wandered.

One could also watch these predators from the reasonable comfort of the privy, also near the edge of the cliff which, for privacy, was walled in on three sides by corrugated iron, the doorless fourth open to the view. The business part of this arrangement was appropriately known as a flaming fury.

Why? You may well ask. It was a forty four gallon fuel drum half sunk into the ground with a hole cut in its top. A smallish chimney was fitted into its rear and, when in use, a wooden seat was placed on top of the drum. The fantastic part comes in the aftermath: a metal funnel takes the place of the seat, after paraffin-soaked paper and wood have been gingerly put through the hole and a lighted match thrown in. How well it was named! An unmissable experience! Flames erupted synchronously with an incredibly loud WOOMP woomp WOOMP woomp which continued until the flames subsided, all passion spent. I'm not sure if the earth actually shook, but one imagined that it did. Sadly, just before we left, the authorities deemed this inappropriate and installed, uninvited, a septic system in the house, adjacent to the back steps.

The construction of the septic tank was an engineering marvel: a truck with boring equipment attached drove up and drilled a hole in the ground. A charge of gelignite was chucked in and exploded. Voila! A septic tank! I hoped that the subsoil water flowed towards the sea, away from the town.

Just as Percy was about to leave a new recruit, Harry H. materialised. This was a great relief. Not only did it lessen the workload, it also meant the appearance of a very congenial colleague, happy to give the anaesthetics. Moreover, he was more interested in Medicine, which left me clear to attend to the Surgery. Sadly, he decided to leave a little before I did.

He lived in bachelor quarters with lay staff members, naturally forming friendships with some. One, a young man, developed appendicitis. Harry gave the anaesthetic. Whiling away the time whilst I operated, as a practical joke: he painted an artistic pattern upon the patient's face with silver nitrate, which turns brown on exposure to light, of which there's more than enough in Darwin. The other failed to see the joke and took legal action: nasty considering that the design was harmless and only temporary. Harry settled out of court, but it left such a nasty taste in his mouth that he decided to leave.

Soon after Harry arrived I had another noteworthy trip South. A semi-urgent call from the Katherine latish one afternoon. An almighty thunderstorm was brewing: there are really impressive ones around the Top End.

It would soon be dark and perfectly suicidal to attempt to fly the fragile Dragon in the dark through the fierce winds always encountered in storm clouds. Stepping on it, a car wouldn't take much longer, allowing for the formalities necessary before a plane could take off, in the unlikely assumption that that would have been allowed.

It seemed a good idea at the time to take the little green Austin 8. That storm soon arrived and it seemed to follow me. Just to the North of the Adelaide River is a low range of ironstone hills that attracted the lightning: a wild world! Rain lashed at the car the fiercely roaring winds repeatedly hitting in gusts, shaking the little car so much that I thought I'd be blown off the road. The pitch blackness was incessantly punctured by the violet blue glow of sheet lightning and, most frightening of all, bolts of red-hued lightning blasting away at the roadside, yards from the car. The thick shafts, scattering showers of glowing globules as they struck, added deafening explosions to the cacophony.

Conditions still rather wet, the weather improved towards the Katherine. Suddenly a strange noise emanated from the front of the car. I initially thought it a trick of the wind—and in retrospect that's probably what it was—but the possibility that wheel nuts could have been loosened worried me. Arrived at the Katherine River which, though now spanned by a high-level bridge, was crossed at low level in those days, it seemed a good idea to brave the rain and have a look. Torchlight and a good shake of the wheel revealed nothing on the driver's side. On the other? As I moved to the front of the car the torch illuminated an enormous crocodile! Had it so decided, it would have been too quick for me to make my escape –extremely quick, believe me! Perhaps the sudden arrival of a strange being which flashed lights unnerved it, but it took off in the opposite direction almost as quickly as myself.

On a couple of occasions I did have to treat crocodile bites, not from those, but a small species: fresh water or Johnson River crocs. Both victims had been swimming in one or other stream. Anybody idiotic enough to do that was simply asking for it.

A couple of risky travel situations have been mentioned. It seems appropriate here to mention two more: one actually made and one that would have been fatal, had it been taken.

Jack Slade was in Canberra obtaining an airworthiness certificate for one of the two Dragons when the brass decided that the aborigines of Mataranka Station should be tested for leprosy: it was endemic there. For this, the nasal septa were swabbed. When the resulting smear is stained and examined microscopically, tell-tale bacilli are readily seen.

There was a choice of two planes: an Avro Anson or a Fox Moth. The latter was the obvious option, both because the Aggie would drop like a stone if its engines cut out and also because its pilot had a liking for strong waters.

The Fox is more or less identical with the better known Tiger Moth, but with a small cabin that could accommodate four people or two persons and a stretcher on two canvas seats facing one another, immediately behind the engine. The pilot, Harry Moss, flew crocodile shooters out to their hunting grounds in those days of sanity when these malevolent predators, now protected, could be shot for their valuable skins. Landing on river banks. He would fly the skins back. Ample evidence, both of the cargo and the rough landings he'd made was afforded both by the not entirely salubrious smell of stale crocodile but also by the noise of the much traumatised undercarriage as we taxied for take-off: a loud warrawarrawarra which ceased when the craft was airborne. I thought of re-naming it the Tigger Moth.

Mataranka Station, some distance from the village we've already visited, was immortalised in *We of the Never Never*, a moving true story of life on a remote cattle property in the early days of the Twentieth Century. Still to be seen there is the gravestone of the Fizzer, Henry Ventilia Peckham, one of its characters, an intrepid postman who lost his life in a flood, heroically carrying out his duties. No persuasion to make this visit was necessary: I'd read and re-read that book.

Gliding in for a landing I was startled to hear, above the engine noise, passionate swearing. A look for the cause revealed a landing strip completely covered with the pyramidal projections of innumerable, concrete-hard termite nests, each six or more inches high. The effects on the plane of hitting these at speed can well be imagined, a vivid picture arising of the plane coming to rest with the engine a few feet behind where my head presently was. Though Harry was skilled at landing in tricky conditions, how he managed to miss all of those close-set lethal obstructions of hardened clay I'll never know. The manager of the station had told a couple of aborigines to knock some down when he heard the plane approaching. What Harry said to Mr. Crowson, the manager, lengthy, fluent and colourful, is best left to the imagination.

As he circled prior to landing, Harry had yelled:

'See those abos heading for the bush? They're the ones with leprosy. They know why we're here. They'll come back as soon as we leave.'

It was so—all excepting one of the smears was negative.

Lunch was corned beef slabs with thick slices of onion, aka cold meat and salad. Returning from these trips in the afternoons was always a rough old affair at the low altitudes at which we flew. The effects of continuous shaking, for hours on end with a stomach full of raw onion are not pleasant. It was years before I could face an onion again. We were offered beer, but in the absence of refrigeration it frothed all over the place when opened, holding no charms at all. There were no electrical refrigerators in the bush, simply because there was no electricity. Those operated by paraffin packed it in when it was really hot.

Mention of Leprosy reminds me that there was a leprosarium on Channel Island, across the water from Darwin. I felt that somebody should take an interest in it, in particular to see if things were up to scratch with no essentials lacking. It was run by the same saintly Sisters of the Sacred Heart who manned the Bathurst Island mission. In both places the utter dedication was extremely moving, but on Channel Island the situation was different because close contact with lepers in every stage of the horrible disease was essential if they were to do their work properly. The sisters would have been very aware that the disease is contagious. Would to God there were more people like them in today's selfish, self-oriented world.

More effective treatments were in the pipeline, not yet widely used. It was terrible having to look at the poor wrecks' disfigurement: horrible faces with nose eaten away; fingers reduced to stumps; palsied limbs, of limited use if any, nerves infiltrated by the relentless bacillus. Sizeable areas of depigmented skin are also a feature. In olden times many sufferers from perfectly benign vitiligo were ostracised and forced to live miserable lives of exclusion and beggary in the mistaken belief that they suffered from leprosy.

As might have been anticipated in this headless monster of a medical service, much was indeed lacking there. The island was obviously completely isolated, excepting that once a week a lay brother who did the odd jobs, rowed across to the mainland to collect supplies and the few letters. What horrified me was the fact that the only water tank was rusted. Part of it had already collapsed, the Sister-in-charge not knowing how much longer the remainder would last. She'd written repeatedly to the Chief Medical Officer expressing her concern but had never had a response. This was only one of a number of issues making me ever more angry.

Oh, yes! The fatal trip that never happened! Early one morning I received a call on Aeradio from Port Keats, a mission station over the Westralian border—a long slog away. A man had been seriously injured in an accident. There were no other flying doctors within range. I rang Jack Slade. He'd just left for the airport, so I phoned the duty officer there.

'He's just this second taken off.'

No radios on the old Dragon! I apologised deeply to the mission.

Finally arrived back in Darwin, Jack saw the message indicating that I'd called, so he dropped in to see me on his way home. He'd had a grim day. Taking off with medical supplies for Elcho Island, which is located towards the Eastern end of the North coast of Arnhem Land, an engine began pumping out oil well into the trip. Dragons could almost, not quite, fly on one engine. With usual cool skill, he decided that he could make it by landing at another mission, filling the faulty engine with oil and continuing, ditto at Elcho Island and the same on the way back. I told him where the call had come from. He thought for a few minutes.

'If you'd called a couple of minutes earlier, we'd have gone down plumb in the middle of Joseph Buonaparte Gulf, miles from land.'

Silence all round. After a time he said:

'You know, I had that problem once before. A motor cut out half way between here and the Katherine. I estimated that I'd go down just before the Adelaide River. There was plenty of weather around, so I thought I'd chance flying into a nearby cumulus. What a ride! The plane nearly twisted itself inside out. I finally emerged at about twenty thousand feet, just enough to get me home.'

Once, with Jack, the updraught from the Katherine River responsible for the DC3's behaviour caused him embarrassment. Passing over the river, the Dragon suddenly shot up high into the air. Jack tried to bring it down, but the hot air rising from the tarmac stubbornly refused to let us land. A colleague of Jack was on the strip and ostentatiously doubled up with laughter, continuing with his histrionics whilst Jack had to pull up and go around again, professional pride deeply wounded.

Life wasn't all work. Clarry would invite me to buffalo shoots on the Vestey property he managed. He'd developed a urethral stricture as a result of unprotected sex at Pine Creek when the railway was being built. He sometimes recalled those roaring days, when Pine Creek was a veritable Babylon. His problem, due to infection with *Neisseria gonorrhoeae*, was potentially serious. There was no cure for it in those days, so a stricture formed and inexorably narrowed until it was difficult for him to pass urine; impossible if left untreated.

Unless the situation's hopeless and necessitates major surgery, the treatment is passage of sounds: curved metal rods of sizes graduated from very thin to fat. These, from finest upwards are passed through the stricture until it's dilated sufficiently. Treatment must be repeated at intervals or the stricture will contract again.

The catch is that the thinnest sound, being passed first, its tiny tapered end can easily push through the friable scar tissue, creating a false passage. Repeated failure means that the bladder, outlet blocked, becomes painfully distended. and must be opened urgently to prevent fatal kidney failure. A tube's then inserted to drain it pending difficult definitive surgery necessary to attempt a cure.

On rare occasions after repeated inexpert treatment the urine finds its way through numerous false passages, producing the horrible 'watering can scrotum'. Luckily for both, Mordo's teaching bore fruit and Clarry escaped any horticultural problems.

Sound, a strange word for a bent metal rod, derives its name from its use in pre-modern times, when one such was inserted into the bladder to diagnose bladder stone by means of the characteristic feeling when the tip touches a stone. Stone can be removed without any cutting by means of an instrument, known as a lithotrite, whose curved lower part has retractable jaws. Inserted into the bladder, when a stone is felt, the jaws are opened and then depressed, so that the stone falls between the jaws, which are forcibly closed. Repeated, the stone becomes crushed sufficiently for the fragments to be washed out in irrigating fluid. I found this procedure useful, always carefully filljng the bladder fist with fluid. To avoid the risk of closing those jaws on the bladder's lining—or even its full thickness. There are, of course, cystoscopes with a lithotrite attachment, but I never found it necessary to use one. Though with these one can visualise what's going on, a good sense of touch is all that's really necessary.

I sometimes felt that my popularity at the buffalo shoots depended in part upon the generator, forerunner of the alternator, in my pick-up: It matched the one in Clarry's ex-army four-by-four which was perennially on the blink. As soon as I'd arrive, Clarry would call out to one of his aboriginal employees:

'Moonlight! You change over them generators!'

And Moonlight would do so, in a matter of minutes. Most impressive.

He and I liked each other, becoming friends. He was very intelligent and, when he knew that I was about to leave the territory, gave me a much prized didgeridoo of his own making.

Buffalo shoots tended to be hilarious, though the buffalo failed to share this view. Rising at dawn, it was de rigeur to 'keep down a couple of rums before breakfast'. After these and a 5am meal of steak and eggs, we were prepared to tackle the buffalo, bare-handed if necessary.

Clarry firmly believed in a straight line being the shortest distance between two points. Bouncing along Deaf Adder Creek's flood plain, if a clump of melaleuca trees happened to be on that line, he drove straight through it. Sometimes we were jolted to an abrupt halt by a larger than normal tree which caused the bumper bar to become very concave. No worries! (Sorry! That expression hadn't as yet been invented.). Clarry would swiftly wrap a stout chain several times around both the bumper and the tree and then reverse violently. With a more or less straight bumper, we'd hurtle onwards until the next jarring halt.

The shoot's objective was to cull excess bulls and collect their valuable hides. using .303 rifles, mine dating from my range-shooting days when at school. A direct hit at right angles was essential: oblique ones merely bounced off the extremely tough hide. One aimed just behind the shoulder for an instant kill.

When a group of bulls was sighted everybody excitedly fired fusillade after fusillade. We were supposed to keep in line, but on one shoot some idiot got behind me and a bullet whistled—audibly—past my ear. An alternative interpretation is that an idiot placed himself in front of another shooter. The rifle barrels became very hot, inflicting a nasty burn if inadvertently touched.

That approach was decidedly *effete* compared with the practice up to the end of the Second World War. Shooting then was executed on horseback, the rider bringing his galloping horse alongside the speeding beast, shooting it just behind the head. Sometimes a skilful shot merely stunned the animal. Clarry told me that he'd once shot a buffalo enjoying the shade of a tree he'd earmarked as a spot suitable for his lunch. His shot transformed it into a convenient seat. Whist he began rolling a cigarette, far from dead, the beast suddenly arose in an unpleasant mood. Clarry took a run, just managing to take hold of the tree's lowest branch, hauling himself to safety. His opponent, however, stood, fixing him with a murderously bloodshot glare, continuing thus for most of the very hot afternoon, until thirst nearly drove him frantic. It was only by chance that other shooters happened by and despatched the animal. He went to that tree on several subsequent occasions and, taking a good run, tried repeatedly; unsuccessfully, to reach that branch.

We all set to, skinning the beasts, whose hides, so heavy that horses could only carry one at a time, were taken back to the homestead.

When lunch called a stay, Moonlight took a gun and one cartridge, bringing back two delicious magpie geese, lining them up before making his shot. Digging an earthen oven, he cooked them native style. Scrumptious!

On one occasion during lunch, a pygmy goose o flew over at quite a distance. Arthur Krieg, a wonderful friend, grabbed his rifle and shot it through the head. It took him a long time to live that down.

Buffalo slaughter ended, the aborigines removed tongues and testicles for an evening celebration. Chatting after dinner, we listened to their music: the hoarse throated didgeridoo; percussive music sticks and bull-roarer, backing very evocative singing. Some repeated semiquaver descending passages were most haunting. I don't know if these were actual corroborees. Clarry said they were. Of course we didn't intrude.

When the party included a few Old Territorians, the stories were fascinating, but sadly, they're either forgotten or unprintable. Some of the guests had actually known the characters in *We of the Never Never*.

As a step towards so-called democracy, an appointed Legislative Council was instituted in the Territory. Prior to this it had been administered from Canberra. One of the members chosen was the doctor from Tennant Creek: he who recommended all Territorians to drink at least two bottles of beer before lunch. Though very many did their best to adhere to this regimen, even better it, it was often difficult or impossible of implementation because the beer ran out at regular intervals. I always knew when this had happened because the casualties from the pubs changed from minor broken knuckles and the like to much more serious injuries.

The result of his appointment to the legislature was that I'd periodically fly down to the Tennant to act in his place. Gold production was in full swing, the continuous thudding of the stampers being heard throughout the night These crushed the ore which, mixed with water was run over mercury plates to which the gold adhered. I watched one morning whilst a retort of small melon size was heated until the mercury vaporised and the vividly glowing liquid gold was poured into a receptacle. Mercury vapour? Health and Safety would have had four-times forty fits.

One old hospital inmate who had an interest in some of the mines would sit outside on the hospital veranda in the evenings, harkening to the glad sound, the rhythmic thumping music to her ears.

Speaking of music, on most nights the local priest would join me at dinner and in listening, wistfully, to Dr. Webster's classical records. We both loved Beethoven and his Pastoral Symphony seemed to be appropriate. The incongruity was lost on neither of us. On one occasion, after the last notes died away he said:

'And here we sit like birds in the wilderness.'

I agreed, but had the advantage: he was stuck there whilst I was able to leave after some days.

It was a wild and woolly frontier town, but nevertheless rather in the nature of a rest, being much less busy than Darwin. A few veterinary procedures, however, do come to mind. There was no vet; at least at that time. The animal patients had injuries for the most part. In particular I remember a parrot with a broken leg. It took a very close interest indeed in my splinting procedure, beak millimetres from my fingers. Poised to punish a false move? A plaster of Paris pelvic spica is surprisingly difficult to apply to a dog. It has many strategies for removing it!!

Back in Darwin, the pharmacist brought in a little local boy suffering from diphtheria. The membrane had spread to his larynx and he was struggling for breath. Hating to operate unnecessarily, we rigged up a steam tent—that sometimes helps—but how to conjure up steam? None was piped through the hospital. Rummaging in the stores I happened on a Primus stove which, with a large kettle would provide some steam. No nurse in this remote and countrified outpost knew how to light one—or had even heard of one. When I began pumping it up, the staff all made a quick, sharp exit, watching proceedings by peeping around a distant door.

Steam was produced, to no avail. Breathing ever more laboured, he turned blue: I had no option but to perform urgent tracheotomy. The violent coughing when the curved metal tracheotomy tube is inserted has already been mentioned. The cloth sponge on this occasion allowed some membrane to escape: on to my face, but with no ill-effects.

I'd heard nothing of immunisation programmes so, operation complete, I rushed up to the CMO to ask him if there was one such, pointing out that the child, a Chinese, lived in one of the more crowded, less favoured parts of the town. One case here was likely to lead to others: the last thing anybody would want would be an epidemic. Nothing had been done, but a programme would be instituted, almost immediately. Thus spake CMO. He lied or didn't know how to organise an immunisation programme.

Weeks went by without anything being done so, when a case of malaria arrived from Pine Creek, I mentioned it to him, but realising it would be up to me, took matters and a canister of kerosene (paraffin) into my own hands. Arrived at the village, I climbed to the top of the large railway water tank, taking a sample of the water. Sure enough, malarial mosquito larvae wriggled in the glass. It being the dry season: no surface water for mosquitos to breed, so the kerosene, tipped on to the water and which spread in a thin film over the entire surface, did the trick. Mosquitos can neither breathe nor emerge through that film.

One day the CMO, sidling up in a corridor, instructed me to admit a woman with a fractured clavicle: both unwarranted, and a waste of hospital resources. Enquiry revealed that the patient managed a prominent local hotel, living in an apartment with her daughter, after whom—amongst other females—he lusted. This was a ploy to get mum out of the way for a few days. It left me feeling an accessory before the fact, with a nasty taste in my mouth.

The wet season was early, violent storms and huge falls of rain flooding much of the countryside. A call came from the Adelaide River settlement: the resident police officer, Tas Fitzer, was very ill with abdominal pain.

The flooded roads were quite impassable and Jack Slade assured me that the land was too soggy for a plane to land. The only alternative possibility for rescuing the patient lay by sea. The cyclonic winds having stirred the seas to fury, the only possibility lay in a vessel large enough to have a reasonable chance in mountainous waves. The Naval Boom Defence ship was the only suitable one there at that time. The officer in charge readily agreed to help. He was disaffected having been marked down by the brass as never to be promoted to higher rank. No doubt because of this and his enforced exile in Darwin, he was a very heavy drinker, with a strange, rolling gait. It was said that the only criterion as to his sobriety lay in his fly buttons. He was sober if they were all done up. He needed no persuading, nor did Father Flynn, who immediately volunteered: it must be said that the risks were considerable. The ship itself couldn't be taken up the river, not the least reason being the chances of it being fatally holed by one of the huge logs, wrenched up by their roots, spearing out to sea in that perilous flood. The naval officer instructed his men to load his own beloved, expensive motor launch on board (he came of a wealthy Queensland family).

Frank Flynn graphically related the adventure. Waiting only until a case of gin had been loaded at the skipper's insistence, they set out into the raging sea. The commander had never visited this part of the coastline before, nor had it been charted recently. The only charts he had were Matthew Flinders' original ones from 1802 but they fortunately proved to be completely accurate.

Lowering the speed boat over the side of the ship and scrambling aboard it as tumultuous waves thrust the two vessels up and down at uneven heights must have been hazardous in the extreme. No doubt the entire crew would have been severely tested, but not being there, I can't tell you their story. The river current was so swift that H, the officer, had to force the launch's engines to their absolute maximum to make any headway at all, ruining them in the event. It was apparently a nightmare, with logs rushing past and the land being submerged: where terra firma ended and river began was anyone's guess. Fortunately, navigation in those impossible conditions being miraculous, the settlement's jetty superstructure was seen peeping above water. The victim was brought back in good condition.

On their return, H did his best to finish up the gin with not a little success. Darwin harbour can be very tricky, with idiosyncratic currents. The strong winds can't have made matters any easier, but Frank said that he'd never seen anything like it. Barely able to stand, the man, supporting himself successively on the wheel and then the engine telegraph, manipulated that ship to come alongside with absolute perfection at the first attempt, even in those nearly impossible conditions.

The patient had a very nasty infection in his gallbladder. Threatening to burst, it presented as a large, firm, acutely tender mass below his rib cage on the Right side. He hadn't rebound abdominal tenderness: he hadn't developed peritonitis. Rebound tenderness: on pressing on the abdomen, then suddenly releasing, sudden pain occurring is an important, indicative sign of peritonitis or, in trauma cases, blood issuing from an injured organ..

Where to make my incision? For normal gall bladder surgery there are several options, though open surgery is performed much less often since the advent of operating laparoscopes allowing of so-called keyhole surgery.

The three most important incisions for open operations are the Kocher involving an oblique cut parallel to and a little below the Right rib cage, abdominal muscles, being all cut straight across. Inevitably, the nerve supply to some of the musculature is cut in the process, so I never used this, in my view brutal approach. As I read this to my writers' group, a member said:

'Oh! I had that incision. It's given me nothing but trouble!'

I also mentioned this to a close friend whom I thought had had keyhole surgery. He immediately harrumphed:

'Tell me about it. My incision's swollen and it's always painful.'

Paramedian and median incisions are the other alternatives. Because the paramedian is more liable to result in wound hernia, I always used a median incision. Properly sutured, this should never herniate..

Kocher performed much thyroid surgery and invented extremely useful tissue forceps. He should have concentrated his operating skill upon the neck.

Tas's case was different. I assumed, hopefully, that the inflammation, which must have developed over many days, had by then caused the gall bladder to adhere to the peritoneum. Cutting carefully through this adhesion directly into the gall bladder would be most unlikely to result in contamination of the peritoneal cavity with resulting peritonitis: always serious: much more so in those days. As a result I opted for a relatively tiny Kocher-type incision, enabling a cut over the apex of the swelling. As I'd hoped, adhesion had occurred, so it was safe to cut straight into the angry red mass. Thick, cheesy pus spurted out under pressure, to be quickly sucked out—a sucker is essential equipment in every operation. Using special forceps, a large gallstone was removed. Draining the wound with a rubber tube was all that was now necessary—apart from sewing up, of course. He recovered quickly, being well enough to return to his post by the time roads were open to traffic.

Just after the dry season began, I was called to Wave Hill station: nothing major, just a riding accident much less severe than was originally thought. One of the largest cattle properties in the world, it employed a large workforce, white and indigenous. The former dined in a stark, cement-walled room around a long, narrow table above which were long punkahs operated manually by ropes passing through holes bored through the architrave into an adjacent room.

Flies there were in millions. As the punkahs swung to and fro they'd spiral upwards from the table, then down again to the beat. Almost everyone in the room smoked roll-your-owns. What puzzled me was that the punkahs stopped when someone lit up: its operator couldn't possibly see into the room. The devastatingly simple answer was that the man about to light a match dragged the heel of his boot across the rough concrete floor. Though making little sound, it was heard by sharp ears next door.

Days, weeks and months had passed, but there was still no immunisation programme—fortunately no diphtheria either. For this and many other reasons, I wrote a letter of complaint to the Grand Panjandrum, Medicine, Canberra. A lesser but nevertheless grand Panjandrum was eventually dispatched to investigate. Apparently a weighty matter, some kind of court was convened. The Territory Administrator, drinking companion of the CMO chaired it. I gave my evidence in open court, if that's what one cares to call it. The CMO gave his refutation in camera, i.e. I wasn't there to hear it.

The Panjandrum duly departed and my good friend, Arthur, he of the flying goose episode, being the local manager of the airline, was there to see him off as he did with all VIPs. The CMO was there too, and, as the former was about to embark, he turned and shook the CMO by the hand:

'Well, cheerio X old boy, you're doing a great job!'

Arthur popped in with this news on his way home and my letter of resignation was on the CMO's desk the next morning.

Arthur, a delightful person, cheery, kind and thoughtful, helped me with my fish trap. We were next-door neighbours

Myilly Point, the site of our houses, overlooked two very different bays. One has already been mentioned; the other was less salubrious. Overlooked by the hospital, it had a rather muddy bottom, most of which was exposed when the tide went out.

I got the idea of building a fish trap: a line of wire netting leading out from the shore to an enclosure with a narrow opening. Swimming along the shore line, when fish met the netting, they would swim seawards along the 'fence' until they entered the narrow opening, whence there was no return. When the tide receded they were left high and dry, waiting for us to collect them. We had many lovely catches of barramundi and a variety of salmon until somebody discovered it and always thereafter beat us to the catch.

Communism flourished in those days and the head of the hospital union, Mrs Randall, though pleasant enough, was a red activist. She called a strike on specious grounds, thankfully ignored by the nursing staff. The main problem was that the hospital laundry wasn't washed. Arthur was the proud owner of a washing machine and kindly offered me its use, so, together, we did the hospital laundry!

Mrs Randall had a daughter, Treasure, who was often at the hospital, as was her fiancé, a policeman. They seemed a nice enough couple. When married, they were sent to a remote outpost. Only weeks later her husband shot her dead.

Arthur made a point of being present at all aircraft take offs and landings.

One morning he received scant notice of a plane's arrival. Hurrying down his stairs, at the landing, he went straight through it, hitting the ground with a painful thud!: termites had been active in the night. Listening at any of his walls, these little creatures could be heard chewing cheerfully away. The name of his abode? White ant Mansion.

His delightful wife gave us a very worrying time with her first baby, who showed a marked disinclination to arrive. For days Bobby lay in some pain but made no progress: so-called primary uterine inertia. A pituitary gland extract that hurries things along wasn't then available. (Later, when in Saudi Arabia you'll hear about gross misuse of this substance). I finally resorted to the application of obstetrical forceps and the charming Kerry arrived intact.

Recent mention of Communism reminded me of another patient. After so many years most patients inevitably are lost to memory unless they were of special interest in some way. This memory is of Bob Markham, who was already an inpatient when I arrived. He was a dedicated Communist and we often chatted together, the conversation inevitably arriving at his favourite subject. As I'll mention in the next chapter, I was aware of my youth and was eager to glean as much knowledge about religion and politics as I could before making any possible commitment. Bob eventually persuaded his wife to bring his most prized possession to the hospital for me to inspect: a massive tome interlarded with fragments of important flags and suchlike mementos from the time of the October Revolution. Though interesting—and probably valuable—one was not entirely overwhelmed.

Poor Bob had an inoperable squamous cancer of the neck which he bore with great fortitude and good humour. One morning it eroded his carotid artery and he was gone in an instant.

Before farewelling Darwin, further mention of obstetrics must be made. Though Harry H liked it and did most of it, I had to do my share. It was usually a middle-of-the-night affair and, on entering the labour ward, one was greeted by a long line of green frogs sitting complacently on the water pipe. Rather charming, one thought. They did no harm.

One day Father Flynn introduced me to a really delightful lady in an advanced state of pregnancy.

'She has a slight problem, Wylie, so I'd like you to look after her.'

This problem proved to be the worst, most florid and extensive varicosities of the veins of her nether region that one could possibly imagine. They were thin-walled, too, so, fearful of haemorrhage when and after giving birth and there being no transfusion or other like facilities, I declined with thanks.

'No' Said Frank firmly, 'D refuses to go South. You can do it!'

So there I was. Thank God, her labour went very smoothly. I didn't even have a heart attack!

My daughter Prue was born there after I'd given notice:

'Prudence has arrived!' Announced the telephone in the middle of the night, so I rushed to see her.

Just as well I did: when I examined her she was covered in blood. A poorly applied tie had come off her umbilical cord and it was still bleeding.

The poor little soul had another early problem. We flew back to Brisbane in a Qantas DC3 aeroplane and though the journey took all day she didn't complain once, even though—or perhaps because—at about nine thousand feet—we were more than a little shaken about.

Because of the rough weather, the pilot took us up to more than eleven thousand, whereupon Prue suddenly turned blue and began to gasp distressingly. I signalled the stewardess and the pilot promptly descended.

Of interest was a halt at Longreach, whose small terminal was adorned with the propeller of the first Qantas plane which had begun its operations from there.

In those days there was an organization, the Empire Medical Advisory Bureau. They'd kindly accepted me under their wing for postgraduate studies, booking me in for a basic sciences course at Middlesex Hospital in preparation for the Primary exam of the Royal College of Surgeons. It wasn't due to start until almost a year hence: I needed a job in the meantime.

Before we return to the tropics, however, something of my thoughts and beliefs which guided me: I think successfully, might be of interest. My serious failures must form part of these considerations.

Religio Medici

At this early stage of my life I was surrounded by a whirl of thought and opinion, political and religious, so I made every endeavour to arrive at beliefs that were as informed as possible.

I had no trouble with the Labour Party, in power in Queensland since 1915. It was totally corrupt and its socialist ventures such as a government cattle station and shipping line were expensive failures enriching their operatives. There were restrictive boards for everything, even second-hand packing cases. Its bureaucracy flourished like the introduced foreign weeds that infested the state unchecked, From one of the most active and enterprising, *avant garde* states it had become a laggard and high taxes had driven enterprises elsewhere.

Socialism has never, ever succeeded. The most spectacular fall was of the Soviet Union, but in elective polities there is a rhythm: socialist government runs down their countries' financial resources; free enterprise party pulls things together. In the meantime, who has suffered the most? The working class to which it has directed its messages: messages, like those of its opponents, filled with lies, distortions and obfuscations. Deng Shou Ping was smart enough to realise that and, still with a Communist pseudonym, introduced a capitalist economy into China.

But, earlier in Australia the Communist Party was very much in evidence and many of my friends in the early forties especially and acquaintances too believed in it or its principles.

The horrors of Soviet Russia hadn't as yet been realised and one whom I—wrongly—assumed would be my future brother-in-law, though not overtly Communist made strong cases for Soviet Russia. He laboured dialectical materialism as though it were a magic formula, so I studied it and Marxism, but decided that the former was merely a trumped-up justification for revolution founded upon a complete *non sequiter*.

Thinking I could be missing something I continued with my subscription to the *Australian Communist Review* until its odious justifications for China's rape of Tibet made me close my subscription in disgust.

At the time, that only left the Nationalist Party which Bob Menzies metamorphosed into the Australian Liberal Party. He did so many things of which I approved that I supported it, finally even entering the Australian Parliament as a member. Once there, I gradually came to realise that the system specifically breeds untruthful self-serving hypocrites concerned solely with self-advancement and power and that there is no real democracy, only an oligarchy which ensures the alternation of power between two political juntas, many of whose power brokers are unelected.

My awakening had been gradual. Though I realised that most of my colleagues left much to be desired, this failed to ring a bell. The first tinklings began when I was elected to the allegedly prestigious Public Accounts Committee. This razor sharp monitor of public expenditure operated as follows: the committee sat around a table and was informed as to the department which we were to keep in financial order that day. When that department's representative appeared, our bureaucratic boss handed us each a question which we were to ask. We dutifully carried out our little tasks in order around the table and Bob was your uncle. I resigned after three meetings of this hypocritical pantomime.

Power and wealth are the two major evils corrosive of human character and elective forms of government not only attract but specifically nurture those who will do anything to achieve it. Because of this, it should be made impossible for anyone: absolutely anyone at all, to achieve power by any kind of negotiation, be it through the all-too-fallible ballot box; by force; by bribery or any other means. The sudden realisation of this meant that when I lost my seat as the result of a redistribution, I made no effort to re-enter that jungle of conspiracy. The world deteriorates in almost every way, year by year because those in power are those least to be trusted to exercise it.

I put a lot of study into this problem and then wrote a widely unread book about it: Jefferson's Disease: the cause and cure for sickness in the body corporate.

Religion also occupied a great deal of my thoughts.

I was raised a Presbyterian because that was my father's faith, so strongly held that he consented to be Clerk of the Session of his church. Sadly it won't stand up to much scrutiny. John Knox was ghastly, his theory of Election worse: we're born inexorably either to go to Hell or to Heaven when we die: nothing we can do about it. Knox, of course, was one of the Elect, heavenward bound.

The Elect had the right to bully and otherwise maltreat their unfortunate inferiors.

If that weren't off-putting enough, I thought their Holy Communion a farce. Instead of wine, grape juice was drunk: and that, sitting up like Jacky. I felt that when dealing with God we should do it in a submissive manner, preferably on our knees.

Then there was Anglicanism: real wine and on our knees was a good start. Moreover, when I was so ill, the only clergyman who visited me was Anglican and he was charming. For quite some years I regarded myself as Anglican though I seldom entered one of their churches. But then I became very friendly with a fellow collegian, John Farnworth, who persuaded me to accompany him to a couple of Catholic services. These attracted me so much that, when in Darwin, I broached the matter to Frank Flynn.

For some reason he didn't answer any of the doubts I had and instead he sent another priest to talk to me. Perhaps he realised that the doubts I had were insoluble: transubstantiation and Papal infallibility. This priest was quite hopeless. So I didn't become a brand plucked from the burning.

At the time I hadn't come to appreciate the absurd irreconcilability of the Holy Trinity, so continued as an occasionally practising Anglican.

Doubts became stronger as I studied Ancient History: many Mithraic practices mirrored Christian ones too closely for comfort. Christ certainly existed: that was evident from one of Tacitus' remarks. But was he actually the son of God? I still believe that he was, but no more so than you or I.

I don't really know what removed the scales from my eyes. Looked at dispassionately, the whole Christian system is a whole load of hogwash. That doesn't mean that some of its principles aren't good. In the harsh environment of the Middle Ages many wonderful people did what they could to ameliorate suffering despite the greed and criminality of their superiors. People at the bottom have always tended to be more humane and honest than those intent on climbing to the heights. Against the charitable amongst the humbler clergy stand the purveyors of indulgences and the like, knowing them to be bogus and people like the Countess Judith, William of Normandy's close relative who not only presided over a convent but also ran a brothel.

The *Bible* is flawed, the *Old Testament* a mix of fairy tales and folk history. Why did Moses grind the Commandment tablets to dust in his wrath? Because they never existed, so couldn't be produced. The *New Testament* was written long after Christ had departed, one way and another and typifies much writing of the first couple of centuries of our era, including much fiction that the authors thought appropriate to the story.

Christ is even a debatable figure. Some historians think that he was complicit in the murder of John the Baptist, whom he perceived as a rival.

So it's all bunk? Probably. Worse, like all organised religion its evil deeds far outweigh its good ones.

When they have the power, organised religions are unrelentingly ruthless and oppressive: every one of the rotten lot.

So God doesn't exist? It's all arisen because people are afraid of dying? Absolutely not. I firmly believe in God, Creator of Heaven and Earth; of all things visible and invisible.

Which reminds me: that bit comes from the *Nicene Creed*, hammered out by a ruthless bunch of 'religious' politicians who, as soon as they'd got their version approved, set about the destruction of those who held alternate views.

A little sidelight: the Western Communion is actually guilty of heresy, thanks to Charlemagne's insertion of the word *filioque* into the wording of that creed.

But enough of this: I see the universe as a wonderfully integrated whole, the Earth in particular as a marvel of systems that work wonderfully down to the minutest level. In particular, consciousness can still only be credibly explained on the basis of the existence of a Creative being. I don't confine that to humans, who, because they can't commune with other animals inner thoughts, wrongly believe that they don't have any: they do, but I shan't prolong my argument along those lines. There is evidence that all living cells possess some form of consciousness in the broadest, not in Jung's sense.

Evolution certainly occurs and in some cases it almost appears that this results from some urge on the part of some creatures to evolve. This, however, isn't a crude Darwinian process. Take the Cypriot bee orchid. The flower is indeed constructed to resemble a bee, which is needed to fertilise it. This shape isn't the main reason for its attractiveness to that creature: it is the secretion of female bee pheromone which does the trick: inexplicable on Darwinian grounds.

Speaking of bees: these little marvels have merely a couple of ganglia for their central nervous system, yet perform miracles of hive husbandry and are able to assess the quality of flowers and their location and can convey that information to their fellows.

There's more, but I'll leave it at that.

More and more people are becoming atheist and the more there are, the more will relinquish any belief, because we are herd animals: either leaders or followers, the curse which has brought politics into existence.

This instinct pervades all aspects of human activity. Even where one might least expect it: in science. Even here aspirants for a place in the sun must conform to the current beliefs of the leaders. If you don't subscribe to the Big Bang theory, for instance, woe is you. Your papers will be relegated to neglected journals. No professorships for you either!

Yet the Big Bang would be impossible without the intervention of a god: mass so concentrated would explode long before it reached that impossible density.

And the Universe isn't expanding. If it is, then why, all over the Universe, are galaxies colliding?

The cosmic microwave background? Fossil of the Big Bang? Or there because of the lost energy from light in its travels across virtually boundless space?

There has to be a mistake in their sums: a faulty assumption or a false approximation.

Perhaps that will ultimately help explain Quantum Theory which runs so against instinct. Surely chaotic behaviour in the very building blocks of matter can't result in totally orderly behaviour in visible matter.

But you've probably had enough of that.

I do believe in God, but also believe that, though He has no intention of instructing us to adopt any particular belief, evidence of His presence is everywhere.

So evil will be punished in the hereafter? There will indeed be a hereafter? I have no idea. I only know that there is a God whom I believe to be good.

Before all operations early in my career and before dangerous and complicated ones always, I prayed for His guidance and I do believe that my results have been well above average.

Over fifty years of practice I have only a few regrets and these still bother me.

I hate obstetrics—though I won the prize for the subject in my final year—but, rejected by my colleagues when I returned to Ipswich I had to bring some babies into the world—and did so for friends later, too, to my dismay.

One patient was Greek and very shy of Australians generally, so I agreed to look after her. Her pelvis appeared to be of normal dimensions, but the largish baby failed to progress far enough: I delivered him with obstetrical forceps. The poor little fellow died after a few hours. I believe that I should have delivered him by Caesarian section, an operation which, in any case, I enjoyed performing.

Only three of my patients died inter operatively: the ruptured aorta already mentioned and a patient who had a heart attack before I had begun the operation. I opened his chest and massaged his heart for ages: it would begin to beat, tantalisingly and then stop again until I finally had to give up. The third was a Fijian toddler who had an enormous abdominal tumour. His frail constitution wasn't up to the trauma of the necessary surgery.

Five also died soon post-operatively. The most puzzling one was a Chinese lady from the far outback whose husband wanted me to perform a hysterectomy—for valid reasons, of course. She was terribly shy and uncommunicative. The operation went well—at least so I believed, but post operatively she gradually wilted away for no apparent cause. An elderly lady upon whom I performed gastrectomy faded in much the same way.

I was good friends with Jack H upon whom I'd already performed anterior resection of the rectum for cancer. This recurred and he wanted me to try radical surgery, which I did, It proved to be too much for his system. This was probably just as well: he was spared the end result of this horrible disease.

Charlie M, elderly, developed cancer of his bladder, which I removed and then transplanted his ureters into his lower colon. This, again, was too much for him, but better, in my view, than dying of that cancer.

One new-born baby had multiple atresias of the small bowel: long segments had failed to develop and had to be resected, Many lengths of bowel had to be joined together. This, again, was too much for the little soul.

I can't think of others and they do stand out in one's memory.

I thank Good for my good results.

THURSDAY ISLAND

After Darwin, a position was almost immediately forthcoming, on rather romantic-sounding Thursday Island, in the Torres Straits which separate Australia from New Guinea. A couple of weeks after departing from Darwin I was on a two day bucketing in a DC3 to my new place of employment. The first leg took me to Cairns, the day following to my destination. That section of the journey is vivid in memory. Once airborne, the captain passed the word down that unfortunately the air inlets to the cabin wouldn't open. Imagine a tin tube exposed to the raging tropical sun: stifling beyond description. Dehydration was inevitable, but when I ordered a beer, the only beverage on board, most of the bottle's contents emptied itself on to the cabin's ceiling.

Thursday Island being predominantly hilly, planes land at Hammond Island. A ferry takes passengers across the water.

We were accommodated in a Commonwealth house and I suppose that's why I was now also a Federal quarantine officer, unpaid, even though my paymaster was the Government of Queensland. If there were medical problems on passing ships, I was entitled to charge for my services. Before long a schedule of fees became necessary. The scale of charges was directly proportional to the distance travelled. If a considerate ship's master hove to not far from the island, my charges were modest. Anchored out in the open seas, in view of the fact that the quarantine vessel was not especially seaworthy (it was known as the floating coffin), my charges escalated considerably.

On one occasion I was called out to a ship, the *Wave Baron*, many leagues away. Leaping on to the ladder from the heaving launch and finally arriving on the deck, one was loudly greeted by the jolly *I'm Looking over a Four Leafed Clover* roaring out of the ship's tannoy: it was the time of the Al Jolson revival.

My reception, however, was in marked contrast. The master was especially unpleasant, obviously angry at having to halt his progress because of a sick sailor. He reluctantly took me down to see the chief cook who'd fallen ill, I suspected, correctly as it transpired, with amoebic dysentery. With a difficult to treat food infection of this kind he certainly shouldn't have been allowed any more contact with the kitchen, so I took him off to the hospital. His off-sider also claimed to be ill, obviously falsely, but because I'd been called out into the raging sea by such a rude, aggressive man, I took him off, too and hoped the meals for the next week or two would be basic in the extreme.

These trips were always fascinating with waterspouts seen everywhere, especially towards the New Guinea coast: dark, swirling fingers poking out of clouds, tips probing around before finally making contact with the sea.

More intriguing was a variation in the sea levels. Water travelling from the Indian to the Pacific Oceans—or vice versa—had either to travel through these straits or far away to the South of Australia. The currents in consequence were strong and unpredictable. Whirlpools were everywhere and when the launch passed over them, it would veer vigorously to and fro, literally doing the twist. In places there was a noticeable step in water levels of perhaps even up to a couple of feet as it swirled in different directions.

When the Festival of Britain was drawing in huge crowds on London's South Bank, there was a clever device purporting to tell tide times for anywhere in the World on any given date. I tapped in high tide, Thursday Island, such and such a date. It produced specific times: all lies! Tides there are unpredictable with often an ebb on the North side; rising tide on the South.

One launch trip was especially memorable. It was to check on sick people on several different mission stations in the Gulf of Carpentaria. The lengthy journey began in the afternoon and when the stars began their brilliant display, wheeling slowly overhead as we gently rolled our way southwards, the boatman, an aborigine and I sat together on deck talking. Such circumstances breed togetherness and we formed a real bond, so much so that he told me a great deal about his tribe and its customs, including secret tribal matters and taboos I'm sure he wouldn't have imparted in other circumstances. It was probably indiscreet of him, so it's only right to be silent about what he said. He was of the kangaroo totem, that I'm prepared to mention.

The first stop was at Mapoon. Like all missioners the manager was most hospitable and lent me a horse so that I could explore the surrounding rainforest, replete with ferns and orchids.

Weipa was well under the control of a Scottish couple who'd retained their well-honed accents even after twenty years' exile. Attendance at a religious service was mandatory and to this day I can hear the voice, standing out above all the others, high pitched, incisive but sweet, of an aboriginal girl behind me:

'....I am all infirmity.'

A universal expression of the human condition, I thought, greatly moved.

The presence of bauxite there was known, but nothing had yet been done to exploit it. Now Weipa's a large thriving settlement replete with huge machines including an enormous wheel which, rotating relentlessly, gouges out vast quantities of little round reddish balls, depositing them on conveyor belts that dump them into the holds of waiting ships. It's then transported, usually overseas, to be converted into aluminium.

Most memorable of all was Arukun, supervised by a most saintly person. When sitting in his library—an extreme rarity in that part of the world—I remarked upon his full set of Bairnsfather's *Fragments* from France: marvellous cartoons humorously depicting the appalling existence led by unfortunate soldiers in France during the First World War. My father had these too and I used to read and re-read them when young. It was obvious that they were amongst his few most precious possessions, but, when I mentioned my appreciation of them, he insistently tried to force them upon me.

The mission is/was some distance from the water and when I left the entire population came down to the boat and sang *Now is the Hour when We must say Goodbye*. Whose eye would be dry?

On the long trek back to semi-civilization one marvelled at the richness of the marine life in those shallow waters; not least the sinuous legions of sea snakes dangling from the surface of the sea.

The joke was on me on another voyage. A cyclone had just passed over. Whether or not this was a contributing factor, the man looking after the repeater station at Jacky Jacky, on Cape York Peninsula, had gone 'troppo'—off his head, in other words. Those were still the days of the overland telegraph. The postmaster asked me to assess the poor fellow and, if necessary administer a tranquilliser before taking him back to the island.

The station was a mile or so from where we'd anchored. As I was disembarking—into water almost waist deep—the postmaster suggested I remove my shoes:

'Don't spose yer want ter get 'em wet, do yer.'

I fell for it. When we were on our way, I was reminded that death adders were prevalent in these sandy parts. Indeed they were, lying concealed under the sand with only their worm-like tails showing. When these are touched, most commonly by an unfortunate creature in search of a meal, the reptile rounds at lightning speed, envenoming its prey. Is one able to walk a mile without feet touching the ground? I certainly did my best!

The patient was calm if incoherent. No violence, fortunately and to our delight he didn't try to jump overboard on our way back.

The Island community is relatively small: people get to know one another. The islanders were friendly and often popped in with gifts of pearl shell or dugong steaks or turtle meat, the latter accepted in the spirit in which they were given. They're very musical and the evenings were beautified by their lovely harmonies, more easily understood by Western ear than those of the aborigine.

The powerhouse shut down at eleven pm, the moon and stars then providing the illumination. One evening a dusky shadow flitted across the hallway as I prepared for bed in the gloom. With a roar, I took off in pursuit. It was an uneven contest, especially when the gravelled roadway was reached: and my tender feet prevented much progress. I found myself, with wild surmise, stark naked, at the adjacent intersection. In the unlikely eventuality of my catching up with the thief, what would have happened? Most islanders are tall and muscular. Probably, chuckling, he was watching me from the shadows.

Though formerly a warlike people, I never once had to treat a case of human violence.

One day, the ruler of some of the outer islands was brought to the hospital. Extremely frail, silver hair contrasting with his dark, deeply wrinkled skin; very ill, he was still able to conduct his court. He lay propped up on pillows in the ward: more or less a broad semi-enclosed veranda. His retainers squatted on the floor around him and, given a gesture of command, one or other would rush off to do his bidding. He was diabetic, one of his legs having become gangrenous, he was dangerously ill. Amputation was unavoidable.

Arrived on the island, I was delighted to discover my old friend, an Oxford Vaporiser, the same semi-primitive anaesthetic machine I'd found in Darwin. Nobody knew how it came to be there but, presumably, it had been left behind by the army at the end of the war. This meant that I'd be able to give my own anaesthetics. There was only one other doctor on the Island and he was often away elsewhere. This old king, however, was much too ill for ether anaesthesia, so I instructed the local plumbers (and Lords High Everything Else!) to make a metal trough to my specifications. Also the icemen, these entrepreneurs provided the cracked ice I needed. The royal leg was placed in the trough and packed with ice. When it had lost all sensation. It was swiftly removed using the time-honoured *tour de maitre*, skin and soft tissues being cut through to the bone in one circular motion.

This was the only humane approach on battlefields in the days before anaesthesia. This, of course had to be followed by haemostasis, easy in my present case. In healthy wounded soldiers in medieval times, this had to be accomplished at great speed because the severed large femoral artery would forcibly eject virtually all of a person's blood in seconds. In those far off battlefield days this catastrophe was prevented by plunging the stump into molten pitch, a far from painless procedure. It wasn't until the Sixteenth Century that military surgeon Ambroise Pare came up with the bright idea of the ligature. In the present instance the Femoral Artery was so occluded by atheroma that there'd been but a trickle of blood into the limb: hence his problem. He felt nothing, but jumped when the sciatic nerve was cut. Skin apposition after the tour de maitre isn't as neat as when skin flaps are raised first, though that rarely presents a problem.

Speed in this case was of the essence. I've noticed that, for some reason, nursing staff react with something akin to horror when bone is being sawn through.

The operation was successful, as the saying goes, but ... he lingered for a couple of days then died. My last view of him, or at least his coffin was of it bouncing around in the back of the plumbers' speeding pick-up truck on its way to the cemetery. They were also the undertakers.

It was apparently the great-great grandfather of this potentate who'd attacked Bligh in his open boat at Attack Reef as he made his way to Timor after being turfed off the *Bounty*.

In the early fifties advertising, less omnipresent but more intelligent than in these dark days, could be amusing. Some of the ads in carriages of the London Underground carried amusing illustrated verses, one of which comes to mind:

> 'Rejoice you scum' cried Captain Bligh:
> Five months adrift, 'the shore is nigh'.
> He seized his log: We owe salvation
> To pluck, to faultless navigation;
> To discipline; to lack of gin
> And wearing wool against the skin.
> The last a most essential rule:
> There is no substitute for wool.'

Pearl diving in the Straits was active at that time: sharks always so. They're one of very few predators man hasn't eliminated as a significant killer, yet a lunatic subculture of our race wants them protected. They're ecologically essential and beautiful, too, they say. Of course that's rubbish and that latter quality is very much in the eye of the beholder. Protect sharks that don't eat us, yes, by all means, but man eaters? What could be more idiotic? The excuse that they're invaluable scavengers isn't valid: there are any amount of creatures, more benign varieties of sharks included, ready to take their place. Moreover, in this world of increasing food shortages, these creatures both consume far too many edible fish and are themselves edible.

In the short time I was on the Island, a little more than five months, there were a couple of fatalities there, thanks to these predators. However, one diver was hauled on board his boat just in time. I had to attend to his leg which had been badly mauled, those rows of razor-sharp teeth having inflicted deeply incised multiple wounds—multiple in this case is an altogether inadequate understatement of the man's problem—which ran all the way down one thigh and leg. After blood loss, the main worry in such a case is sepsis, which is always very much a problem with wounds sustained in coral seas. With appropriate treatment: constant irrigation and debridement of necrotic tissues as they appeared, infection was fortunately a minor problem.

Patients from one or other of the outlying islands often arrived for treatment. One day a lass from Saibai, which is very close both to New Guinea and to disappearing beneath the waves, presented with an old Bell's palsy. This rather disfiguring complaint often follows a chill, a condition rather unlikely so close to the Equator, or to an infection or other cause which produces a swelling in the Facial Nerve as it passes through a narrow hole in the skull. It can be transitory, in which case supporting the sagging face and lower eyelid with strapping is, in my view, a good idea. This case was permanent and she finally prevailed upon me to operate.

A dense layer of fascia overlies the Temporalis Muscle: it can be felt tightening at the side of the head when teeth are clenched. I cut the fascia into a number of 'fingers' and attaching this to part of the muscle, brought each finger down to a different part of the face: below the eye; to the cheek, upper lip and beside the chin by tunnelling through the facial tissues with a long pair of artery forceps (Harrison Cripps), anchoring them with sutures through the skin. There was less bleeding than expected in an area so rich in blood vessels, though I did use a drainage tube. I was quite pleased with the result. So was Temkisa Wiiya—I think!

Scotty, the matron, phoned me whilst I was having lunch one day. She sounded distressed and asked me to come to the hospital ASAP. She had a quiet word before taking me to see two completely distraught Anglican nuns, just arrived in a small open boat from Lockhart River mission, a couple of hundred miles to the South. A man at the mission had developed tetanus, so this gallant pair had put him on board and started out for Thursday Island in something little bigger than a dinghy: in the open sea! Each time the boat rocked, or a larger than usual wave struck, the poor victim would develop tetanic spasms. Agonising is a totally inadequate word for the resulting pain: imagine cramp, affecting the entire body, magnified many times. The inevitable screams of agony must have traumatised those gentle creatures. They'd almost reached their goal when the man sadly died. Putting ashore on Cape York Peninsula they buried him.

Arrived on TI they naturally reported immediately to the Anglican Priest. This representative of Gentle Jesus, meek and mild ordered them to sail back to their mission immediately, yes, then and there, after days battling the seas to the accompaniment of screams of the afflicted man. Moreover, being gentle nuns they were distraught at having lost one of their community in such heart rending circumstances, I ordered them into hospital for observation—and the loving kindness of Scotty and her staff of loving, conscientious sisters. I never spoke to that swine of a clergyman again. As one might expect, I believe he later became a bishop.

One morning an infant was brought in to the hospital in a moribund state, suffering from severe diarrhoea, I was unable to save her life. More children, from all quarters of the island, began appearing, a number of whom died. The widespread distribution of the illness indicated that it was waterborne

The island's water supply came from a dam in the centre of the island surrounded by hills. I took the hospital secretary's car, not being important enough to be allocated one myself and inspected the dam. To my horror, numerous islanders were camped within the catchment area, without any sanitary provisions. Rain sent their excreta straight into our drinking water.

I rushed to the quaintly denominated Protector of Aborigines to tell him, rather breathlessly, of my discovery. The Lord High Bureaucrat in his department, I'd wondered why he'd been located here rather than in Brisbane: a disciplinary matter, or by his own preference?

When Whitlam introduced his brainless turtle farming project there, the manager was located, as one would naturally expect, in Canberra, thousands of miles away. Perhaps in this instance it was his own choice, after all: he had at his disposal a comfortable yacht, the *Melbidir*, courtesy our generous taxpayers.

This doughty bureaucrat expressed surprise, dismay and, indeed, every appropriate emotion, promising immediate action. With admirable consistency he did this each time I pestered him. Nothing happened. Surprised? Fresh from Darwin, I'd been here before, very recently. I allowed ample time for something to happen—remember: this was a serious epidemic—so when nothing happened I made the only move that could possibly eventually result in some improvement: I resigned.

A Labour Government had sullied the State of Queensland for about thirty years, doing it a lot of no good. Corrupt, it retained office by gerrymanders, the Catholic Church and intimidation of trade unionists through numbered ballot papers. It was extremely nepotistic and I knew that appeals to higher, i.e. parliamentary political levels would have no effect. I returned by boat and someone must have tipped one of the local newspapers off: on disembarking, I was met by a reporter. My tale was published next day.

My father was an old school chum of the Chief Bureaucrat, Health, for Queensland. Reading the newspaper report, he promptly phoned my father: to express contrition for this disgusting state of affairs? Just to say Hello? No, to express extreme displeasure, to say the least. One learns more about bureaucracy as time rolls on, little is ever favourable!

The P&O steamer *Strathaird* was due to leave for Tilbury, so I booked my passage and spent the interim studying, excepting for a delightful couple of weeks at the seaside with dear Arthur Krieg and his little family. Funnily enough, guess who the quarantine officer was when the ship was quarantined at Fremantle? None other than my erstwhile Darwinian CMO! Why this tumbling to earth? Perhaps he'd blotted his copybook once too often:

'I'll quarantine you on your way back!' he smiled.

Postgraduate England

The Empire Medical Advisory Bureau had arranged a very nice apartment for us in Kent, an easy train and tube journey to the Middlesex Hospital, and a course to improve one's chances at the Primary exam for the Fellowship. Students were there from all over the past and present British Empire from Oz and New Zealand, Canada, South Africa, Egypt and India (the abject, lamentable, mistake of dividing the Indian subcontinent had just been made). All were bright and eager to learn. There can have been few courses more brilliantly conducted, staffed with more gifted lecturers. Anatomy was under the aegis of one Dr. Wall who, at the course's conclusion traversed the entire anatomy of the human body, central Nervous System excepted in one single lecture. There have been few more exhilarating experiences than following him in that lecture.

The initial Physiology lectures were given by Samson Wright, author of a famed textbook: entertaining and witty to say the least. The main body of that course was delivered by David Slome, a Jew of such imposing presence that one fancied him an incarnation of Zadok the Priest. Brilliant fails to describe his ingenious, witty, entertaining and thorough lectures. His mnemonic for Thyroxin's formula: two little mice, one of whose tails has been bitten off was superb; still remembered after seventyty five years.

On one occasion he said:

'The results of any action whatsoever are: local and general; immediate and remote, but you are all such idiots that you'll forget that forthwith.'

'I won't!' piped a know-all from Western Australia:

'Ten pounds (a great deal in those days especially for students) says you will.'

'You're on!'

Of course Slome won. One day he worked us up to fever pitch on a fascinating topic at the then growing edge of knowledge.

'And what's the result of that (a particular manoeuvre)?'

Seething with excitement he pointed to his victim. The answer required rapid thought. He gave a short answer.

'Ten pounds you owe me: it's always immediate and remote; local and general!'

How we laughed.

Slome was an inveterate gambler and with a surgeon, Mr. O'Shannessy, was a pioneer in experiments to restore the circulation to diseased hearts with coronary artery disease. They used racing greyhounds for their experiments, tying off their Coronaries, then bringing a fold of tissue from the abdomen, attaching it to the heart. The procedure is now obsolete, of course, but their dogs won races.

When our exams loomed, he had some means of discovering whom our examiners would be, dividing us into groups accordingly, taking each through those examiners' idiosyncrasies and usual questions. More than that, this man of extreme enthusiasm would subject each student to an individual, private *viva*, pretending to be the appropriate examiner.

These were the glorious days before political correctness and some questions were humorous but in doubtful taste. One of my examiners, Professor Harris of Cambridge had three favourites:

'Can a cat eat cartilage?

Can a cow walk down the middle of the road?

Why is the bladder lined with transitional epithelium?'

The answer to the last is: because it's piss proof. The others are a bit esoteric.

As it happened, he asked me none of these, but as I waited my turn at the periphery of the exam room, I did hear:

'Because it's piss proof!'

Booming across the room. He proved to be charming but, as you've guessed, eccentric. We got on extremely well, and he asked me if I could, on my return home, send him some fruit bats:

'Yes, sir, you mean flying foxes?'

'Yes sir, I mean fruit bats.'

If I could (as it happened I couldn't) yes sir, yes sir, three bags full!

My next examiner, in anatomy, was one Mr. Mitchiner who, with gaol cropped hair and steel-rimmed specs stood grimly like some convict 99 behind Prof. Harris whilst this exchange was going on.

'Bribery and corruption!'

This without a smile, proceeding to give me an unholy grilling. He had a cadaver beside him and every organ, nerve or blood vessel I had to identify was an abnormal one or in an abnormal position. Worse, when I gave the correct answer to a question, he cut me off with a curt No! Then proceeded to give the correct answer word for word to my own.

I knew about this man and was sure that he'd failed me. He'd just come out of the army with the rank of Major General. Once, on manoeuvres with his troops, he over-nighted with another regiment. He sat down to dinner in battle dress on a dining-in night, officers being required to dress in formal finery. The Mess Secretary approached with some trepidation:

'Excuse me, sir, but this is dining-in night. I'd be most grateful if you wouldn't mind removing your battle dress.'

'Certainly!'

He took it off immediately and dined in his underwear.

I didn't like him at all because of all the trick questions and went to receive my results in chastened mood.

These were given out on the same evening in Examination Hall, Queen's Square. Here we were herded together in a room, overlooked by a huge Queen Victoria in supercilious mood. All escape was prevented by two functionaries who, after an eternity, stood at the exit, one calling out our numbers in turn. They were practised sadists:

'Number so-and-so!' A victim shuffles forward.

'Number so-and-so?'

'Yes.'

A long pause, though he must have known what came next.

'Dr. X?'

A tremulous 'Yes.'

An even longer pause, everyone present goggling. The verdict was either :'Sorry sir, you've failed.' Or 'You're through.'

After which, with near unseeing eyes, one tottered on to the street, looking for the nearest pub. As it happened, I was lucky and found a pub.

Hammersmith Hospital

This hospital, with its Royal Postgraduate Medical School isn't in Hammersmith, silly! It's in White City. I got there thanks to the ever helpful EMAB. Getting into this hospital was a most tremendous boost.

Promptly after passing my primary I'd successfully applied for a senior House Surgeon position in a large town I shan't name. The letter confirming the appointment came on the same day as the Bureau put on a bun fight for its protégées. The Director welcomed me, so I asked for a word:

'I've just been accepted for a senior houseman's position in X. What's the town like, sir?'

His voice shook with emotion:

'The last place on God's earth!'

Food for thought indeed. A little later, a tiny, unimpressive man edged up to me:

'Care for a job in Hammersmith Hospital?'

The brain did computations. The other hospital was more than a hundred miles from London, whereas Hammersmith was right there, though I'd never heard of it. It had to be better!

'Why, thank you very much.'

'Your first position will be in the Radiotherapy Department, thereafter in Surgery. Come along next Monday.'

I didn't know how such an insignificant person could have that amount of authority, so asked:

'Whom shall I ask for?'

Drawing himself up to his full height of five feet nothing:

'Why ME of course!'

It transpired that he was the Lord High Everything Else, Medicine, for the entire North West region and Hammersmith Hospital incorporated the (now Royal) British Postgraduate Medical School. What luck!

Furious study of radiotherapy for the next few days. The Medical School turned out to be the most intellectually stimulating place I've ever experienced: incisive thought with lots of most enjoyable cut and thrust. It was then at the forefront of a number of disciplines. More importantly, from a personal point of view, the professor of Surgery, Ian Aird, had written the main surgical textbook I was using.

Students and junior staff, varied in age, included not a few grey hairs. One member of the grey haired contingent fascinated. Working as a medical missionary in Kashmir, he'd written a monograph on Khangri cancer. Kashmiris endeavour to keep themselves warm in their freezing winters by wearing a Khangri, hung from string around their necks: pottery vessels which burn chinar leaves, rather like sycamore in shape. Smoke and heat from these cause a special kind of skin cancer on the chest.

At the end of my first week, still thoroughly nescient about place and staff, the department held a demonstration day. I was allocated a man with a fibrosarcoma in the Right armpit. He'd been given more than 6,000r radiation already: a large dose. The hard lump hadn't been affected, though his skin was darkening and beginning to show the first signs of weeping: reaction to the treatment. r stands for Rontgen, named after the discoverer of X rays and is a unit of radiation dosage. Various tissues and different cancers differ widely in their response to these deadly rays.

The demonstration was going well when another grey haired student ambled up, took a look, examined the lump and said in his best Scottish burr:

'Tha' would be a lymphosarcoma.'

He referred to a commoner cause of lumps in this situation that's very radiosensitive. It was clearly necessary to put this ignorant student to rights: teach him a thing or two:

'Now, please just tell me: how this could possibly be a lymphosarcoma. 6000r? Marked skin reaction already and the lesion hasn't responded one little bit.'

And so on and on. The student nodded and trotted off. Minutes later a registrar hurried up;

'Where's Professor Aird? We need him urgently. You were talking to him a moment ago.'

Muggins had been ticking off a most influential man. I was terrified lest he should do something unpleasant, perhaps even have me sacked for insubordination. Nothing happened. He probably laughed at the brash Australian.

The position was most interesting, affording many insights into a wide variety of cancers. The mood in the wards was never gloomy, some of the patients being very cheery indeed. One old dear, fresh in the memory, asked every morning how she was, invariably replied: smarshin', even though dying of cervical cancer. On the other hand, nobody ever actually asked me about their prognosis.

Some think that cancer sufferers should be apprised of their fate, citing all kinds of reasons: all specious. The victim will know soon enough and if they choose to live in a temporary state of happy ignorance, why shouldn't they? If they ask, then tell them of course, as tactfully and positively as possible.

The wards were very busy and all lung cancer patients from the region ended up here. Professors Doll and Bradford-Hill had just brought out their seminal work on the association of smoking with that grim disease. I asked all of my lung cancer patients about their habits: all smoked.

Interestingly, this distinguished pair sent a questionnaire to every doctor in Britain inquiring about their smoking habits. Five years later they sent another, similar one. The results were amazing: the death rate—from all causes—of smokers was astoundingly higher than for the virtuous group.

There were a couple of patients with advanced thyroid cancer who'd needed tracheostomy to enable them to breathe, the cancer having encroached on either their larynxes or wind pipes . In other words, they needed a permanent tube into their tracheae, made of metal. (hence ... ostomy, making a mouth or permanent opening as contrasted to ...otomy, cutting the organ open with a view to closing it later) They couldn't wear these when receiving radiotherapy: metal would concentrate the radiation, causing severe burns around the tube and alter the distribution of the rays. Someone—Muggins—had to be close by when treatment was in progress in case the patient's airway became obstructed. I thought this silly. A newly introduced plastic, polyethylene, could be made into tubes and the like and wouldn't affect the patient or the radiotherapy dosage distribution. I went down into the bowels of the hospital to talk to the technical staff. Yes, it could be done—and was. From that time onward both patient and doctor breathed easy during treatment.

One interesting patient was an old dear who'd had her scalp injured by bomb fragments in a first World War Zeppelin raid. The wound had never healed and now her entire scalp had been replaced by a basal cell cancer. The other name for this is rodent ulcer and it's common. The good thing about it is that it never metastasises, i.e. spreads to other parts of the body.

Strong in the memory is a young woman with two young daughters, brought in with a ruptured ovarian cancer. Even today this condition has a bad prognosis, mainly because it tends to be diagnosed late in the disease. Her cancer had embedded itself all over her peritoneal cavity, causing ascites: free fluid in her abdominal cavity, which, swelling inexorably, was causing great discomfort. Her worry was that she'd never see her girls grow up. We immediately developed strong rapport.

Her treatment began in the usual way—there were few alternatives to radiation in those days—and her abdomen was irradiated (Manchester Bridge method), a procedure usually associated with unpleasant vomiting and diarrhoea: the lining of the bowel is especially sensitive to gamma rays. After only a few days she vomited uncontrollably and was kept alive with intravenous fluids.

From the first day of vomiting I'd been protesting that there was an alternative: radioactive colloidal gold, being produced at the establishment at Harwell. My nagging finally paid off and the consultants agreed to its use—if I administered it.

The solution was extremely beautiful: a glorious purplish-blue, but the entire department stood at the far end of the ward whilst I inserted a needle into her tummy, drained off some of the fluid, ran the gold solution into the peritoneal cavity, then placed her in a number of different positions in the hope that the gold would occupy most if not all of the nooks and crannies.

Their fear was completely illogical, as the distance over which this substance acts isn't much more than one centimetre—a cause of worry from the point of view of its effectiveness. Surely they were aware of this?

It wasn't only effective, it was miraculous and before long the swelling had disappeared and she went home to her little girls. There was no sign of recurrence for the remainder of the time I was in the department.

I grew attached to those wards and amongst fond memories is recollection of my evening ward rounds. In one ward, a kindly sister always left out a large bottle of stout for me which I consumed whilst reading the daily papers of which there was always a good selection. In those happy days the Health Service made alcoholic drinks available to these patients.

Because of these feelings, just before returning to Oz I asked if I might do a ward round, both for old time's sake and in the hope of chatting with any old patients who still happened to be there. Nowadays, of course, they would all have been turfed out long ago. Though there was, indeed, a general shortage of hospital beds at that time, the position was controllable. On entering the female ward I suddenly stood stock still: there was my ovarian cancer patient. I greeted her fondly and sympathetically, but discovered that there had been no recurrence of her ovarian problem. She'd developed breast cancer. I doubt if she managed to survive this, because, largely as an experiment, Hammersmith was treating all breast cancer patients with radiotherapy only, without surgery: never, in my view, an effective approach.

Nowadays there are vast numbers of ways in which cancer may be treated, many extremely sophisticated and causing less harm than the old shot gun radiotherapy. At the time we're considering, apart from surgery, radiotherapy and that precious gold –very rarely used—there were few alternatives and in fact I am only able to remember two: cyclophosphamide and nitrogen mustard.

The origin of the latter is quite interesting. During the ghastly first World War, one unsavoury way of killing and maiming involved the use of mustard gas, a little more vile than chlorine.

Inventors of killing devices: do they go home at night to wife and kids and say:

'I've had a wonderful day today inventing a brilliant new land mine: it'll blow both legs off and the gizzard out of anybody within fifty yards!'

'Oh, you are so clever papa: perhaps they'll give you a knighthood.'

'No, probably only a CBE.'

Nitrogen mustard becomes liquid at relatively high temperatures, tending to persist in low lying places. Some sufferers from leukaemia found themselves in the neighbourhood of old battlefields soon after the war when the weather warmed up in 1919 and were affected by it. It was noticed that their condition improved, leading to research into the substance. Nitrogen mustard was something of an improvement on the gas itself.

As a consultant surgeon I treated a large number of breast cancer patients. My preference for treatment was a regimen developed by Professor McWhirter of Edinburgh: local mastectomy, removing the breast only, but all of it, taking the skin incision well wide of the nipple and the cancer itself, then sending the patients for radiotherapy as soon as possible after the operation—almost always after seven or eight days. The wound, of course, had to be healed. Admittedly I cheated on occasions. Despite McWhirter's recommendations, if the glands in the armpit had become affected, I'd not extend the incision but, disturbing tissues as little as possible, remove them.

One of the marvellous things about Hammersmith was that not only could one often manipulate the times one worked and thus attend many of the lectures and conferences, always in progress, but timetables were arranged to allow us to participate in them as much as possible. On days off, one could attend the operating sessions, ward rounds and outpatient clinics of the great and good in surgery in any and all of the London hospitals. Some were indeed great, but some had feet of clay. Some told awful porkies. For instance, Sir Gordon Gordon-Taylor (not a surgeon at Hammersmith) maintained that his breast cancer patients had well over ninety percent survival over five years, which just could not be. He had no magic formula.

I was also shocked by some of the techniques employed in bowel surgery by one surgeon, later ennobled. His Christian name was Hedley. His house staff called him 'Deadly'. My old teacher, George, had cautioned me about several errors which his lordship habitually made. Risking boring you, I repeat:

> 'The race is not always to the swift, nor the battle to the strong.'

Another surgeon there, Sir Heneage O, was known as Sir Haemorrhage O. In another hospital, a 'world authority' on parathyroid disease couldn't answer even one of my questions about surgical problems connected with that gland.

On the other hand, word of mouth led me to some superb surgeons who didn't have posts in the famous teaching hospitals.

Funnily enough, on moving over to surgery at Hammersmith, I found myself on Prof. Aird's team. He was a great lecturer and a charming person, but it was soon apparent that the poor fellow was a manic depressive. It was hair-raising when he operated when manic, his gestures and movements being exaggerated as is usual in this disorder. Once, when removing a gall bladder, he cut the common bile duct—a decided and definite no no.

Of course, he wasn't the first, nor by any means the last to do so, but that's no excuse. At about the same time, Walton, supposedly a giant of abdominal surgery, performed the same trick on then Prime Minister, Anthony Eden who had to be flown to America to have the potentially lethal problem fixed by a real expert.

That episode changed British political history a little because though, like so many politicians at the top, his mental state at the best of times was questionable, after his ordeal Eden's emotions became altogether too labile, hastening his erasure from the grubby political scene.

Because of his emotional vagaries when operating, I found the practical aspects of my apprenticeship with the Professor too traumatic and of no help where technique was concerned, so in some way which I've forgotten, I managed to get myself on to what I still believe to be an exceptionally gifted team: Mr. Franklin, senior general surgeon, Mr. Gray, senior orthopod and a junior vascular surgeon whose name I forget. Vascular surgery was then in its extreme infancy.

Mr. Franklin's fully deserved reputation was of the highest, his technique superb. He was at the same time quiet, kindly and full of humour. The latter could be rather sharp at times.

Work on cardiology was at the World forefront at Hammersmith under the aegis of Professor Mc Michael. His reader was a New Zealander, one Russell Fraser and we rather looked on him askance as, in furtherance of his research—and bubble reputation—he catheterised the hearts of newly born babies in the Obstetric Department—healthy or no.

One night Fraser developed acute appendicitis so, being smart, he elected to have my chief do the job. As he lay in the anteroom awaiting his anaesthetic, Mr. Franklin approached:

'Oh, by the way, Fraser, I'm sure you won't mind if we catheterise your heart whilst you're under the anaesthetic!'

Red-haired Fraser's colour, like Phyllida's

'Trembled to a lily and wavered to a rose.'

There was something to be learned from Mr. Gray—apart from looking out for his vicious temper—but orthopaedics was still in its infancy. For instance, the surgical treatment for arthritis of the hip was barbaric in the extreme: the head of the femur, in one favoured operation, was simply cut off, full stop, or, as a refinement, the top of that bone was splayed out at an angle in a forlorn attempt to minimise the inevitable lurching gait that followed. A special contrivance of leather was often strapped around the waist in a doomed hope of increasing stability when the patient walked.

A notable advance was made at that very time: we listened in wonder at this new departure and studied the X rays of the operation intently. The inventor of this procedure was one Smith Petersen, the inventor of the nail I used to fix fractures of the hip. He reamed the femoral head to remove the arthritic knobs and excrescences and inserted a metal cup over it before replacing it in its socket. There was less lurching than with the Girdlestone method mentioned above, but still an unacceptable unsteadiness, nor was the end result uniformly pain-free. Near perfection still had some years to wait. Gray performed none of those. Instead, faced with unbearably painful arthritic hips or knees he would arthrodese the joints, removing all of the cartilage covering the articular surfaces of the bones, then immobilise the joint until the adjacent bones had fused together. Varying kinds of bone graft were usually necessary as well. Knees in such cases were fixed in a slightly flexed position to aid a more normal walking gait. The hip was a different matter and this was probably the reason why Girdlestone and others had devised the wibbly wobbly approach already mentioned. When the hip joint has been stiffened, movement must now take place between the pelvis and vertebrae, leading to arthritis in the backbone and thus back pain, often so severe as greatly to impair quality of life.

Mr. Franklin, on the other hand, was a fount of most important knowledge, especially where gastrectomy is concerned. In the absence of effective medical treatment, a high proportion of peptic (gastric/ duodenal) ulcer patients had to have a greater or lesser portion of their stomachs removed. In cases of cancer of that organ, a very lethal disease, the entire stomach should be removed.

The operation for benign peptic ulceration is now performed much less frequently now that more is known about those conditions and reasonably effective medical treatment is available.

There are many different surgical approaches to the problems. In the later eighteen hundreds, a German surgeon, Bilroth devised two different types of operation which in principle cover the various perms and coms of doing the deed. Both assume that a capable surgeon has removed all of the necessary tissue required by circumstances: usually a greater part of the stomach and a greater or lesser part of the first part of the duodenum, depending upon where the ulcer is. Orthodoxy had it that, after that step, the cut end of the duodenum was closed and the jejunum—the small bowel next along from the duodenum—should be connected to the stomach. The popular version, the Polya, is a type of Bilroth's second operation.

When I was learning about these, b.f. (before Franklin) I was given all of the reasons in the world why the Polya was superior to the Bilroth 1: the opening in the latter would be too narrow; the suture line might leak; in order to join the two ends without tension it isn't possible to take away enough of the stomach; the world might come to an end if a Bilroth I is performed and so on. My time with Mr. Franklin changed my views completely. It is vastly superior in every way. It's the Polya that has a dodgy suture line. I've seen a number of unfortunates where the now blind end of the duodenum has fatally burst. Moreover, the food after that operation now travels in an abnormal direction, going straight into the jejunum, imperfectly mixed with bile and pancreatic juice. There's also an increased chance that the stomach/small bowel junction will ulcerate. Many Polya victims suffer from the 'dumps', a very unpleasant sensation experienced after eating.

The Bilroth 1 connects the two cut ends directly, the only snag being that the diameter of the cut end of the stomach, many times that of the duodenum, must be narrowed. That's surely enough about those pros and cons; suffice it to say that this wonderful surgeon conclusively demonstrated that the alleged advantages of the Polya over the Bilroth I are completely without foundation, a fine example of the herd instinct so deeply embedded in all of us and all aspects of our lives. Leaders of the surgical herd issued the edict that Bilroth II operations are the ones of choice and it is so—in the minds of the following surgical herd. Joining the pack has its advantages of course: it always pays to cultivate herd leaders if bubble reputation is what one aspires to.

Another surgeon in the hospital who'd adopted this game plan and was on his way up—I have an idea that he even managed a knighthood—performed the Polya. He was hopeless in any case. I saw him, during ward rounds one day, spend a little extra time with a youngish woman upon whom it had been—shall we say executed? It was obvious, at least to yours truly, that her duodenal stump had blown, but our doughty ST felt that he was dealing with a psychological problem and jollied her along with motivational talk. She was dead before his round had ended. Such clinical acumen!

Herewith a Jeremiad on the decline of clinical acumen, that essential element in good medical practice, already mentioned in connection with my old surgical professor. Nowadays this attribute appears to be in the discard, partly due to the Legal profession's greed—well, it's not a profession any longer, is it? Professionalism? The Oxford dictionary doesn't help much, overlooking as it does the ethical constraints that once governed the practice of Law, Medicine and other professions.

Greed has always been with us, no professions ever having been exempt. When professionalism was at its height, however, I believe that many of its members, took pride in their skills, deriving pleasure and satisfaction in using them to benefit mankind. Money? Of course it was important, but not all-important.

Pardon me for saying that my father's great exemplar has coloured my views. Principal of a busy legal firm, he literally slaved away at his work, bringing it home with him after a long day in his office. If any clients were ill or infirm, without hesitation he'd visit them in their homes—after work, of course, often bringing me along, largely I suppose, to witness wills. Sometimes my mother and brother joined us and I have the acutest feelings of nostalgia when thinking of the three of us waiting in our car on some country road, singing songs in the encroaching gloom.

My father often spoke of the people he was about to see and, this being in the time of the Great Depression, many were struggling for existence. Sometimes it emerged that he had saved one or other from having their home repossessed. Moreover, if they were very poor he'd never even consider charging a fee. That's not the stuff of making a great fortune, but we were comfortably off and really wanted for nothing, but the deep satisfaction my father derived from his professional life was always evident—and we were a very happy family.

Nowadays greed reigns supreme. Professionals are free to advertise themselves and most certainly do. I strongly believe that this cheap commercialism is demeaning. When a customer—I use that word advisedly—walks into the office, lawyers don't see a person with a problem to be fixed but instead not just a fee, but one to be maximised—and so do far too many members of my own profession. Material gain is everything.

This has had terrible consequences. The effects of greed, now universal and not confined to professions, will be final and fatal. The upward spiral in extracting earth's all-too-finite resources has inevitably led to an upward one in atmospheric pollution and a downward one in the amount of available resources. This absolutely can't go on and it's my view, for several reasons, that Earth will have seen the last of its human incubus by the end of this century

Greed in the Legal profession has totally destroyed the wonderful old doctor/patient relationship. Egged on by venal vultures, patients now sue doctors successfully on most ridiculous grounds. Lawyers, including judges, rarely medically qualified, cannot—and, apparently, will not—recognise the extreme variability of the human body and its reactions to differing conditions, including treatment by varying means. First class clinicians have been taken to the cleaners despite impeccable practice which, nevertheless, has led to bad, but completely unavoidable results. This has had at least five dreadful results: it's led to such a colossal increase in the cost of indemnity insurance that in some countries it's caused many doctors either to emigrate or seek other jobs; it's necessitated an unconscionable increase in the number of pathology tests and X rays, to the extent that medical costs have rocketed. It's also led to alienation of the medical profession and, at the same time, loss of clinical acumen.

The fifth adverse result concerns obstetrics. In the good old days, a very rewarding part of a family doctor's duties involved bringing new life into the world, further cementing the doctor/patient relationship. Nowadays few if any GPs would be brave or foolhardy enough to buy into that can of worms. HK, whose work I know and respect is being sued over a confinement he conducted twenty years ago. The child concerned is of low intelligence. In search of a quick buck, the parents suddenly hit on the wheeze of blaming HK and suing him for a million dollars.

Returning to the matter of clinical acumen, a patient on presenting with a problem nowadays is subjected to a barrage of tests, some of which actually cause harm, many of them unnecessary if the doctor used his brains. Fear of greedy legal operators has done all this and more. It goes without saying that these investigatory media are marvels of science and invaluable if used properly and in due measure.

Whilst the heat under my collar abates I'll mention briefly a victim of this medical fad for catheterisation of hearts and great vessels in

Hammersmith's Medical Department. The name of one of my patients, appropriately enough, was Mrs. Slaughter. She had a congenital problem, polycystic kidneys, its name surely self-explanatory. The medicine men heard about it and persuaded her to allow them to catheterise her inferior vena cava, the great vein that drains virtually all of the blood from the lower half of the body including the kidneys, directly into the heart. Murphy's Law reared its omnipresent head and her great vein clotted, with dire consequences.

A third surgical team at Hammersmith was led by Mr. Shackman. He was an enterprising soul and when Brock, a surgeon at the London Hospital, began to operate upon the heart, something hitherto impossible, thanks to technical constraints, Shackers followed suit, but with less good results, to say the least.

It must have taken Brock a great deal of courage to undertake that pioneering work. Lung surgery was just coming into its own: there'd been a tremendous psychological barrier to opening the chest and more sophisticated anaesthesia, which made it much safer, hadn't long been developed. The heart, however, had an even more powerful taboo against it being opened. Fame is indeed that last infirmity of noble mind, seeking the bubble reputation an infirmity of much less noble ones. The leaders of virtually every social pack snap,snarl and bite—usually metaphorically— at anyone with the temerity to embark upon anything which could be interpreted as a challenge to them.

Take Lord Lister before he got to the top of the heap. In his early days, the accepted treatment of compound fracture was to leave the wound open. Thanks to the prevailing ghastly conditions in the wards and complete ignorance of the causes of wound infection, the wound inevitably became infected and poured pus. If it didn't, there were instruments designed to generate what was then known as laudable pus. The end result was almost always amputation, continued sepsis and the ultimately fatal amyloid disease—but see Sir Percival Pott later in this book. Surgeons in the not-so-good old days operated in frock coats: the stiffer from soiling from blood and pus, the more it was treasured. A very senior surgeon had a rigid coat. Is it any surprise that the infection rate was high?

Lister had the temerity to treat one particular child's compound fracture with his revolutionary antiseptic method, closing the wound and keeping it covered. Professional outrage amongst his colleagues—or competitors?—was so great that, had the patient come to any harm, he would have been drummed out of his profession. Fortunately for him and countless thousands of people since, the wound healed by first intention.

Similarly, if Brock had lost his first few patients, his name would have been mud, to say the least. Lister and Brock were winners, an equally brilliant man called Semmelweiss a loser. An Obstetrician/Gynaecologist who practised as professorial assistant at the Vienna General Hospital, he was one down for starters because he was just a silly Hungarian, not a brilliant, world bestriding Austrian. The death rate from childbirth was astronomical, so he put on his thinking cap.

At the time, staff and students performed autopsies on the many victims of puerperal sepsis, then immediately proceeded to the delivery room. Though Pasteur hadn't as yet made his seminal discovery, it occurred to our friend that some factor might be carried from autopsies to the delivery room. He suggested that people wash their hands before going from the former to the latter. His professor pooh-poohed the idea despite the fact that when hands were washed the death rate declined by a factor of about ten. He stuck to his guns so was sacked. He knew that he was right, so wrote increasingly angry letters to his colleagues. He'd have to be mad, wouldn't he? I mean to say, what a silly notion he had. None of the herd leaders in his profession believed it. There was only one thing to do: lock him up in an asylum. He died about a fortnight later, probably beaten to death.

Don't smirk: that attitude's still alive and well and Brock must have been aware of it. Viewed from today's perspective, his operations were crude and the dangers of opening a heart in the way he did present fewer risks than one might imagine. He parted Mitral valves which had become stuck together because of a rheumatic infection. This valve, between the left atrium and its ventricle, prevents blood from leaking back into the atrium when the powerful ventricle contracts, forcing blood around the entire body. If its two leaves stick together and thus narrow the opening between the two heart chambers, blood tends to back up into the lungs with ultimately fatal results. The problem is magnified by the fact that the flow of blood in to the ventricle is also diminished, leaving less to be pumped around the body.

Though an enormous volume of blood constantly flows through, its pressure inside the atrium isn't terribly high, making it relatively easy to control blood loss when it's opened. Brock sewed a purse string suture around the auricular part of the Left Atrium, incised it, put his finger through, quickly tightened the suture to minimise blood loss then unstuck the valve with his finger, giving enormous temporary relief and extending the patient's life span by a year, often much more. Ultimately the valve cusps stuck together again. In any case they were still deformed. But it was the great breakthrough and encouraged more and more advances, especially as anaesthetic techniques became increasingly sophisticated.

Shackers was always one for heroic surgery. This usually meant copious blood loss. To counter this he used—and I think actually devised—a huge glass reservoir into which vast quantities of blood were poured. The tank contained a number of tubes with a rotating pump in the middle: hence it's colloquial name, the whirling spray. He always needed several hands on deck and this sometimes included me. The operations went on for hours and when his field was the pelvis he needed every drop of that blood. Pelvic veins are thin-walled: easy to tear. I remember him battling for hours trying to staunch bleeding caused thus, ultimately unsuccessfully, despite his whirling spray.

Everybody who'd passed the English Primary exam was entitled to sit the finals held by any of the other British Surgical Colleges and my employers benignly allowed me time off work to go to Edinburgh to sit their finals. I passed. The examiners were kindly and gentlemanly. One question was on the treatment, in immense detail, of pyloric stenosis in infants. I'll tell you more about this later, but it's a blockage of the outlet of the stomach in new-born babies—usually males—due to an overgrowth of the muscle regulating the flow of food from stomach to duodenum. I'd seen many cases at the Royal Brisbane Children's, even operating upon a couple. I felt that that got me through. The results were tactfully given through a side window, in contrast with the custom at the English College.

The dread finals there reared their ugly head and I passed these too. The examiners were courteous, the method of delivering the results brutal. A crowd gathered in the College hall where, thoughtfully, a bar, well patronised by those awaiting their fate, operated. The moment of doom arriving, a uniformed functionary positions himself at the foot of the staircase, ascent of which leads to the Elysian Fields of Fellowship. A name is called. The hopeful leaves the protection of the throng, including his sisters, his cousins and his aunts, apprehensively approaching the stairway. The functionary enquiring the candidate's name consults, entirely without haste, his list. He looks at the victim:

'Sorry sir, you've failed.'

Humiliated, the figure dejected but smiling bravely, totters back to the crowd. But if it's 'You're through, sir!' The happy soul floats up the stairs to be congratulated and given a glass of sherry.

The only other memories of Hammersmith are the wonderful lectures and conferences, stimulating to the point of exaltation. I didn't apply to stay longer because the Korean War had broken out and there was everywhere talk of World War III and the effects of atomic bombs dropped upon London. I had a little family and thought it unfair to subject infants to that terrible risk. I was offered a locum position with Mr. Franklin at one of his other hospitals, so accepted with gratitude whilst organising a return to Oz. It was quite a thrill to be called Mister rather than doctor, though that wore off after twenty four hours.

Still no bombs, so I took a registrar post with Mr St.John Buxton, another irascible orthopod. Hip replacement techniques had advanced slightly and my chief was the pioneer in England of the Judet hip. In retrospect, this was doomed from the very start: the arthritic head of the femur was cut off and a substitute fixed in its place by pushing the stem of the new head through a hole bored through the middle of the neck of the femur and then across the thick, cortical bone. The results were most gratifying—for a very short time. The new head, made of acrylic, couldn't possibly withstand the wear and tear of every day walking. Moreover, there was nothing really effective which would prevent the stem from working loose. The poor patients probably didn't think so, but this was a faltering step in the right direction—to be continued.

But the threat of World War III and atomic bombs still hung in the air. Family booked home, I signed on as a ship's surgeon to save a little money.

Just before I left, Miss Spence-Sales, Mr. Franklin's anaesthetist rang and asked me if I'd like to be his assistant at another hospital. How dearly would I have loved to, but the die had been cast, so one fine sunny day I set sail on the good ship *Delphic*, a cargo vessel bound for Australia via the Panama Canal.

Ship's Surgeon Bundaberg

It was some days before I met the master: the sea was rough and he, like Captain Corcoran of HMS *Pinafore*, was hardly ever sick at sea. This was an exception. The waves soon settled, however, and a hardly exacting routine began. This consisted of a morning round of the ship with the skipper; a morning surgery lasting perhaps half an hour, the majority of patients being lead swingers, some most inventive; pre-luncheon drinks—the hardest part; lunch; sleep; deck croquet with Number One; pre-dinner drinks; the movies or Twenty Questions with the crew; more drinks; slumber.

Gin and tonic was *de rigeur* before lunch. It proved too much, especially as it has never been my preferred beverage. It was far more pleasant to opt out and read a book instead.

'Oil and water don't mix.' So quoth the Captain and Chief Engineer, each on numerous occasions. The engineering staff took no part in the social activities, so, to be fair—as I saw it then—I'd often have a pre-dinner drink with the Chief Engineer.

Oh! I nearly forgot about the animals: I also had to look after their health and well-being: sheep, cattle and many dogs, including a giant mastiff. The latter animal was huge and probably could have bitten my hand off without noticing—and I had to treat a canker of his ear which evidently caused quite some pain. The first grip of his ear was tentative indeed, accompanied by any number of good boys but he submitted gracefully to my ministrations, probably understanding the good intentions.

At night it was wonderful to sit up on the top deck on clear nights and listening to the soothing puttering of the engines; watching the brilliantly coruscating stars as they wheeled slowly around the sky, patterns slowly changing as we moved South.

I can't remember how I came to be on the wharf at Panama before the ship finally berthed: I believe I must have jumped off the gangway as the ship slowed, but not enough. As I watched with disbelief, I saw the doughty *Delphic* plough its way inexorably into the timbers of the wharf a couple of feet from where I stood. A glance up at the bridge revealed a highly agitated captain dancing around and waving his arms—to no effect. Apparently one of the engines snuffed just as he rang full astern. The ship suffered some buckling of the hull, but not enough to render her unseaworthy, so there was no delay. It was a very pleasant thing to gaze at the lush vegetation passing slowly by as we traversed the Canal.

Once into the Pacific, it was non-stop to Sydney. We did sail close to Pitcairn Island whence some of the crew of the *Bounty* lived with their paramours to escape the lethal wrath of Bligh and the Admiralty. One morning I awoke to a stationary ship and a chorus of nasal twangs. Sydney!

One must eat, so my brother, appreciating this fact, had applied on my behalf for the position of Medical Superintendent, Bundaberg General Hospital, an institution attaining notoriety fairly recently, thanks to the maniacal ministrations of one Dr. Patel—and the failure to take any notice, during his tenure, of a lone whistle blower who was so appalled at his treatments that she overcame her amply justified fear for her job.

Whistle blowers are very brave people who receive no credit for their gallantry. Sacking, even serious persecution is the almost invariable result of their calling attention to serious problems, even criminal misdemeanour as messrs. Assange, Snowden et al. have discovered.

The UN and EU are well known hotbeds of corruption and incompetence. The invariable result of any employee calling attention to it is prompt sacking. The most recent sacking is of someone who highlighted multiple rapings by UN troops in the Congo. How dare that person spill the beans! There's no escape for those honest persons. The mills of both execrable organizations grind exceeding small.

The position at Bundaberg was, for the most part, very pleasant. The daily ward rounds with the matron, efficient and compatible, were always congenial and one could, if one wished, read all of the X rays and perform such tests as barium meals. There was any amount of surgery, too and once a week an Orthopod would come up from Brisbane to help. There was lots of this, mostly of the traumatic variety. In particular there was a dangerous combination: a straight stretch of road North of Bundaberg bridge and more than a few youngsters in and around the town who rode their motorbikes along it at the maximum speed they could coax out of their vehicles: ninety miles an hour seemed to be the average, from what they told me. When things went wrong—as they inevitably did—hours and hours would be spent surgically picking up the pieces. Few if any died so far as one remembers. I recall one, Baldwin by name, who was discharged just after I arrived having broken a leg and who popped up again not long afterward with another, very bad break which kept him in for some time. He waved away all counsels of caution and was admitted once again not long before I left.

Sadder was the case of Ken D, who'd collided with a tree in such a way that his Right Brachial Plexus was torn asunder, leaving him with a virtually denervated arm which had lost all feeling and movement: a useless appendage. He naturally took this badly, and finally persuaded me to try to do something surgically, even though assured that the odds were practically nil. I exposed the plexus, which is in the neck, carefully excised the ends of the torn nerves, suturing them together, preserving as nearly as possible their original orientation. He did get a twitch of useless movement which raised his hopes, but I understand that he later committed suicide.

There were also many fractured necks of the Femur, i.e. of the hip. The head and neck of the femur break in several ways. The treatment of choice is, in my strongly held view, the nailing or screwing of the fragments together unless the blood supply to the head has been destroyed. It's actually a fun operation, especially now that one can view one's efforts in real-time by using an X Ray image intensifier, which hadn't then been invented.

The standard approach is to reduce the fracture, then, after gouging the hard outer bone from a small area on the femur's upper outer aspect, making the next step practicable. A guide pin is passed through the fracture as nearly as possible through the middle of the neck of the bone. In the days before the intensifier, X rays had to be taken, developed and then assessed by the surgeon; tedious and time consuming. It's necessary to take views in two directions: fore and aft and laterally. A pin apparently in superb position in one view might be sadly astray in the other. In those days, Smith Petersen's tri-fin nail, hollow to pass over the pin, was the method of choice for immobilising the fracture. It was hammered over the guide pin when one was satisfied that the latter was in good position. Some of these fractures also required the addition of a plate, further to stabilise the break.

The snag at Bundaberg was the boringly long time it took the radiographer to take the exposed films in their rectangular aluminium holders, scuttle downstairs, develop them, breathlessly essay the stairs again and hold them, still wet, over the viewing box for me to assess.

There was the added problem that the hospital boasted but one portable X ray machine. This meant a great deal of messing around, altering surgical drapes and so on, whilst the machine's position was altered for both views to be taken. Sterility could easily have been compromised whilst the drapes were rearranged and the X ray machine moved: a constant worry.

Lord Lister came to the rescue. When he introduced antiseptic surgery, he had a carbolic spray in constant operation. Every instrument, before use, was passed through this spray. The X ray Department was a busy one, with lots of traffic passing through, inevitably carrying lots of germs. Lord Lister had little or no sepsis in his wounds, so what was good enough for him was good enough for yours truly. So, to minimise the delays when a fractured neck of Femur arrived, I'd close, then personally spray the X ray room with carbolic as thoroughly as I could and use that as an operating theatre. The patient lay on the X ray table. For the A-P view, the large, fixed machine was used, whilst with the good leg cocked over the portable machine the lateral view was obtained. No running up and down stairs; no fiddling around with the patient's position: it was a doddle!

It rather disgusts me that all too often today this operation isn't used, total hip replacement taking its place. Though that's a good, indeed marvellous operation, it should hardly ever be used here. It's not always done well and too often the results only last for a limited number of years before the replacement has to be repeated. It's also an operation which is far more traumatic, putting a strain, not infrequently fatal, upon a frail patient—they're frequently elderly, tending to fall more readily, breaking an osteoporotic bone. My brother was such a victim. My scheme worked well with no wound infections. At this distance in time I can't remember many unusual cases from Bundaberg, but two do spring to mind, both surgical. One was a very unusual lymphosarcoma—a type of cancer—of the small bowel. I resected it and could see no abnormal lymph glands so did nothing radical. It was towards the end of my stay and I don't know if the patient was actually cured.

Another patient came in bleeding profusely from the bowel and, as I couldn't even guess at the cause, I did what's known as exploratory laparotomy. There, in the small bowel, were innumerable polyps, busily bleeding away. It was necessary to resect a largish portion of the Ileum, the part of the small bowel that empties into the colon. If one has to resect more than a certain proportion of the small bowel, diarrhoea and nutritional problems arise. Fortunately he escaped these, but might not have survived had I not chanced to visit him in the wee small hours. He'd lost a very great amount of blood and a negligent sister—unusual in that hospital—had failed to supervise his transfusion and the blood flask was empty: had been, the patient said, for some considerable time.

Bundaberg was a friendly place; pleasant, too, with fishing and an indifferent surfing beach nearby. Sadly, from my point of view, it had two fatal faults: the pay was derisory and the job led nowhere. As to the pay, my opposite number in Townsville, on the same salary, estimated that if the hospital gardener worked for the hours he put in, he'd be paid at least twice as much.

I wrote, offering my surgical services, to all of the doctors in my home town of Ipswich. The answers, if any, were a snub: NO! But my parents had stood by me when I'd gone to England for further studies. In filial piety, I thought, I'd go there anyway. In other words, the next stop was:

IPSWICH

Just at that time, a general practice in the town was advertised: the very one from which my old chief George Brandis had practised before moving to Brisbane. Overcoming a disinclination to enter general practice, I thought that this might be some kind of answer: that a beginning here, as in George's case, could lead to a specialist surgical practice.

I remember speeding down to Ipswich in my little grey rear-engined Renault and in particular listening to Josef Schmidt singing *Der postillion von Longumeau* in incisive, silvery tones on the car's radio. I thought how ghastly it was for anyone, but especially one with a talent like his, to be snuffed out because of some bizarre—in this case Nazi—credo. Strange, isn't it, how such minutiae remain in the memory?

The vendor, poor old Donald C, showed me over the premises—with which I was already familiar—repeating that I'd be very successful there. His mood was extremely odd and he made no mention of sordid financial details or, indeed, much else. I went back to Bundaberg to think about it. Donald cut his throat two days later. Superstitious, perhaps, but I didn't like the idea of bringing myself and family to a suicide address, especially as I'd known the poor fellow from my previous work in the Ipswich Hospital.

At this time I was also offered a partnership in a busy practice, but declined with thanks as this would almost certainly mean that I'd be a GP for good and all. Surgery was my thing, so I decided to 'squat'.

My father found suitable premises which, it so happened, were, unintentionally, almost opposite to the surgery of the practice in which I'd been offered a partnership. News gets around. Just before I left Bundaberg, the Queensland Director General of Health, aka the one-armed bandit partly because he did only have one arm, phoned and asked if I'd like to become a surgical consultant at the Brisbane Chlidren's Hospital. Of course I did!

On my first day in Ipswich, latish in the afternoon, I had my first patient, a non-surgically acutely ill man who'd presented at the practice opposite. Doctors at that time in Ipswich worked very leisurely hours, so the answer to his plea to be seen as a matter of urgency was: NO.

'Do you know of anyone else who might see me?'

The answer was the same, even though I'd paid a courtesy call to the doctors in that practice that very morning. My paranoia now had something substantial to work on, albeit a little triumphantly. It was given a boost a couple of days later. There was only a British Medical Association in those happy days: no Australian one. I'd had my professional name plates prepared by them—one for Ipswich and one for Wickham Terrace, home of the specialists, in Brisbane, where I'd also set up my shingle. If there'd been anything questionable about those plates the Association would certainly have suggested that I change them. The Brisbane plate had my qualifications in the usual abbreviated form, but as the local yokels of Ipswich were, at that time, innocent of any experience with specialists, on this plate, I had them printed in full. One evening as I say, a couple of days later, Stuart, one of the local GPs, not of the lot opposite appeared:

'You'll have to have your plate changed. You shouldn't have your qualifications set out in full.

 Because, of course, it would be bad for his business. He was actually the doctor whose knowledge of my previous illness—his parents and mine were old family friends—spared me a wartime of skirmishing in the wilds of Western Australia. I both said and did nothing. Well, I might have said

'Oh, yes?'

Virtually all of the local GPs were appointed as honoraries to the hospital in those days on the tacit understanding that Dr. Trumpy had full control. I was appointed likewise, but with this difference: I performed all of the major surgery. Heretofore this had been sent to Brisbane. Now cases rolled in, three bags full. I'm sure that almost all of the GPs loved the idea because, of course, it kept me from my consulting rooms. I didn't care.

In the first place, I loved surgery; in the second, it pleased me to perform a service which allowed patients to have visitors who didn't have to trek all the way to Brisbane, essaying the difficult task of finding a parking place (an incident highlighting this problem comes soon); thirdly, I was fully aware of the hostility I'd created and believed that the enemy had demeaned itself by referring patients to me in the public hospital when they'd die rather than refer them to me privately. There was one noteworthy exception and, if you're still alive, Merv. and chance to read this, my hearty thanx and very best wishes.

As a matter of fact, two of those perishers called me in consultation when their children became ill and I operated upon one. No referrals followed. Of course those machinations didn't keep me from my rooms: I merely worked longer hours and in my first month of work in Ipswich I earned more, gross, than in my whole year at Bundaberg.

Remember my parenthetical reference to parking near Brisbane General Hospital? Here's a story from a few years subsequently: An excellent artist in his early thirties struggled into my Brisbane rooms. He'd been diagnosed as having the dread MS. He wanted confirmation. His trouble struck him suddenly, whilst driving his car near to that hospital. He felt very ill and had lost some of the use of his legs. Even in those days, that establishment was of more than two thousand beds, so one can imagine how many visitors' cars were parked along the various surrounding streets. There was no space for well over a mile. Really ill, in desperation he drove into the precincts, into a doctors' bay. He was admitted immediately and had a lumbar puncture performed. Just as this had been completed, a hospital bureaucrat stormed into the ward:

'Anyone here who owns car number so-and-so?'

'I do.'

'Remove it immediately or it will be clamped and towed away.'

'But I've just had a lumbar puncture.'

Patients must always lie in a recumbent position for some time after this procedure.

'You heard what I said.'

So the poor fellow struggled downstairs, drove for ages until he found a parking space more than a mile away and then struggled back. At the very least he'd have had a bad headache for long afterwards and, indeed, it's possible that his problem could have been aggravated. I diagnosed incomplete transverse myelitis of the spinal cord, a diagnosis vindicated, I believe, because, more than thirty years later, he still paints most brilliant and sought-after paintings, several of which I can see on my wall as I write.

But let's return to my early Ipswich years. One episode saddened me. Soon after commencing practice, a patient needing urgent cystoscopy: examination of the interior of her bladder, presented. Her problem was not uncommon in those days: having taken sulphonamide antibacterial drugs without drinking enough water, her ureters blocked with crystals of sulphadiazine, causing anuria, i.e. was not producing any urine. I phoned Trump, asking to borrow the hospital's instrument. He refused. Very disappointed—I thought we were friends—I hurtled to Brisbane and bought one. Carefully catheterising each ureter in turn and irrigating them with great care. I managed to clear the tubes enough for urine production to resume. Not long afterwards, Trump asked me to cystoscope a public patient. When I arrived in the theatre, there was the hospital scope, ready to be used.

'What's that, sister?'

'Why, the cystoscope, of course.'

'Take it away. I'll only use my own from now on.'

Whether this rebuke ever reached Trump's ears I don't know. I realised he was only reacting to pressure from my enemies and we did become friends once more; nothing said.

The Children's Hospital did keep me away from my rooms, however, but the work was full of interest—and pathos. I was there for seven or eight years. I'll tell you about some of my little patients.

Perhaps the most hair raising op. was on a lad who suffered from von Recklinghausen's disease: neurofibromatosis. The famous elephant man was an extreme example of what can be a most distressing disease: lumps grow on nerves, occasionally in one, more often in many different places. Associated with this are *café au lait* blotches on the skin and occasionally gross overgrowth of patches of skin and underlying tissue as in the case of that poor elephant man. In this case, the overgrowth was—for as long as I followed the boy—confined to the Left Vagus nerve. He presented with a disfiguring series of lumps in his neck and, more importantly, pressure symptoms, obviously from one or more neurofibromata in his upper chest.

At operation, there was little trouble in removing the chest extension of the disease. The incision in the child's neck had to extend from top to bottom, as there were many tumours entangled with the great vessels and nerves, demanding care and patience in that tiger country. With such ample exposure it was also possible, by meticulously stripping back the pleura and retracting the lung, to obtain a sufficient view to mobilise the lumps and then, with slim long handled scissors, breath held! Snip the nerve below the lesions in the chest. The big problem arose when I'd followed the mass up to the base of the skull: the uppermost extension fully occupied the jugular foramen, the opening in the base of the skull that exits the internal jugular vein. That vein carries an enormous volume of blood from the brain. Within the foramen it has virtually no walls: only an endothelial lining: nothing to be tied off. Danger!! When removing or tying off the internal jugular vein it's important to be sure that the one on the other side is working. At this point in the operation I thought of the unfortunate experience of one of our senior lecturers, a very well regarded surgeon. It was, more precisely, his patient who'd been unfortunate.

The surgeon was sometimes unkindly called Jugular Joe, because he'd operated upon a patient with secondary cancerous glands of the neck, performing what's known as a block dissection. This involves tying off the internal jugular vein as a rule and then removing the cancerous glands and surrounding tissues in one piece. The only problem here was that his patient didn't have a jugular on her other side. The result was fatal. My little boy had a blocked vein on the side in question, so the vein opposite must have been functional. But what to do when the tumour was to be removed from this recess in the base of his skull? He'd bleed to death in extremely short order if nothing were done instantaneously to staunch the inevitable torrent of blood. I raised a flap from the adjacent sternomastoid muscle. When the lump came out, so did the expected bloody cascade. Saying my prayers, I jammed the muscle flap into the foramen, holding it there. After an interval, I removed my finger—thank God! He soon recovered.

Another boy with the same condition had his problem in his abdomen: pain with palpable swellings. The neurofibromata were relatively easy to remove and the parents were grateful, but what of the future? All too often these lumps become cancerous, so-called neurofibrosarcoma, a fatal condition. The man with whom I made a faux pas when demonstrating him to Professor Aird probably suffered from the same illness.

Most congenital abnormalities arising in Queensland requiring surgical treatment came to the hospital, affording invaluable experience. One fairly common one was meconium ileus, a form of bowel obstruction caused by a lack of digestive enzymes in the gut, which remains full of meconium: detritus built up in the bowel during the baby's development in utero. This produces a blockage and so, of course, it's fatal if not treated promptly and the greatly distended large bowel emptied surgically. Unfortunately, the child goes on to develop fibrocystic disease of the Pancreas and associated pulmonary problems.

A very common condition is pyloric stenosis—a misnomer, really, because the pylorus, the stomach's point of exit, isn't stenosed but blocked by an overgrown, overactive pyloric muscle. The child, at least in my time—things change—is usually a male, often the first-born. Food: milk, is taken avidly—the patient's both hungry and dehydrated, pinched little face abnormally alert—only to be vomited, in a special way, so-called projectile vomiting. You see the problem? Babies can vomit for several reasons. One of the clues, though, is the actual process of vomiting: it comes out in a great rush, hence projectile. Sometimes the diagnosis is obvious; sometimes difficult. Careful examination often reveals a small lump in the tummy, above the umbilicus. The operation itself is utterly simple: one opens the abdomen and inspects the pyloric region. A swollen pyloric muscle is evident. One merely has to cut the muscle across its fibres, i.e. in the long axis of the organ, exercising great care, firstly to ensure that all fibres have been severed and secondly, even more importantly, to make sure that the bowel lining isn't cut through, usually resulting in a fatal peritonitis. It's easy to make this mistake: a fold of the duodenum's lining comes close to the surface here. These kids do well when, as is usual, the operation is performed carefully.

Another kind of blockage results when, during foetal development, part of the bowel doesn't develop at all. This can occur in different places along the bowel and there's a limit to the number of these which can be corrected if the infant is to survive.

Another congenital bowel problem was Hirschsprung's disease, otherwise known as congenital megacolon, caused by a defect in the nervous control of a greater or lesser length of the lower part of the large bowel which, contracted and inert, produces a blockage. In consequence the large bowel above the obstruction dilates more and more, eventually causing the tummy to swell enormously. The treatment at this hospital was resection of the faulty bowel segment, then joining the healthy part to the anus. Some perform a colostomy first to more or less normalise matters and lessen the chance of infection. There's another approach, with a number of variants, the so-called pull through, the healthy part being pulled through the affected segment. The idea doesn't appeal to me. I never used it.

There are many abnormalities of the urogenital tract in both sexes—why in the name of all that's decent do the mind police insist on the word gender these days? Many are distressing. One such was Tommy R. His bladder was always distended with urine. He had to press on his tummy before he could pass any at all. An IVP showed that the resulting backpressure had dilated his ureters and caused his kidneys to atrophy. He wouldn't live for much longer untreated. The cause proved to be valves at the neck of his bladder: not easy to diagnose, as, if, for example, one passed a sound, or catheter, it would go into the bladder without any resistance. It was urine coming the other way whose exit was blocked. The diagnosis was made on clinical and radiological, grounds: the Children's Hospital didn't possess an operating cystoscope for children. Had there been one, the valves could have been removed without cutting the boy. As it was, I opened the bladder and excised them with long, narrow, curved scissors. I had serious doubts as to whether the kidneys would regenerate. They must have. When, years later, I was working in Sydney, he phoned me. We met and had a coffee together. He was in the army.

Not so lucky was another little boy, Michael H. His mother said anxiously:

'I'm so worried, doctor. When he passes urine his thing swells right up.'

I looked whilst he performed, something no other wretched quack had done before. She wasn't wrong: his prepuce swelled just like a balloon, and the urine came out only in the tiniest drips. Simple circumcision would have saved his life. I actually performed a. lesser operation, a simple dorsal slit to open things up because he wasn't at all well. X rays had showed the same picture as Tommy's, only his kidneys had been reduced to a shell. The poor little boy died soon afterward of uraemia.

Possibly the commonest abnormality in this region is undescended testes. These organs develop in the abdomen and, not long before birth, migrate to the scrotum, guided by strands of tissue known as gubernacula: rudders. These splay out, sometimes leading the testis into the groin or elsewhere where it shouldn't be: the so-called ectopic testis. It's also possible to mistake a retractile testis for the real thing. The muscle raising and lowering it is most sensitive in many youngsters, keeping that organ persistently up in the groin. It often takes some time before one can finally make up one's mind as to whether the testicle is really undescended or not.

When undescended they can be located almost anywhere on the route of descent. A hernia is usually present, too. It's often difficult to bring the testis into the scrotum and this is/was often accomplished by various means employing force or strong traction, the desired result being achieved at the cost of lost function: a well-placed but useless organ. So, why bother? Because an undescended organ is more likely to become cancerous and, if they're bilateral, the child will be infertile.

A happily married woman once presented with a mild hernia associated with a lump she'd just noticed in her groin. At operation this proved to be an undescended testicle. I removed it largely because of the cancer risk. The woman in question was genetically a man. I told nobody. Imagine the emotional trauma ensuing from such news, to say nothing of the probable eventual break-up of the marriage. Fortunately the pathologist who confirmed the diagnosis was also circumspect.

Two well-known but relatively uncommon abnormalities in especially the second, which is, decidedly uncommon—are hypospadias and epispadias.

In the former, the urethra doesn't extend to the end of the penis, often opening just in front of the scrotum: the patient wets himself whenever he wees. He's virtually infertile. Australian aborigines performed the operation of subincision of the penis as a means of birth control.

Recent investigations suggest that some cases can be due to the maternal use of hair spray in early pregnancy. This would be far from being the only cause.

Epispadias occurs when the upper surface of the penis lies open, bad enough for the patient, but when this split extends as far as and includes the bladder, it's terrible. The highly sensitive surface of the bladder lies more or less flat on the tummy wall, so that the patient constantly leaks urine for the rest of his life if nothing's done. In addition to this, the pubic bones don't meet, leading to instability when walking. Curvature of the spine often results. I'll tell you the remarkable story one of these unfortunates later. Treatment of this condition is difficult in the extreme and usually involves the removal of the bladder and transplantation of the ureters—the tubes leading from kidney to bladder—into the lower bowel. The patient soon grows accustomed to the new situation, but dies early of repeated ascending kidney infections.

On the subject of ureters: another Jeremiad coming up!! One day over morning tea at the Children's Hospital, the psychiatrist asked me if I'd be interested in seeing a little girl who'd been referred to him for bed wetting—a very common condition, of course. He said that he wasn't satisfied that it was in fact a psychiatric problem, even though she'd been seen by countless doctors who'd all come to that conclusion. The answer was of course, yes.

A few days later the patient appeared at my outpatient clinic with her mother. Here it might be slightly understandable why so many doctors misdiagnosed the case and it took a good clinician, a psychiatrist who doesn't see many physical problems, to realise that all of those so-called doctors had erred. You see, the mother had a severe tic and every time she spoke, her head twisted around most distressingly, making her appear to be the idiot she most certainly was not. She was in fact quite intelligent.

'Pop up on to the couch and I'll see what's going on.' I said.

It was bad and very good: bad because her bottom was covered in innumerable revolting warts; good, triumphantly good because, as I watched, a spurt of urine came from one of the lips of her nether region.

'I'll do my best to have kidney X rays done tomorrow (The X ray Department was always obliging) and I'll operate on A. on Friday.'

'But doctor, that'll be her twelfth birthday.'

'And the operation will be the best birthday present she'll ever have.'

And it was so. The X ray (intravenous pyelogram) showed that the left ureter had duplicated during development, the aberrant one being the cause of twelve years of distress, not only physical by being constantly wet. The effect upon a child's self-esteem of being told by one doctor after another that she was a bed wetter can only be imagined. Just think about those doctors: not one of the swine took the time or trouble to look at the poor child, simply prescribing drugs and/or bells that rang in the night when she became wet, when all of the time the patient was psychologically sound and, indeed, mature.

I didn't enquire into the mother's circumstances, but doubt if they were very good, but, on the final consultation, she gave me an expensive gold fountain pen. I still have it; prize it; wouldn't part with it. I've had other gold pens given to me. This is the only one whose donor I distinctly remember. It must be obvious from this that very many doctors don't care enough about their patients, whizzing them through as quickly as they can: the more they see, the more money they rake in. Many serious problems including cancer are missed in this way.

Take a dire development suffered by my mother. It prostrated her. A highly qualified physician consultant was called in:

'I'm sorry to have to tell you that your mother has serious cardiac failure. I think we can pull her round this time, but I'm afraid I can't see her lasting more than another eighteen months at the very best.'

He then prescribed thiazide diuretics: water tablets, together with orange juice to provide the potassium that the tablets remove from the body. She became violently ill, nearly dying until I angrily roared in and cancelled the juice, to which my mother was very sensitive. This wonderful lady had expended her strength during the war, having organised everything in Ipswich that could be organised from the female point of view: Red Cross; Women's National Emergency Legion; Bundles for Britain; camouflage net making: you name it. She received no recognition, only hostility from the bystanders. Her hours were long; meals, if any, irregular. The result at war's end: an abdominal emergency, wrongly diagnosed as gallbladder trouble, but, in fact, peptic ulcer: Hence, in part, the vomiting. This doctor should have known these circumstances: he

was in the town for all of this time. I went to school with his brother: his
father was the Gilmore already mentioned—but he didn't trouble to take a
full case history. This would have included any sensitivities, in this case to
orange juice.

In the night I'd pay a visit and inject my mother with vitamin B group
in large doses. This Fellow of a couple of Royal Colleges of Medicine had
missed a case of beri beri. It nonetheless took that dear person months to
recover. Incidentally, on the day she was allowed out of the hospital did
she go home? Oh, dear no: she went straight to a bridge party. She lived
for sixteen more years.

Other common abnormalities amongst infants were imperfect
development of the spinal cord and its coverings, varying through all of
the possible permutations and combinations having regard to the manner
in which their development occurs. The mildest anomaly is spina bifida,
where the vertebra—sometimes vertebrae—don't develop properly at
the back, leaving a gap where there should be an arch of bone. In worse
cases, the spinal coverings: the meninges, cause a bulge through this
gap in the lower back: meningocoele. If part of the spinal cord is also
involved: meningomyelocoele, there will be serious nerve defects resulting
in a greater or lesser degree of paralysis; often incontinence too. In
meningomyelocoele—I don't believe there have been significant advances
in this distressing problem—all one can do is to excise the redundant
covering, possibly also dissecting adherent nerves off the structure with
meticulous care, then covering the tissues with skin; possibly also muscle.
But there is often an associated problem: the drainage of cerebrospinal
fluid has also been affected and the child may develop water on the brain:
hydrocephalus. There are a few things which can be done here. One is to
insert a Spitzer valve, which enables—until repeated refluxes of blood blocks
it—the cerebrospinal fluid to escape via the jugular vein. Another approach
is to drain the fluid by means of a fine tube, either into the pleural cavity or

the peritoneal cavity. The latter approach tends to give better drainage, but adds the danger of meningitis if the patient develops peritonitis from, for example, appendicitis at some later date. I used both methods, but favoured the latter: the spino-peritoneostomy.

The most extreme scenario is when the spinal cord is imperfectly developed and its truncated end lies, bare, on the victim's back. This is, or should be, incompatible with existence. I don't know what the situation is today, but for many years the incidence of these distressing developmental defects of the spinal cord was unduly high in Ireland and a number of studies were carried out in an effort to pin the blame on to one of that country's favourite repasts: the potato, which eventually emerged unblemished. It's now known that there's indeed a nutritional factor involved and that mothers-to-be taking Folic acid has a protective effect.

There's one other abnormal development in this region which appears later in life: a cord extends from the tip of the spinal cord to the sacral bone. As the child's body elongates, increasing tension on the cord produces a variety of neurological signs and symptoms that can be confusing. It's uncommon: I only saw a couple of these at the Children's. Once diagnosed, the problem's easily corrected.

You'll have gathered that, in my early days in Ipswich I did a certain amount of general practice. I knew of no other approach than to examine a patient thoroughly after taking an adequate history. I can't see that, trusted to deal with a health problem—more than a cough, cold or that kind of thing—any less care should be taken in attempting to arrive at a diagnosis whether one's a general practitioner or a specialist. This approach, certainly more time consuming, does limit one's throughput. I suspected that my enemies sent spies posing as patients to suss me out. This was confirmed one day when one of the doctors who'd asked me to attend his child, -a senior consultant physician, also acting as a GP, a situation possible in those days— suggested to me that when doing GP work I should see my patients more quickly:

> 'After a couple of minutes I make a guess. If it's wrong, the
> patient will turn up again and you can take it from there.'

I can't tell you how shocked I was. What if the patient didn't
come back and subsequently died of cancer? There's far too much
off-handedness in my profession. Perhaps there'd be a more generally
sympathetic approach if more doctors had themselves suffered from a
major illness. Only yesterday I heard of a lass who caught her hand in a
hedge cutter. She presented at hospital, complaining that, apart from a
messed-up hand, her fingers were numb.

'Oh, the feeling will come back in a couple of days' lied the uncaring
doctor, lazy mentally, physically or both. The skin was sutured, nothing
else. She had to go elsewhere for the necessary nerve and tendon repairs.

Years ago, at medical meetings, the phone would ring:

'Oh, well, another L.O.G.'

The doctor would sometimes remark as he went off on an after-hours
call. L.O.G? Love of God, i.e. a charity call: The patient would have been
poor. That's all gone by the board now, but in those days there was a strong
doctor/patient relationship, a good doctor knowing the medical history
and health idiosyncrasies of an entire family. That family in return gave
their doctor trust, even love. Not any longer. Many nowadays are alert
to any opportunity: pretext, for suing their doctor, an attitude inevitably
breeding wariness, to say the least, on the practitioner's part. Now, after
hours calls are usually directed to some profitable firm whose employees
know zero of the history or medical quirks of the case and that patient's
doctor may never realise that that event had occurred.

Medical unions, too, use energies not taken up by politics to
maximise the income of their members. In Australia, as only one example,
the AMA schedule of fees for services is nothing short of greedy. Make no
mistake, there aren't any professions now: only businesses, L.O.G. replaced

by L.O.M. M: Mammon.

Becoming busier, I contacted one of my erstwhile junior doctors, still working in Bundaberg. He'd anaesthetised all of my surgical cases there, very well. I asked him to join me in my practice. He agreed. Henceforth, excepting for a time when he was absent overseas obtaining his higher professional qualifications, he anaesthetised all of my Ipswich patients. I was thus able, to hive off most of my general practice; all of it when a well-qualified physician and another GP joined the group. I merely kept my own fees and the others could do what they liked about finances.

Soon after commencing in Ipswich, another of my resident Medical Officers from Bundaberg who'd set up practice in Goondiwindi asked if I'd care to operate there upon his patients needing surgery. He'd look after the patients after the first postoperative day. He was kind, caring and intelligent so, though it was a long trek, this appealed to both nomadic instincts and wallet.

It also appealed to my mother, who took a keen interest in my patients, in emergencies, standing in as a receptionist in my rooms. She regularly catechised me about private operations I'd performed: I'd sometimes forget to tell my clerical staff. For both reasons she jumped at the idea

Everything went well with this project and I only had to return there on one occasion: a man continued to bleed from a kidney from which I'd removed a so-called staghorn calculus: a large stone, the 'horns' of which had extended itself into the kidney's calyces, several channels which, when conjoined, form the pelvis. The pelvis leads to the ureter which empties into the bladder. The patient settled without further treatment.

The only problem was weather: in that semi-arid region it invariably rained, heavily, whenever we set forth and my car, the first post war model Lanchester, was by far the worst vehicle it's been my misfortune to own. In particular, it stalled whenever it went through water, even though driven slowly at the time. Water in dips on that road there was aplenty when it rained. When that happened—always in the dark—my mother, totally, abysmally ignorant of anything to do with cars, driving excepted, would, after the bonnet was opened, wave a cloth vaguely in the direction of the engine until it fired. Rain and visits to that town coincided so often that our hotel proprietor once said:

'Oh, so you're here again. No wonder it's raining!'

Once it rained for days on end and that afternoon I had to perform an operation in Ipswich which couldn't possibly be postponed. We had to get back, but all of the roads were blocked. Somebody suggested a possibility: the so-called Heifer Creek road. Arrived at the creek, there was a queue of cars, drivers morosely studying the swirling waters.

If a car with normal transmission stalls in water, engaging low gear and using the starter motor usually gets one through. Not so the epicyclic geared Lanchester. I asked my mother if we should give it a go. She nodded. At least a heavy car, in we went! The bonnet dipped further and further—and further, the force of flow causing water to bank up against the car, which slithered slowly downstream. I looked back: one car, attempting to follow was stuck, nose down in the flood. My stupid car's engine didn't miss a beat. Don't ask how! The spark plugs, let into the side of the engine, must have been below the waterline, but on the downstream side. I know the water had risen above them because of water in a headlamp holed by a flying stone. The hole was above the level of the plugs. A minor miracle, I thought, duly thankful.

There was an aftermath: many years later, I had a dream. My mother and I, on our way to Goondiwindi once again, she looked across at me:

'Well, Wyle, this is the last trip we're going to make together. You see, I'm going to die now.'

The phone rang. It was my brother: 'Mum's just died.'

Senior Consultant Ipswich

Modern ways finally caught up with Ipswich Hospital: the honorary system was abolished. It was probably natural that I'd be appointed Senior Surgical consultant. I was busy enough as it was, so resigned from the Children's Hospital.

The only other surgical consultant position was theoretically reserved for orthopaedics. However, the appointee, well known, unfavourably, to me, was appallingly slow, *inter alia*, increasing risk of infection. This being against patients' best interests, I ordered all major orthopaedic work to come to me. Though mutually courteous, no firm friendship was formed!

My sessions were supposedly three half days a week, but I was on call every alternate night of the year. I had very capable registrars and house officers, so they spared me as much as possible. Operating sessions, however, got right out of hand, so I added one half day unofficially, i.e. unpaid, to my commitment.

I must pay tribute to my senior theatre sister. Margaret Harper, a gem precious beyond price: anticipating every move, slapping instruments into my hand the nanosecond I'd asked. I couldn't have achieved whatever was managed without you Margaret, wherever you are. God bless you!

My Brisbane practice, though reasonably modest, did present a steady stream of patients. Very busy, I'd burn up the road to Brisbane, infinitely less traffic-laden than today. It would be absolutely impossible today, thanks to speed cameras and the huge volume of traffic. I was only caught twice, escaping unscathed—nearly—on both occasions.

A Brisbane patient with retrosternal goitre: an enlarged thyroid behind the breastbone, pressing upon the wind pipe as it grew, was causing serious breathing difficulties: an emergency if ever there was one. She was scheduled for operation in the early afternoon, but, just as I was finishing my Ipswich list, a patient was admitted with a ruptured ovarian cancer—the problem at Hammersmith, remember? The lass treated with radioactive colloidal gold?

The English patient's problem had arisen insidiously without causing acute symptoms. This patient was ill, in great pain; rather shocked. More, I was anxious to clear her tummy of all of the leaked fluid, hopefully before the contained cancer cells embedded themselves in the peritoneum.

A nurse ring the Brisbane hospital asking for a deferral: an hour, yes. More: no. An emergency had been admitted and all theatres would be fully occupied for the remainder of the day—and evening.

I removed the ovary and washed out the peritoneum with dilute Eusol, a substance cancer cells don't like, had my assistant sew up and flew out of the theatre. Near the town of Goodna was a sign: 40 miles an hour speed limit. I was, literally, doing a ton (I'd obviously scrapped the Lanchester!) when a stroppy policeman appeared out of the woodwork. I explained the reason for my haste, so he delayed me for as long as he possibly could whilst slowly, methodically, writing out his ticket. By the grace of God both patients did well and that ovarian cancer never recurred. But I was summonsed.

Incredibly, I'd not been charged with doing a hundred miles an hour in a restricted zone, but merely with exceeding the speed limit there (no radar at that time, obviously!)

My brother suggested that his friend, Doug McGill, QC, take my case. Doug embarrassed me no end in court, stirring up the cop who'd booked me to what I thought to be an entirely unnecessary level of anger. Eventually the road signage came up for consideration. After much arguing and derision on Doug's part, the forty mile restricting sign had to be described in detail. By this time the cop was so angry he didn't really know or care what he was saying and wrongly described the derestriction sign.

'No case, your Worship. The signs clearly don't meet with the requirements of the Act.'

Case dismissed. The magistrate had obviously been on my side anyway.

'I'd better not catch you speeding again.' Growled the cop ominously as I left the court.

A few months later, poor Doug was driving home with his daughter when a drunk sped over the brow of a hill on the wrong side of the road, almost severing his car in two. His anguished daughter, almost unharmed, had to see the mangled body of her father beside her, then and no doubt many times thereafter: in nightmares.

Ipswich, whose original name was Limestone, began existence as a convict settlement where that stone was burnt into lime. At the time we're considering it was quite a large city. In the nineteenth century it made a strong bid to becoming State capital, on the valid grounds that a bar of hard rock in the bed of the Brisbane River prevented large ships from entering Brisbane city. Ipswich had a rail connection with a fine deep-water port, still unused. When State Governor McIlraith was being carried ashore to inspect the projected port and adjacent land, he was accidentally/purposely dropped in the mud. End of Ipswich's prospects!

The city's fortunes now flag and it's almost been subsumed into the sprawling city which it once rivalled.

Ipswich, surrounding villages and the agricultural district provided a great variety of surgical cases, many cancer, especially of the breast and bowel. Quite a number of old boys with enlarged prostates, unwilling to go to Brisbane and wanting families around them postoperatively now came out of the woodwork. There was no diathermy machine at the hospital, so transurethral resection, the hot wire method mentioned earlier, was impracticable. They nevertheless preferred the older, cruder supra—and retro pubic operations if they were to be performed locally. Later, when I managed to prise a diathermy machine out of State Stores, parsimoniously guarded by the Director General, I could borrow an operating cystoscope from one of the Brisbane hospitals.

How did I dislodge a diathermy machine from State stores? The local Magistrate always had as one of his duties Chairmanship of the local Hospital Board. Alf S had chaired my Board in Bundaberg. Not long after my arrival he was transferred to Ipswich. We had always had a most cordial relationship, so he became a patient. Eventually developing gallbladder disease, that organ had to be removed. I regaled him with a description of the operation in great detail, emphasising the increased risk involved if one had to tie off all the bleeding points around the liver rather than sear them with the coagulating current of a diathermy machine. Miraculously, an excellent model arrived just in time for his operation.

These machines also have a cutting current, occasionally of use. I only employed that sparingly: I believed that inevitable burning associated with the procedure represented unnecessary additional tissue trauma.

Benign prostatic swellings are due to non-cancerous growth, an adenoma which enlarges, finally blocking urinary flow. The hot wire—now laser—removes this bit by bit, almost always leaving some of the adenoma behind. The older, cruder methods removed the entire adenoma in one fell swoop, but the actual removal results in sudden, copious bleeding which must be dealt with instantly. It's always a critical situation and the patient's blood pressure drops, sometimes precipitately. I fortunately had no deaths, but the procedure is less pleasant for the patient—and can be hair raising for the surgeon. Convalescence is somewhat longer. The suprapubic procedure involves opening the bladder via the abdominal wall, the adenoma being enucleated with the forefinger by touch. Bleeding is virtually instantaneous, so a pack is quickly thrust into the resulting cavity. This is a long way down in the pelvis, making access very difficult \nd demanding special instruments. Those almost universally used were devised by one Harry Harris. The worst bleeding comes from two arteries entering the gland from either side, postero-laterally. I preferred to tie these individually, with the help of very long, curved artery forceps and a special instrument which carries the suture down into the depths: not always easy. As a last resort, Harris' boomerang needle is brought into play: a thick, traumatising needle, more or less of the shape described, with a notch just behind the cutting edge, mounted on a handle with a button at its top. When this is pressed, the needle is pushed forward through the tissue, only after one has a well-founded mental image of just where it's going. Using a special carrier, the suture is engaged in the notch and, when the button is released, the needle's pulled back out of the tissue. The suture, now in place, is tied. Any bladder mucosa happening to be flapping in the breeze is anchored likewise.

I had the good fortune to be ambidextrous when operating, especially useful when operating to remove a gall bladder, as in Alf's case. I've already mentioned the various options one has with incisions. Incredibly, the day before this was written, a very good friend complained to me of a worrying discomfort—and slight bulge in his Right upper abdomen. He'd had his gallbladder out a year or more ago. That execrable Kocher incision was the cause of his problem. I invariably used a midline incision. That never, ever,

ever, caused subsequent trouble.

The ambidextrous part: a Right handed surgeon would normally stand on the patient's Right side, but the gallbladder sits snugly under the liver, which slopes upward from right to Left. The bladder therefore faces away from the surgeon—unless he stands on the Left.

The median incision encounters peritoneal folds which cause triflingly insignificant inconvenience. The wound's edges are retracted and there's the focus of attention. Any intruding gut is kept at bay by means of muslin packs wrung out in hot water. The vital next move: identify where the gallbladder's cystic duct meets the common bile duct which carries bile from the liver to the bowel. Vital's indeed the word. If the surgeon is lazy he might take pot luck on exactly where that junction is—and, thanks to adhesions and other annoying obstacles, that vital move isn't always easy. Negligence at this point puts the patient's life in jeopardy. I've already mentioned Anthony Eden. This area's then cleared and the cystic duct and nothing but the cystic duct—is clamped and tied almost at the junction. It's a good idea then to deal with the cystic artery or arteries supplying blood to the gall bladder: varied in location. The bladder's then carefully dissected off the liver and consequent bleeding dealt with. Some dissect up flaps of peritoneum and suture them over the raw area; some don't. There's often a bit of blood and occasionally biliary leakage, so a drainage tube's placed in the neighbourhood, the wound closed and Bob's your uncle.

Bowel surgery had progressed since my days with George: it was only infrequently that one had to perform the abdominoperineal operation he so brilliantly executed. Risks to the patient of this severe operation had also become less, thanks to advances in anaesthesia, blood and fluid replacement, antibiotics—and, of course, the diathermy machine.

In many operations it's greatly to the patient's benefit—and rewarding to the surgeon, if respect is accorded tissue planes. Often these can be peeled satisfyingly apart, bloodlessly, greatly facilitating matters: right hemicolectomy for example, usually performed to treat cancer of the caecum, the blind proximal end of the large bowel. This has a lower five year survival rate than some other bowel cancers, because it can be symptomless until late in the disease, by which time it's often spread to lymph glands or the liver. For the astute clinician, anaemia may afford a clue, as the lesion silently bleeds away often rendering the patient anaemic. Tests readily reveal the presence of blood in the faeces and a careful examination may detect a soft lump in the lower right abdomen. Given a rather liberal incision, a touch of the knife along the outer side of the Right large bowel will, with due care, enable the entire ascending colon to be freed, together with the tissue containing its blood supply and lymphatic drainage, entirely without blood loss. There's a slight complication when one rounds the corner to the transverse colon which we needn't go into. Thus the entire bowel in question can easily be removed.

The small bowel is attached to the large one here. Its cut end is now joined to that at the end of large bowel left after the diseased bowel, blood supply, lymphatic drainage and metal clamps at either cut end have been removed and dumped into a kidney dish. It's obviously necessary to avoid any contamination of the peritoneal cavity, so the bowel is cut between clamps, much of the sewing together of the ends being done with the clamps in place. Some use staples to do the plumbing. The idea never attracted me.

When gut surgery is performed, the bowel tends to go on strike for a greater or lesser time. For this reason, a nasogastric tube should always be inserted to suck out fluid collecting in the inactive gut. The appropriate intravenous fluids must also carefully be administered to replace what has been lost and add the additional requirements. So that one knows what's going on, a fluid balance chart must be kept. Sometimes, however, but very much less frequently now, thanks to ever-growing knowledge, the gut continues to languish, a serious condition known as ileus, accompanied by what's been described as a dull, wearing ache. That's surely enough about gut surgery!

Talk of peeling away tissues reminds me of a problem suffered by my father and also of a different one entirely encountered by my mother, both at about the same time. Tissue peeling first!

My father developed a nasty-looking lesion on his face. Not liking to treat family if it could otherwise be helped, I referred him to him of the junior dustcoat—remember? I should have known better after the episode next in line. This oh, so eminent surgeon told my father that the matter was serious. After excision, extensive plastic surgery would be necessary to reconstitute his face. When father stoically retailed this news, I took a pair of forceps and peeled the core out of the growth. It healed, leaving behind no mark. ET was either dishonest: this would have been an expensive exercise, which possibility I doubt, or pig ignorance, which amazed me. The lesion wasn't cancerous, it was a keratoacanthoma and the correct treatment was as above.

Not long previously, my mother had been diagnosed with kidney stones, a result of the long period of recumbency when so ill in 1956. Mordo would have been my choice, but he'd shuffled off this mortal coil. In view of her frailty, I wanted a trustworthy surgeon. ET refused to operate, probably because he thought he wasn't up to the job. Mortality rates are important from a venal as well as a humanitarian point of view: if these are high, business suffers. It was hopeless trying to persuade her to go to anybody else, with the result that her declining years were marred by increasing uraemia as the stones, one way and another, gradually destroyed her kidney function.

It must be obvious by now that I never restricted myself to general surgery. If one has a sound knowledge of anatomy and enough of the medical sciences and is a careful operator there's no reason why, for instance, one shouldn't also essay the fields of Gynaecology and Urology. The reason for entering the latter field has already been mentioned. As to the former, the local standard as I saw it was low. If a patient required gynaecological surgery, I could see no reason moral, ethical or otherwise why I shouldn't take care of her.

Though abjuring obstetrics, gynaecology had always been an interest. I actually won a prize in the subject in my finals. A family emergency had taken me to England in 1956 so, whilst there, I availed myself of this great opportunity of learning the best techniques for vaginal hysterectomy. I'll return to this in a moment. Whilst in London, because of my association with George, Laurence Abel, an eminent if eccentric surgeon in the great Ernest Miles tradition took me under his wing and had me assist him at operations at the London Clinic. It gave me rather a start to realise that the tortoise shell hair brushes I used to spruce up post operatively actually had Ernest Miles' silver monogram on them. They'd been bequeathed to my mentor as he proudly told me, waltzing around the theatre precincts in underpants variously designed, all with pictures of many, varied ants.

'I've got ants in my pants!' He'd cry.

The best indication for vaginal hysterectomy, prolapse in a menopausal woman, a most distressing condition often associated with a degree of urinary incontinence. The protruding organ is always most uncomfortable and tends to ulcerate. There are risks associated with the operation, as for all others, if it's not performed with skill and care. It's also associated with recurrence if the greatest attention isn't given to every detail. I shall spare you them!

This and mastectomy for breast cancer became probably my most frequently performed operations at Ipswich. Bowel surgery came a good third with orthopaedics breathing down their necks.

So jealously guarded are the various specialties today (filthy lucre would have nothing to do with that, of course!) that it would probably be extremely difficult, indeed impossible, to exercise this freedom today.

One evening I was working on the inevitable official bumf—it's multiplied by a hundred times since—and was alone in my rooms when there came a knock on the door. The man was in obvious pain and without any doubt had a severe disc lesion at the lumbo-sacral level: the bottom of the back. After a thorough examination I told the man that, though I was always reluctant to operate unless it was absolutely necessary, there was no room for conservatism in his case.

'You should be admitted immediately for rest in traction and I expect to operate before the end of the week.'

The man exploded and, with a few obscenities, hobbled off into the night. The subsequent development completely changed my views on disc lesions. Some weeks, perhaps a couple of months later he knocked again at about the same time.

'I've come to apologise for my behaviour. I'm terrified of operations and couldn't control myself. Anyway, I'm cured.'

'Oh, yes, who operated?'

'Nobody. I went to John Jefferies.'

With his permission I got him up on a couch and examined him. Absolutely all of the signs, abundantly present at my previous examination had gone. Absent reflexes had returned. There was no sensory loss or muscle wasting. Movements were free and painless.

That gave me something to think about, but just a couple of days after that episode another man appeared with the same, severe, problem.

'Can you do anything without operating, doc, please? I'm a small crops farmer, have to do a harvest over the next weeks and if I lose this crop Mr X—a greedy man whom I knew—will take my farm away.'

The poor fellow was in debt.

'OK then' I said, 'I will, on one condition.'

'What's that?'

'That you come back and tell me how you got on.'

I referred him to a no doubt astonished John. Chiropractors were anathema in those days, especially to orthopods. In due course an exceedingly happy, symptom free man returned.

I love surfing and once bumped, head first, into a woman who'd strayed into my path as I body-surfed a wave. The aftermath was bouts of severe headaches, so bad that, if alone, I'd roll around in agony on the floor. I'd sought expert advice without any joy, the unspoken diagnosis probably being neurosis. After the surprise I'd received, it now seemed to be a good idea to risk treatment at John Jefferies' hands.

Lying comfortably down, my head in his hands, I wondered if, in seconds, I'd become quadriplegic. Instead, sounds, almost musical, emanated from my neck and, more than fifty years later, there's been no recurrence of those fearsome pains.

'Would you mind if I looked at your back?' John asked. Who could object? As I stood, he said;

'Your right sacro-iliac joint is out.'

There'd been no mention of it, but, after standing for a quarter of an hour, it had always, because of the pain, become necessary for me to sit. This problem, too, he corrected.

As a prisoner of war of the Japs and a sergeant—apparently the highest surviving rank in his part of the conflict—he'd attended the sick and suffering that were all about him. This aroused his interest in things medical and, on his return, he was attracted to and became a disciple of one Mr. Sjelburg, a Swede who'd come to Australia prior to the first World War. This remarkable man evidently practised an ancient form of chiropractic indigenous to his country and with great success in Sydney until rising hostility—he was taken for a German—drove him to a small town in North Queensland where he continued to practice from that time onward. News of his success spread and eventually he established a sizeable colony where, with his helpers, he treated enormous numbers. Good news travels far as well as fast. John eventually succeeded in having himself apprenticed to the great man and was himself exceedingly successful.

One night, a little before my experiences with John, we dined with a friend acquired during Darwin days and now living opposite to him:

'I don't want for entertainment. I often sit in a front room and watch people hobbling in and walking out of that place over the road.' Said she, a prime example of human folly. Even in Darwin she'd suffered, albeit mildly, from Raynaud's phenomenon: fingers which blanched and became painful in cold weather, firstly because of spasm in the digital arteries and then, as time went on, a progressive narrowing of those blood vessels due to proliferation of the cells lining them. Her problem became much worse when she went to live on the twenty-eighth parallel, where it can become quite cold in wintertime. The whole thing, though, is that her problem was greatly exacerbated by addiction to smoking, despite ample warning. In cooler weather her fingers began to shrivel. She lost them all, bit by bit.

My prescient Professor of surgery, Nipper Sutton, spotted the connection between smoking and circulatory problems years before they were highlighted by Doll and Bradford-Hill. As a student I saw a man with threatened gangrene of his foot. Nipper read the Riot Act about smoking and he ceased this noxious habit. His foot improved remarkably. One year later he presented with actual gangrene: he'd begun to smoke again.

But back to John and then a tiny bit more about chiropractics. John and I became friendly and when he encountered a problem he considered to require actual surgery rather than his ministrations, he'd send the patient to me. Many of these were very interesting. One in particular, less interesting in some ways more in others, springs to mind.

A man came to him complaining of agonising pain in his Left thigh. He'd fractured his femur about a year previously, and was treated by an Orthopod at a large nearby public hospital. John couldn't see any reason for a continuance of such excruciating pain. A simple X ray soon revealed all: the fracture hadn't united. This man had gone to John because his complaint of pain had been dismissed by the specialist. Unbelievable! I pray to the Almighty that I never committed such a sin. I had him admitted; exposed the fracture; removed the fibrous tissue that had formed between the bone fragments; chiselled away the solid bone that had grown across their ends and then applied a metal plate. John generously took him into his home whilst the bone healed itself. It did so in a matter of weeks and this is the really interesting part: finding it hard to believe that the healing of a previously ununited fracture had taken place so quickly, I remarked upon it to John, who told me that he'd been giving the man comfrey, otherwise known as knit bone. It obviously worked, but there's a slight problem here: comfrey is a cancer-producing agent. To my knowledge: John kept a firm tab on all patients. This man probably didn't develop cancer.

Our mentors had always emphasised the dire failings and, indeed, the dangers chiropractors were capable of inflicting. This most certainly didn't apply to John or, indeed, very many others. There are many types of chiropractic. John was called by his opposition a leg puller with, of course, the overtones, but that greatly simplifies his technique. Suffice it to say that many of the alternative forms of treatment performed under the banner of chiropractic involve the twisting and turning of various parts of the body—and the use of some force. There's a Latin tag: *non vi sed arte*, not by force but by art which is most applicable, not only to the surgical art but also to chiropractic. Sadly, I believe that John's version of his particular art is now extinct, superseded by less gentle methods which, to say the least, are no more effective.

I made it my business to learn many of his techniques, especially where backs and shoulders are concerned and since that time have had only to perform a couple of operations to remove ruptured intervertebral discs: those causing serious pressure effects. It is a fact that the results of expertly performed manipulation, excepting in the severest forms of the problem, are much superior to surgery. Moreover, multitudes have had their lives totally ruined by inexpert back surgery, sometimes even when capable surgeons have operated. I've seen and ultimately, for the most part, had to disappoint countless people who've consulted me with intractable pain caused by unsuccessful back surgery.

A very rewarding part of my life now came to an end. The time had come when I was required to pay for my sins.

Canberra and Sydney

Not a lot of surgical interest occurred in this phase of my life, though I did a trifle of practice. I didn't feel up to the full rigours of surgical life immediately after losing my parliamentary seat, so when the position of Executive Director of the drug manufacturers' organization came up at this very time, I applied. I've always been rather naïve, with no exception in this realm, being starry eyed at the truly wonderful advances in therapeutics, thanks to the beneficent research-based drug companies. It slowly dawned upon me that they're far from kindly, operating for the benefit of mankind. As in every company nowadays, the bottom line's all that matters and must be maximised by hook or by crook, mattering not at all which of those two it is. Business plans issued by the various overseas headquarters of the firms had to be achieved—or else, irrespective of whether or not the products were safe and/or effective. Pricing was a work of art, one discovered. Transfer pricing to conceal the true—often minimal—cost of raw materials and manufacturing was the order of the day; the price to the public whatever the traffic would bear.

This industry has indeed brought great benefits to mankind but could have done much, much more. For instance, it could have made its products available at greatly reduced prices to the suffering poor in undeveloped countries: AIDS medication immediately springs to mind.

Some companies are now waking up to the fact that selling a high volume of drugs at a lower mark-up in poor countries makes good business sense. Nevertheless, they could and should also do more research into treatments for less common diseases or those presently largely confined to poorly developed countries. They haven't, because of the probably mistaken idea that it would be less profitable. Some appear to be changing their minds.

There's far too little research into new types of antibiotics with terrible possible results. If none appear we could be back to a pre-Listerian scenario. There are presently on the horizon some which might give humanity breathing space.

For some obscure reason I was made a councillor of the International Federation of Pharmaceutical Manufacturers Associations and, partly as a result, met the heads of most of the major international companies. Some were pleasant; most arrogant bullies primarily concerned with the very real power they possessed. I was unable to detect much of the milk of human kindness.

When a UN conference on psychotropic drugs was held in Geneva, it was felt that I should attend. The only real interest there was the manner in which the Soviet Russian delegates controlled those from the countries over which it held hegemony—and did so in such a way as to rub their noses in it.

Mine was largely a lobbying job—the wrong man for that! But it frequently took me to Canberra to liaise with the bureaucrats. I also had to be chummy with pharmacists and various aspects of the medical profession. The bureaucrats, as one would expect, were at the same time arrogant and incompetent, losing whole suitcases full of drug submissions. I also had to communicate with the general public, via both TV and the press.

The necessity of frequent travel, not only between the states but also overseas, to Switzerland and the US in particular, appealed to the nomad in my genes. Trips to New Zealand in particular were both pleasant and convivial. One of the advantages of the position was the fact that I could, should and did study a wide array of professional journals and monographs.

BACK TO QUEENSLAND

The urge to return to full-time practice increased in proportion with increasing boredom with my job. I had a grazing property in the Hunter Valley, so almost set myself up in a surgeonless town there, but Queensland and family in that state called. There was no chance of a decent hospital appointment at this relatively late stage. There's a ruthless rat race in surgery as everywhere else and, having been out of it for some years, even if I applied for a post—and I didn't—the best one could expect would have been a junior consultant position. Accordingly, I set up my shingle in a bay-side suburb of Brisbane, doing some GP work again but soon dealing with a considerable volume of surgery, augmented because some Ipswich people, learning that I was there, came down.

Unfortunately there were no hospitals in the vicinity and grinding up overcrowded roads into the city centre was hardly enjoyable. Moreover, many patients, especially the elderly, didn't want to be hospitalised where relatives and friends would be discouraged by transportation problems from visiting. Parking by non-medical people anywhere near the hospitals was the nightmare I've already mentioned. In consequence I performed as much surgery as possible where local or regional anaesthesia could be used, in my own rooms, kept scrupulously clean by an excellent receptionist. There were no cases of sepsis. I even opened a knee joint to remove loose bodies because, for various reasons that time and place were the only suitable ones for the patient whose knee continually locked.

My biggest op. there was the reconstruction of a hare lip. The patient had presented for another problem, but the repair that had been done was appalling: the scar wide and the apposition terrible, leading to a repellent disfigurement. I pleaded with the woman to have it re-done. Such disfigurement must have had severe repercussions, personally and socially. It was the usual story:

'I'm not going all the way to Brisbane to have it done.'

I told her it would hardly be pleasant to sit and have it done under local anaesthetic but she insisted, sitting silently, without moving whilst I excised the brutal scar, mobilised the entire upper lip and brought the edges together again.

Next day her husband presented with piles:

'I'll 'ave 'em done here.'

And it was so. They lived not so far away so that, if he bled post operatively I could be there in good time. He didn't.

I also performed many operations to relieve Carpal Tunnel Syndrome both in my own and in Neville's rooms—more about him in a moment. This condition can be distressing with pain, tingling and numbness in the fingers, especially at night. It's commoner in people who use their hands a lot. Repetitive movement can cause swelling in the tissues: tendons in particular, as they pass, with the Median Nerve, through a tunnel at the entrance to the palm of the hand. The tunnel is bounded on three sides by wrist bones and on the other by a very tough ligament. As tissues within the tunnel swell, pressure is exerted on the nerve, which indicates its objection in the ways mentioned. The op is simple: all one has to do is expose, then divide that tough ligament, then ensure that the nerve is freely mobile; not constricted in any way.

The incision, preferably slightly curved, is made more or less in the midline, the far end of the incision ending at about the level of the base of the thumb. This is counter intuitive: I've seen lots of incisions that have been made. lower down, even into the palm of the hand. The operation's conveniently performed under a Bier's block, a type of regional anaesthetic. The limb is elevated and a tourniquet—preferably pneumatic—applied. Local anaesthetic is then injected into a vein. The arm below the tourniquet becomes numb. Bleeding is inhibited at the same time. This method is dangerous if the wrong anaesthetic or too much of it is used, especially if the tourniquet is removed too quickly. In the hands of a competent surgeon it's very safe.

When I opened my practice, I was contacted by an old friend, Neville Breitkreutz, one of my housemen in Ipswich , who had a busy practice in Caloundra. He kindly offered to refer all of his surgery if I'd go to that town once a week. Postoperative care would present no problems with a doctor of his fine capabilities.

He recently reminded me of an operation we performed together to remove the suprarenal glands of a breast cancer patient in an effort to relieve her symptoms and perhaps prolong her life. He was particularly taken by the name of one of the tissue planes important in this op: the fascia of Zuckerkandl.

Incidentally, people can't survive without these glands. After the operation she was put in the hands of a physician for carefully monitored corticosteroid therapy.

Speaking of suprarenals, a serious life threatening condition, Addison's Disease, is caused by malfunction of the suprarenal cortex: that gland's outer layer. Untreated or improperly treated, sudden death is a feature. Patients nowadays have access to very effective replacement therapy. Forty years and more ago that wasn't so well established yet, prior to his election as President of the United States, J.F.Kennedy, swore blind that he didn't have it. He did. He might have lost the election, despite the Mafia's help, if he'd told the truth.

Disaffection with my job with the drug companies had increased when I was asked to lobby the drug Advisory Committee on behalf of a drug which, given intramuscularly, controlled Addison's Disease admirably, with one minor drawback: sudden death in a significant proportion of patients. I hope you don't think that I did as bidden.

I took rooms in Caloundra one day a week, glad I did so in more ways than one: Nev's wife Yvonne introduced me to my own life's partner.

Soon after we were married, I was performing some chore or another with a knife.

'Oh, do be careful!' said she, 'I don't want you to cut yourself!'

'Not very likely' I replied, 'after all, I do earn a living with one of these!'

We both laughed.

There's nothing unusual to report about my ops. there so far as I remember excepting for a tummy tuck upon a quite enormous female. She had had gallbladder trouble but I refused to operate until she lost weight. She did manage it, but her weight rebounded to such a degree that I allowed myself to be persuaded to remove her lard surgically. She, like so many, protested that she kept to a most rigorous diet. Fiddling with her handbag, a packet of Kitkats fell on to the carpet.

Nev. phoned me one Friday, i.e. busy, afternoon because his father-in-law had become very seriously ill and the nearest surgeon, who'd been called in, was hopeless. The patient's condition was deteriorating. Could I please hurry? I could and did and was caught by the usual speed trap. Once again, my pleas and further pleas fell upon deaf ears; I had to write to the Premier, Jo Petersen, before I escaped a penalty.

Arrived at the private hospital in which my patient was gradually expiring, I read the surgeon's notes: long, packed with palaver and codswallop, without sensible substance. I've read similar notes from time to time. When I do I'm never in any doubt that their author has been completely in the dark. A quick sigmoidoscopy revealed a severe acute flare-up of ulcerative colitis. All the old boy. needed was appropriate treatment.

Speaking of codswallop, my dear daughter Ros suffered grievously from an example of it. Her outcome was less happy. I was in England when she developed a lump in her right breast. Her local GP talked a whole lot of drivel and said that the lump was benign, losing valuable time. Her siblings urged her to seek a specialist opinion, so, unfortunately she consulted our old friendly enemy ET. The lump was large and admittedly not typical of the usual breast cancer, so he, too, spouted acres of tommy rot, also pronouncing the lesion to be benign. A person in his position should have known that breast cancer of the medullary type presents in precisely that way. Weird feelings began to develop in the lesion, so she finally saw a surgeon who made the correct diagnosis, too late.

A little previously I mentioned Jo Bjelke-Petersen. He's come in for much criticism on a number of grounds, so I'd like to record this: a little fellow who'd visited me some time previously for a forgotten problem had rather thrust down my neck the fact that he was a faithful follower of the Australian Labour Party. I'd been quite unmoved; politics being well in the past. Many months later he wrote me an anguished letter. He'd been transferred to Mackay and allocated an uninhabitable house. Rain leaked everywhere and he and his little family—he was a widower—were constantly damp; always sick. No bureaucrat would lift a finger to help. At that time Jo was the State Housing Minister, so I phoned him:

'I'll actually be up there shortly. I'll look into it.'

I thanked him but wrongly believed that he'd do nothing. A couple of weeks later he phoned:

'It was just as you said. His accommodation was dreadful. I saw to it that the man was given a decent house.'

He didn't have to do that, having nothing to gain, but he did. Good old Jo!

One day Norman R came to see me with a malignant melanoma of the right foot with obvious extensions in his calf—a lethal situation. Just prior to this time, a very good friend had developed Q fever with sudden, severe cardiac failure. He refused hospital treatment and he probably wouldn't have made the journey to Brisbane in any case, so severe was the attack. His wife phoned one evening to say that he was suddenly much worse. I rushed to my car. It wouldn't start. My wife and I pushed the thing out of the garage and off the driveway and leapt into her Mini. It was too late.

Most unfortunately his funeral was at the precise time that I was operating upon Norm. Though the latter's outlook was grim, I felt I couldn't put it off. Post operatively and with only a little difficulty I managed to persuade the then Director General of Health to let me have some Small Pox vaccine, rightly very carefully controlled. This I applied to all of the areas affected by the disease. As I expect you know, smallpox vaccination produces a pustule. In Norm's case, where the reactions occurred, I was able to pull out long, dark strings of melanomatous tissue. Quite incredible. A year or so later he phoned me in Fiji: he had a recurrence. Of course I could do nothing at that distance, but the fact that it had taken a year to recur suggested that his life had been prolonged, symptom-free. The only other treatment which could have made any sense in such an advanced case would have been amputation of the entire leg. Since a melanoma reaching this stage is invariably fatal, this was not in any way warranted.

Devastatingly, my wonderful son Harry suddenly died of a ruptured aneurysm of his cerebral artery. Familiar scenes and their associations were too painful. I applied for and obtained the post of Consultant Surgeon to the Colonial War Memorial Hospital in Suva, Fiji.

FIJI

We were allocated a cottage in this green and not unpleasant land in a large, unfenced, park-like area, with other expat habitations dotted here and there: very much to our taste.

The political constitution in that country has always been unjust, power being kept in the hands of the Islanders even though the Indian population almost equals theirs. It's understandable in a way because, after all, they were the original inhabitants. On the other hand, the Indians do by far the most work, contributing much more to the common weal. History is important, but shouldn't stand in the way of equality. There's political trouble there still, but this book isn't about Fijian politics.

The senior Fijian surgeon, Etika, was stroppy and uncooperative, another reason for my lack of respect for the Australasian College. They'd granted him an honorary Fellowship which, in my opinion, he didn't deserve. A licence to kill? Perhaps some sense of inferiority because he hadn't obtained his fellowship the hard way was one cause of his prickliness. I gathered that his relationship with my predecessor—a genuine Fellow—had been so stormy that the latter told him what he could do with the job and went into private practice in the town (Suva). On my first day at the hospital he grudgingly showed me around the wards. At the end of the tour, he took me to another part of the building.

'This is the private section.' Pointing to a door. 'Someone in there might interest you.'

With that, he faded into the forest dim. Mystified, I poked my head inside.

'Who the Hell are you?' Came an acerbic voice.

'I'm the new consultant surgeon.'

'So what are your qualifications, if any?'

I told him, then asked about his problem. Manager of a tourist complex some distance West of the capital, he'd fallen from a high ladder whilst making decorative alterations, badly fracturing his left hip. He'd been lying in the hospital for more than a week without anybody doing anything about it.

He lived with a Fijian girl and she'd explained to him that he'd broken some taboo in a way I forget. He firmly believed this and actually, one year to the day of his first injury, hurrying, he'd tangled his legs in plastic material, fallen heavily and badly fractured his elbow.

It was easy to pin the fracture with one of the trifin nails already mentioned, this time adding a plate applied to the upper part of his thigh bone to ensure stability. He was grateful and we became friends, occasionally weekending in his resort.

Mine was a teaching position and there being a lecture that first evening, it seemed the jolly old thing to attend. The lecture was given by Haydn, a Dominican (From the island of that name, not from the Dominican Republic), Reader in Obs/Gynae. His subject was cancer of the cervix, an affliction which is rife there: an impressive, well-researched talk.

When I'd entered the lecture theatre, it was impossible not to be aware, acutely, of suspicious, even hostile, eyes focussing on me, assessing me and coming up with an unfavourable conclusion. After the talk, I stiffened the sinews and introduced myself to the speaker and a number of

Indian consultants who'd gathered round the podium.

Ah, bitter chill it was!

It transpired that both races were suspicious of me and my intentions: which side would I join? Islander or Indian? The answer was, inevitably, the Indians, but it wasn't a deliberate choice. We neither of us harbour any racial prejudices. It simply had to happen that way. Xenophobia, well-illustrated here, is one of mankind's curses: infantile. We socialised with the Indians because they became friendly. We never saw the inside of any Islander or mixed race home. I left that meeting wondering how on earth I was going to manage relationships with my colleagues, so dark were their suspicions.

Behind our house was a bure, a hut for native servants and it was hinted that it would be the decent thing to employ a native girl. Our happy choice was Mere, a cheerful charmer who, whilst she occasionally pinched things, was a welcome addition to our household. She cooked well, especially local dishes such as Vundi, a stubby plantain casseroled with coconut: scrumptious! Another delicious viand was Duruka, made from young shoots of sugarcane.

The waters here abound in fish, but one dare only eat surface feeders of the mackerel family known as Walu. Other deeper-living varieties can cause Ciguatera, a poisoning which regularly caused deaths to a significant number of people on the island who dared eat the other, delectable, varieties. Walu strips soaked in lemon juice made a delicious entrée.

Sometimes Mere would organise a lovo, pork or some such meat wrapped in paw paw leaves and cooked by hot stones in an oven dug into the ground. Her friends, of course, joined in, helping dig the hole and building a fire around the large stones placed in it to provide the necessary heat.

She kept a weather ear open, night and day, for the thud! of a falling coconut. First thing in the morning she'd pick up the haul, deftly remove the husks, chop the shells open, then fragment the coconut flesh with an iron scraper at the end a board: a great adjunct to most of her cooking. After a few days of summing us up, she asked if she could bring her younger daughter, Nunia, to live with her: a vivacious, most delightful child; no trouble at all at any time.

My workload was very heavy. Usually there's a delay between operations whilst the theatre is freshly prepared and the next patient anaesthetised. My throughput was facilitated by a first rate anaesthetist, a Fijian who told me to call him Henry. He saw to it that there were no delays between cases: as the operation for a major case was concluding, he'd leave a nurse in charge of the patient whilst he anaesthetised the next, lesser case by injecting Ketamine. This acts as an anaesthetic, obviating the need for an anaesthetist's constant presence, at least in this rather dire situation. A nurse looked after that patient whilst he readied the next for a major procedure. For this I needed the use of two theatres, a luxury not by any means always available in our own major hospitals. This worked especially well because of the superb qualities of the sister-in-charge of the recovery/intensive care ward, a rotund little Indian, Sister Vir, who comes high in the list of the all-time greats of nurses I've met.

When recovering from ketamine anaesthesia silence is all-important, or a very bad trip will result. There was never a peep in that ward when recovery from this agent was in progress. Because of her skill, the paraplegic cases were nursed here, with never a bed sore. Can any hospital in this country make such a proud claim? I strongly doubt it.

One horrendous morning a desperately injured traffic accident casualty was admitted and I was between cases in the adjacent theatre. Racing thence and with her help I did my best, operating upon the patient in her bed. Opening the abdomen was achieved in a trice, but at that point the patient died of massive haemorrhage from a terribly lacerated liver:

her abdomen awash with her entire complement of blood.

My anaesthetist had a roving eye and one day his wife, catching him at it, with a great swipe of a knife badly damaged his hand. He managed to get back to work quite quickly, before his wounds had really healed, but it seemed like an eternity. The senior anaesthetist was a Rotuman: from an island of that name.to the North of Fiji, The inhabitants aren't Melanaesian like most Fijians, having ruddier complexions and a slightly oriental appearance. This character rarely, if ever, gave anaesthetics, partly because of laziness but possibly because he was spaced out most of the time, on what I don't know: Ketamine?

Instead of stepping into the breach, he allocated a female who had most imperfectly realised pretensions to being an anaesthetist: the most dangerous one it's ever been my misfortune to meet, every case a nightmare, patient always at death's door thanks to her incompetence. I don't think any of her victims actually died, but that was purely by the grace of God. Consequently I performed as many operations as humanly possible under local, regional or block anaesthesia. If a general anaesthetic was absolutely unavoidable, I had to devote attention to the state of the patient. How I rejoiced when our heavily bandaged friend reappeared!

There was a terribly unsettling development in one of the surgical wards. A poor fourteen-year-old lad was dying of sarcoma of the bones around the knee joint. It had grown huge and Etika had given consent for a witch doctor to try to effect a cure. He must have been in an awkward position and one can't criticise that decision. Refusing any of the straws people grasp at on these occasions can be inhumane. I often had to walk past that enormously swollen knee. The boy should have been transferred elsewhere because of the witch doctor's hideous, unearthly yells and cacophonous screams, together with a loud thumping of wood on the floor in an attempt to frighten away the evil spirits causing the disease. The noise echoed and re-echoed throughout the hospital; doubtless the surrounding district, too: dreadfully upsetting for the adult patients; terrifying for the children.

Fiji is a poor country, though, as usual, this didn't prevent the politicians from swanning around in black Mercedes Benz cars. Lack of money meant that less essential items such as facilities in the hospital were lacking. One had to make do. This had repercussions, revealed to you in all good time.

By no means was every Fijian poor. Their tribal system vests ownership of all the land in Islanders' hands, divided between the various tribes, existing boundaries no doubt having been determined upon the battlefield. This results in at least two injustices: firstly, hardworking Indian farmers who'd occupied and worked a farming property for many years might be cast adrift with little or no notice; secondly because the income arising from the land is divided amongst the tribal members unequally, the top dogs arrogate most of the loot to themselves, very little trickling down to ordinary members.

The lack of facilities meant that some procedures, for example hip replacements, couldn't be performed. In fact there were no prostheses of any kind available and amputees had to struggle around on crutches.

There's a high incidence of diabetes amongst both Fijians and the Indians, so loss of a leg was, unfortunately, common because of frequent gangrene of the lower extremities. Where this only affected the forefoot something could be done which gave me considerable satisfaction on three counts: it obviated the use of a crutch because people could walk almost normally afterwards; it was technically pleasing and, finally, it meant that an old, obsolete operation could be used again to great advantage: the Syme amputation. One removes the diseased area, then all foot bones excepting the Calcaneum: heel bone. This is trimmed and rotated so that it's in line with the leg bones, also trimmed at the ankle. The Calcaneum attaches to the lower end of the Tibia by natural healing. The patient can then walk remarkably well. This operation's criticised because a shoe prosthesis could be bulky and awkward, but that's no problem in a poor community where shoes are a luxury. It worked magnificently well. Syme was Professor of Surgery in Edinburgh, Lister's father-in-law.

Other orthopaedic operations meant the use of older style bone plates and screws, but these were perfectly effective.

In a remote country one had to do everything, including neurosurgery of which, mercifully, there was little—with one noteworthy exception, mentioned shortly. Poor people can't afford air fares and really acute emergencies don't allow of any delay. The operations simply had to be done on the spot.

Nowadays, lesions in the brain can be identified, located and assessed by means of CAT scans and, better, Magnetic Resonance Imaging. All we had in Fiji was the old X ray tomography, where the machine generates pictures, as it were in slices through the tissues, in this case the brain. Here it was performed dramatically and extremely well. The lights are low, the radiographer, master of ceremonies, stands on a platform whilst the senior physician below inserts a needle attached to a syringe of radio-opaque dye into an artery, in this case the Carotid in the neck. The physician nods in the darkened room. With a wave of his arms the radiographer shouts: 'NOW! The elderly tomograph erupts into ear-shattering clack-clack-clack-clack whilst the physician injects. A great show!

The results were unbelievably good and one was able to trace the course of the cerebral arteries with ease, any deformation of their course pointing to a lesion and its location. Dealing with it after the diagnosis had been made was another matter. Fortunately I had to grapple with but one case of cerebral tumour, too ill to be sent to New Zealand, both the nearest sophisticated country and one which kept a paternal eye on Fij.

Though very ill, the man was conscious and both he and his family wanted me to try to do something. The tomograph showed quite plainly where the lesion lay, obviously a malignancy. Palliation was the best that could be hoped for. I'd raised a largish osteoplastic flap– a quadrilateral portion of skull which could subsequently be replaced -and opened the dura mater, described later, when the man suddenly died.

On the other hand in traumatic neurosurgery I always, happily, succeeded. There was plenty of this because Suva was a port for refuelling and relaxation for fleets that do their best to denude the Pacific Ocean of fish. Most of these were Taiwanese and Philippinos and they hated one another with deadly loathing, creeping on board one another's boats at night to hit each other over the head with iron bars: civilized behaviour! I don't know how many had previously died in this way, but many of the victims developed potentially fatal extradural haematoma: blood collecting under the tough outer layer of the brain's coverings. An interesting phenomenon, useful in assessing a patient's condition after this head injury is known as Hutchinson's pupils: as bleeding occurs, the pressure in nearby brain tissue increases causing the pupil on that side firstly to contract, then, as matters worsen, dilate. At this stage, the pupil on the uninjured side contracts. When it finally dilates, death is near.

The operation is simple: one opens the skull over the affected area using that ancient instrument, the trephine. Where necessary, further bone is nibbled away with an instrument known, surprisingly enough, as a nibbler. The bone over the temple, the site for these injuries, is thin. If one must open other parts of the skull there's considerable bleeding from the so-called diploic cavities, worm holes, replete with blood, which riddle the space between the inner and outer layers of the skull. This may be controlled by the use of a special kind of wax, spread and pressed into the skull's cut surface: Horsley's wax.

The tough dura mater, the outer membrane, having been pushed aside, the blood is evacuated from the cranial cavity and the bleeding, from the Middle Meningeal Artery, stopped where it pops up into the cranial cavity via a small canal in the base of the skull. If all other means of stopping to the bleeding fail, a sterile match stick has just the right diameter to fit into the foramen. Drainage of the wound for a day or two post op. is a very good idea.

Opening the skull to relieve pressure once offered a dramatic example. A little boy, deeply comatose, was brought in by his weeping father. Careful examination soon indicated a cerebellar abscess caused by a mastoid abscess bursting into the posterior fossa of the skull: the bit at the lower back. With neither time nor need for anaesthesia, using makeshift arrangements, the child was sat up at the operating table, head bent forward, chin on chest. Muscle cutting at the back of the neck immediately below the skull, done in seconds, exposed its relevant part, which was opened. Gentle probing almost immediately resulted in a sudden gush of great quantities of pus which was evacuated and the wound closed quickly. The amazing thing was that the child was conscious before he left the theatre. His father wept again, this time for joy, as I carried the subdued but conscious patient back into the ward. He was, of course, given antibiotics. A team of ENT surgeons, arriving from Canada in timely fashion treated the mastoid.

The relationship to pressure in the posterior fossa and consciousness is strange. There was a constant trickle of these cases in the surgical wards of Brisbane Children's Hospital. One case in particular (not mine) lay in the ward, unconscious, for many weeks, unresponsive. Suddenly one day, for no apparent reason, he awakened.

The CWM was periodically visited by kindly specialist surgeons motivated by what one could perhaps call Christian charity. A cardiac surgeon performed excellent open heart surgery. Fewer and fewer as time progresses, there are still some good altruistic people in the world.

Middle ear infections were common on these islands. My wife helped at a charity devoted to children whose hearing had been impaired because of middle ear infections.

The Fijian Islands are often visited by violent hurricanes. Not long after our arrival, a major one paid a visit. It's well to be inside when they occur, what with all manner of flying debris, including trees and corrugated iron roofing which, skimming along at high speeds, can be especially lethal. International aid's always forthcoming after Nature's violence and a local joke had it that every hurricane passed over the island of Ratu Mara, the Prime Minister. Nobody we knew had been allowed to visit this, truly precious stone, set in the azure sea, but stories had it that it was paved, wall to wall, if not with gold, then at least with ceramics.

However that may be, large areas of our island were cut off by flooding. One morning, rounds just completed, I was approached, very tentatively indeed, by one of the Indian consultants whom I'd met recently, at Haydn's lecture. A little knot of his fellows huddled in the middle distance. They wondered if I'd be prepared to contribute to a fund to bring food, water and aid generally to the cut-off areas. I of course said yes, provided I was allowed to come too, to assist. My wife insisted upon joining the expedition: a marvellous experience. Collecting water and groceries at a discounted price from an Indian grocer, we set out in two four wheel drives which took us as far as possible into the flood. We then transferred to boats, following submerged roads and inundated valleys to leave precious water, food and first aid kits where necessary at the various houses, Islander as well as Indian. Differences in the diets of the two races were taken into account: rice is an Indian staple, whereas Fijians eat dalo, Taro root.

We marvelled at some of the tiny Indian dwellings, neatly painted despite prevailing poverty. Many people had already begun cleaning up. A woman struck by flying roofing was the only casualty needing hospitalisation. This expedition, made two days before the government's effort began, included two other consultants and led to a loss of mutual suspicions between us and, indeed, a cementing of relationships.

It also led to the misapprehension on the indigenes' part that we'd joined the enemy camp. This, of course, wasn't true, but as time went on it became increasingly evident that the Islander registrars, though always polite, were becoming a little surly. Xenophobia is a genetic human disease.

Virtually the entire surgical teaching curriculum was entrusted to me, the only exception being the weekly teaching ward round, joined by Etika. It was soon obvious why my predecessor had quit: the round was marred by his incessant sniping. I kept my cool, but countered his attacks.

The students, especially the Indians, very bright, almost always answered my questions correctly. The Indians in particular studied incessantly. Islanders didn't do so well, so the government asked me to study the situation and make a report on the problem. This took some months, but I could have told them the reason at once: the Islanders were lazy. This applies especially to the males. The women folk by and large are industrious and better human beings than their opposite numbers. This, of course, is cultural. It must also be said, being honest and uninfluenced by so-called political correctness, that the Indians were more intelligent. This, again, could possibly be cultural or perhaps due to Islanders' penchant for drinking Yangona, of which more anon.

Medical graduates were badly treated, underpaid and sent to remote regions to practice despite minimal postgraduate training. Orthopaedics wasn't included in the curriculum, yet fractures in particular were a common occurrence in those primitive island parts to which newly graduated doctors were banished. The only time I had spare was seven am, so I made this an optional hour's lecture every day that wasn't an operating one. They all attended.

European cultural events were few and far between, though, on one occasion a skilled violinist gave a Bach recital which included his unaccompanied partita in D minor, not easy listening for the untrained ear. For entertainment, therefore, we often went to, and enjoyed, the— Bollywood, movies; occasionally a Taiwanese war movie, enjoyed less. One evening, after eating one of the truly delicious ice creams on offer at the theatre, my wife became decidedly ill—and hated the thought of ice creams for years afterwards. It was soon apparent, however, that those delicacies weren't responsible. I called in the medical consultant, Tom, an Englishman who lived close by. He'd thrown in his lot—as he supposed—with the Islander faction and often regaled me with tales of the Indian 'Mafia' in the Fiji Medical Association: guilty of dastardly but unidentified deeds. For him, Fiji and the Fijians could do no wrong. He therefore ruled out dengue fever as it didn't exist on this particular royal throne of kings—though that was, in fact, the problem.

The next couple of weeks were Hell for her. The disease, also known as breakbone fever, has a number of variants. Eileen had it in one of its worst, haemorrhagic, forms. Fortunately, though she came out in haemorrhagic spots, it didn't affect dangerous regions. Nevertheless, she was in absolute agony, the merest touch causing intense pain. The only position she found in any way tolerable was lying, cushioned, on the floor with her legs resting up on the bed. Mere produced a vile tasting native remedy which we do believe shortened the period of distress.

One night, early in that illness I was sitting reading. Looking up, I thought I was hallucinating: crouching in the window, was the figure of a Fijian which continued to move, ever so slowly, into the room. It was no figure of my imagination, though the notion that he was about to knife me was. He was actually about to steal the handbag Eileen had left on the floor before she had collapsed. I hadn't realised that it was there, hidden from view by a piece of furniture. Believing that I was in danger and attack being the best form of defence, I grasped my chair and made for the robber. Unfortunately it was a very heavy wooden type of armchair and the delay in getting it into the attack position allowed the man to lean over, grab the bag and make a quick, sharp exit though I did catch him a fourpenny one on the leg as he made his escape.

This wasn't an isolated case of dengue fever. The disease is endemic there, but this was a full-blown epidemic. Many people developed an extreme haemorrhagic form, a high proportion dying, probably from cerebral haemorrhage. I had to perform several emergency gastrectomies because of severe bleeding from the stomach, only controllable by removing the stomach.

Yaws is another endemic disease that allegedly doesn't exist on those islands: a very unpleasant condition caused by a spirochaete not unlike the one causing syphilis. Amongst other of its effects, this disease may eat away the nose and face in an often horrendous way. Kesho, the senior Paediatric physician, another member of our 'Mafia', took me on a tour of the island to prove to me that it did, in fact, exist there, albeit in remote areas.

Poor Turleygood, poor Tom: his would-be affinity with the Islanders was doomed. He'd hoped to have his contract renewed and, indeed, he was—is?—a good physician. All bureaucrats tend to be bitchy, amongst other unlovable attributes; Fijians no exception. For no other reason I can think of, they didn't renew his contract, much to his disappointment

Meantime, I agreed to join the 'Mafiosi': the committee of the Fiji Medical Association. It wasn't entirely constituted of Indians: Timoci Bavandra, later Prime Minister of a more just, power-sharing Parliament, rapidly deposed by a coup, was a pleasant, constructive member.

We didn't waste much time before actively trying to improve the conditions of the badly treated junior doctors. Negotiation proved hopeless. All of our representations falling upon deaf ears, we called a strike. This worried me. I don't believe medical care should ever be jeopardised. In Darwin, when the Communist head of the hospital staff union called a strike its effect was decidedly minimal: I was the only working doctor there and most of the nurses continued to work too. As already mentioned, dear old Arthur and I did the hospital laundry, using his washing machine.

I expressed serious doubts to the President, the senior pathologist. He only laughed.

'It'll never come to that: just you see.'

We set up stalls in various places where strikers could come and drink Yangona. This extract from the roots of a member of the pepper family looks and tastes like brownish-red mud. It has a soporific effect and plays an important part in Fijian ceremonies. It's poured into a coconut shell, the participant claps loosely three times then downs the draught. I didn't take to it and Karam, the pathologist told me that his research showed that it causes severe cirrhosis of the liver. Our 'strike' neared its climax and, almost at 'D' day itself, the Health Department caved in and negotiated with us. The strike was off.

A less agreeable habit of some Fijian males is a tendency to murder their wives/girl friends when they tire of them or have a real or imagined grievance. Humoured thus, they throw a kind of Molotov cocktail into the bure of their 'loved'-ones, inflicting horrible burns. A whole ward full of these unfortunates was under Etika's 'care' and I had frequently to walk through it. It didn't take long to realise that every patient there died. On making further enquiries, I was aghast to be shown a huge jar of petroleum jelly, of an unpleasant brownish colour. This horrible reservoir of bacteria, smeared on the burns, was the only local treatment employed.

Severely burned patients lose vast amounts of fluids and one's first care in treating them is to ensure that these are rapidly replaced. If this isn't done properly, death ensues rapidly. The next cause of death is septicaemia and this is where that frightful dressing came in: it positively guaranteed death. As soon as I realised this, I asked Etika, as tactfully as possible, if I might be given the care of these patients. He agreed, somewhat to my surprise. I immediately set up a regimen for fluid replacement and hurtled around to the pharmacy to see if any silver sulfadiazine, then the dressing of choice, was there. Of course it wasn't. There were, however, many styptic pencils. These are made of silver nitrate, which works quite well on burns, too, so I got them to scrape off the wax coverings and make up sterile solutions of the result, at the same time exhorting the Chief Pharmacist to try to get silver sulfadiazine—without much hope. I developed an active dislike of that idiot, who acted in as niggardly a manner as possible. The country was poor, yes, but not so poor that some life-saving drugs couldn't be procured. In the meantime an Indian pharmacist in private practice who'd been very helpful—and generous—donated a lot more styptic pencils and undertook, if necessary, to supply the other silver at a very cut price. Of course, this would come out of my pocket.

That hospital pharmacist was a jobsworth who wouldn't fight for his corner: patients mattered far less than his job. The repercussions of this are coming up.

Funnily enough, however, there seemed to be any amount of anti-cancer drugs—a donation at some time?—and it fell to my lot to use them. My wife says that anybody who can read can cook. The same applies to the use of these powerful drugs, the only differences being:

1. That one must be well medically trained.

2. That one must read a very great deal.

There were no catastrophes. Sometimes, in the case of breast cancer, one had to use slightly unconventional combinations of drugs, depending upon what was on offer.

One Saturday afternoon I was called to the hospital to see a footballer who'd been tackled so ferociously that his neck had been broken. Luckily for him, a neck brace had been applied immediately. Otherwise he might well have become quadriplegic. In Saudi Arabia I had the use of a Stryker frame for such cases. It allows of the head to be kept quite still and, if necessary, the patient may be turned over without risk. Nothing like that here! Some of my assistants were very good and attentive to their charges and this made matters easier. Using local anaesthetic whilst Jagdish, a middle grade registrar, held the head completely steady, I drilled holes in either side of the patient's skull and inserted the business ends of ice tong callipers, amazingly so-called because they closely resemble the tongs once used by icemen. A seven pound weight having been attached to a cord connected to the tongs and running over a pulley, my assistant carefully saw to it that that tension was consistently, applied whilst the patient was brought to the theatre.

There are two main approaches to fractures of this kind. I prefer the anterior one, other things being equal. It affords a beautiful example of virtually bloodless surgery. A long incision is made across the neck, the fascia covering the muscles divided. One soon encounters the Thyroid gland and, by simply dividing one artery to it, it can be retracted and the cervical spine exposed without cutting any other tissue or causing bleeding. One must then very carefully cut a trough in the front of the fractured spine (the vertebral body) and those immediately above and below it. With a little difficulty—no Stryker!—a bone graft of the appropriate size was cut from the Iliac part of the pelvic bones and—with the utmost care—pushed into the trough already cut. It's easy to break the graft at that juncture, so great care must be observed. Again, no Stryker and I didn't trust to any bodgie pulley arrangement, so the poor fellow had to endure his head, neck and shoulders immobilised in a plaster cast until the graft had healed.

I wasn't terribly happy when, a couple of days later I discovered that a patient had been admitted to the next door bed suffering from a Pott's abscess in his groin, also known as a cold abscess, because, unlike most abscesses, it's cool to the touch. The condition is named after Percival Pott, probably John Hunter's most brilliant student. He did describe the disease, but so did Hippocrates, very well indeed, more than two thousand years before him.

Perhaps a few words about Pott are appropriate before telling you about this patient. I'll let you off Hippocrates who also described tuberculosis of the spine, which is associated with that abscess. Being due to tuberculosis, these conditions were becoming quite rare at the time we're speaking about, excepting in poor countries. Unfortunately that disease will be with us more frequently in future, thanks to AIDS, which, lowering bodily resistance to infections, is helping tuberculosis make a come-back.

Pott also described other conditions which needn't detain us, but it's worth mentioning the fracture he sustained when, in the course of his rounds, he fell off his horse. There is a fracture bearing his name, but he almost certainly didn't sustain one of those. His was a compound fracture: bone fragments being exposed through the skin and the bone in question was almost certainly his femur, whereas Pott's fracture is of the ankle. There was a construction site nearby, so he bought a door from there and had himself carried on it to his home, where his colleagues recommended amputation—remember Lister's troubles? Well, Pott, though about a century before Lister, was no idiot. He refused amputation opting for splinting and covering the wound, eventually making a full recovery. Surely this, an undoubtedly well-known case would have suggested something to his peers, but they and their successors were hidebound with orthodoxy until Lister woke them up. The herd instinct so deeply rooted in all of us may well do more harm than good now that we've moved on—a little—from our original state of savagery. .

But back to Fiji and the man, in his late twenties, with tuberculosis of the spine. He came in primarily because he was finding it increasingly difficult to walk, thanks to a progressive weakness of his legs. X ray showed a whopping great abscess extending from his lower chest to his groin. This would have been causing pressure on his spinal cord and hence the weakness. I took him to the theatre and, putting the fellow partly on his side, shingled a few of his lower ribs. There wasn't a need to strip up the pleura (chest and lung lining) thanks to the great size of the accumulation of thick, white pus which I sucked out, subsequently irrigating the extensive cavity. I didn't open the abscess where it was pointing at his groin—at least I can't remember doing that. Radiologically there was no apparent disease in his spine, nor could I find any at operation. Not wanting to risk trouble that I might have missed—there must have been a small focus somewhere—I condemned the man to lie in a body plaster cast for three months, giving him an intensive course of anti-tubercular treatment fortunately available. He appeared to be well at the time of my departure, but more than that can't really be said. It's more usual in this situation for the spine to be affected considerably, to the extent that the front of the spinal bodies in the chest collapse, the sufferer becoming a hunch back, the usual cause of that distressing condition. Hippocrates describes hunch back in connection with groin abscess and some of the other complications of the disease. Completely ignorant of the fundamental causes of disease, he didn't miss much clinically.

At the conclusion of this operation, Jagdish rather self-consciously told me that he'd been granted leave. I think it was for a week.

'Taking a holiday?' I asked.

'No, I'm preparing myself to take part in the fire walking.'

I hoped that I wasn't looking too incredulous. This was a manifestation of his firmly held Hindu religion. Jagdish spent his leave being prepared for his ordeal. At the end of it all, he did walk over burning coals without sustaining any burns. I did have to treat one participant for burns of the feet: one of insufficient faith, no doubt—or perhaps he was too slow over the coals.

Swelling of the neck due to non-toxic goitre was a fairly common problem in those living in the inland part of the island. The swelling can be quite enormous and is caused by lack of iodine in the soil and drinking water. Some of these patients were subthyroid, needing replacement therapy—thyroxin—in addition to iodine. Surgery was only needed if the swelling was too unsightly or, rarely, had caused pressure problems. In these circumstances one would expect to see cretins: victims of a lack of thyroxin production at an early age, but I saw none. Perhaps they were kept indoors, like spastic children I saw, in Saudi Arabia.

Cancer of the cervix was very common on the island, remember? Much of it was, sadly, in its late stages. Though there was a consultant in Obstetrics and Gynaecology, conspicuous by her absence from the operating theatre, she didn't appear to do much work. Haydn, the Reader, took her place there and it was my privilege to assist him at the ultimately radical operation for later stages of this disease: pelvic exenteration: the removal of all organs and lymph glands from the pelvis, including uterus, ovaries, bladder; often the lower bowel too. Only late developments in blood and fluid replacement and good anaesthesia had made this possible and, indeed, the operation had been first described only about thirty years previously. It leaves the patient alive, but in a parlous plight, with a colostomy and leaking urine. The ureters may later be implanted into the colon, a special collection bag now being necessary. Even this, of course, didn't necessarily cure the patient: late stage cancer is pitiless. I've already mentioned the dangerous nature of veins in the pelvis and it's a tribute to Haydn that none of his patients bled to death—or even excessively.

Cancer of the oesophagus is also remorseless, though survivals are improving. Very few victims survive even now, probably because symptoms appear after the lesion has spread too far. I dealt with a lucky one. Tom was performing a large series of gastroscopies on behalf of a drug company which had invented a drug which, indeed, proved to be successful in the treatment of peptic ulcer. He was a good, well trained medicine man with a higher diploma. Therefore, in performing gastroscopies he examined the oesophagus on the way down. I was between cases when he called me in to his theatre:

'Take a look at that and tell me what you think.'

There was no doubt about it. At mid-point of the gullet, on the rear surface, was a pearly white nodule perhaps one centimetre across.

'Yes. I know what you're thinking' I said, 'but let's biopsy it first.'

Tom did so there and then and the result proved it to be a carcinoma.

The saying: the smaller the growth, the bigger the operation has much to recommend it: if the growth—cancerous, of course—is small the chances of cure are better and one should employ radical surgery. Like everything else, each case must be judged entirely upon its circumstances. These include its location, degree of malignancy, the age and condition of the patient, etc. There are exceptions to every rule but this wasn't one of them. His oesophagus had to be removed. It's a big operation. Because the entire gullet is removed, the stomach must be mobilised sufficiently to bring it up into the chest and joined to the lower end of the pharynx. There must be absolutely no tension at this junction because the pharynx has very poor tensile strength. In other words, stitches pull out all too readily. If they do, the patient will certainly die. The oesophagus is closely associated with a number of nasties: the aorta, the heart and great veins running into it and the intercostal veins draining blood from between the ribs and another associated vein. The diaphragm must be opened to allow the stomach to be brought into the chest. Many: not too many, arteries supplying the stomach must also be divided to mobilise it sufficiently, but good blood circulation must be preserved. Though the opening incision must be very extensive, some essential parts of the operation must be carried out deep down, well away from the surface. Everything had to be done just so: here was a good chance of effecting a cure. (Cure is now a no no word where cancer's concerned. One must say remission). Assisting was the senior, senior registrar, of mixed race, Elliot by name, a fine person and first rate, grossly underpaid surgeon. It saddened me that he'd been too poor to go overseas to obtain his Fellowship. Unfortunately, too, he suffered from mitral stenosis, a condition mentioned previously in connection with London surgeon Brock. Almost immediately after he'd helped me with this operation he underwent what must have been a Brock type procedure on his heart. After quite a long convalescence he returned to work optimistic but puffing whenever he climbed stairs. I understand he died, quite young, soon after we'd left the country.

The oesophagectomy patient was still alive and perfectly well by the time I left. I was a little proud that he brought his little son across from another island where he lived to meet me at our last consultation.

Towards the end of my stay, Kesho, consultant Paediatrician, took me on an interesting tour of the island's interior. He didn't say why, but it was obviously to demonstrate that yaws did indeed exist in the Fijian Islands. The native villages appeared to be clean; the inhabitants as happy as any. Sure enough, my friend pointed out a few cases and I also identified a couple of cases of goitre, suggesting they come to Suva for treatment.

A young girl, about fourteen or fifteen years of age came up to our Land Cruiser wearing Wellies which concealed her problem remarkably well: a club foot. Because of her age, the condition was well established. She needed no convincing that an operation would help her. Fortunately, as it can be very difficult to achieve a really satisfactory result in late cases, the bones having grown into a deformed state, a fairly simple trimming of the bones of her foot achieved a good result with little if any loss of movement. In trimming them, it's vital either to leave the joint surfaces intact or to fuse adjacent bones if absolutely necessary. Ignoring this will result in an intractably painful, probably stiff foot.

For a long time we of the 'Mafia' had been cultivating the mixed race Health Minister, in his sublime position for political reasons: to placate mixed race electors.

The Indians were most hospitable, their formal meals and barbeques always a delight; the food invariably scrumptious. The only slight problem was the personal development of an addiction to chillies. We invited the Minister along to some of these and he apparently became friendly to the point where we persuaded him to attend a meeting of the consultants to discuss some of our serious grievances.

He chose a lunchtime meeting. I was on take that day and three shockers enraged me and I strode up to that meeting fuming.

With only two days' supply of the appropriate penicillin derivative, I was forced after that to use the only available antibiotic: chloramphenicol, a cheap as dirt generic drug on a child with staphylococcal septicaemia.

As an aside, this drug tends to cause serious blood problems, at least in Europeans. It caused no trouble in any of the Island's races, at least whilst I was there. In any case there was no option but to use it. Unsurprisingly, the drug was useless and the child developed septic pericarditis, pus in the envelope surrounding the heart, because the causative organism, the dreaded golden Staph, circulating throughout the blood stream had settled around the unfortunate boy's heart. A very serious matter for the physicians, I had him transferred. As I was preparing to attend that meeting there was a call from the medical side: the child was ready to be transferred back but the infection had spread to another part of his skeleton and the head of his thigh bone (femur) had been obliterated. Negligently, they hadn't notified me of this development, not that I could have done much about it in the circumstances. What enraged me was the fact that this child, with no hope of a hip prosthesis, would spend the remainder of his life as a cripple, always in pain. Almost immediately there was another call: another burns patients had died. Then a message from the pharmacy: no more silver nitrate solution.

The minister was all smiles as he addressed the meeting. The chairman asked for any questions or comments. I waited a full nanosecond for someone else to speak before making a passionate plea for more money to be made available for drugs.

'At this very moment patients are dying for lack of suitable drugs.' I said.

There was more discussion and the Minister, still all smiles, departed.

The discussion was supposed to be confidential, but someone whispered in my ear that Karam had tipped off the press. That night at about three am the phone rang. Eileen usually took such calls in other countries to spare me a little. This was exceptional: the hospital switch usually closed down by six pm. She could make neither head nor tail of this call. I took over:

'Geebs? Geebs??'

'No, this is Mr. Gibbs speaking.'

It was, of course, the Minister and, as I, likewise, couldn't understand what he was saying, though I had a very good idea of its general tenor. I hung up.

A bearer would call to take me to emergencies when the hospital switchboard was unmanned, his appearance always heralded by the brrr,brrr, brrr, but but but of the elderly, once white, Suzuki he drove. It was no surprise to hear it, before too long, puttering along our road. On this occasion, as usual, the bearer presented a note, this one different:

There will be a meeting of all consultants at five thirty this morning.

I wrote back: It is immature and inconsiderate to call a meeting at this hour of the morning. As I have a very heavy work load in the operating theatre today I shall not attend this meeting as it might impair the quality of my work. For information, I have played no part in any newspaper story.

When I arrived in the theatre that morning some thoughtful person had laid out the morning paper for me. In giant characters occupying more than half of the front page was:

DEAD FOR LACK OF DRUGS.

I was named in the second paragraph. Furious, I wrote a letter to Ratu Mara, Prime Minister and monarch of all he surveyed, pointing out that the Health Minister's reaction to this episode and the administration of his portfolio were such that he'd proved himself unsuitable for the job. To my gratified amazement he was sacked.

The new appointee, an Indian: Mr. Ramzan had been a patient and we'd got on well together. This gave me pause, especially as, at about this time I'd received a letter from the Indian ambassador thanking me for my treatment of the Indian people. Sadly, I could truly see no fundamental improvement in anything in the hospital I'd found so distressing overall. Moreover, the most senior registrar now that Elliot was on leave; no doubt because the mixed race Minister had been sacked and he was also of mixed race, now became antagonistic and somewhat uncooperative. Why put up with that? I sent in my resignation. The Health Minister invited us to dinner and asked me to reconsider. It was a difficult decision, but I felt that the die had been cast.

England En route to Saudi Arabia

I've always loved England, its beautiful countryside—there's still some left!—with her civilized people with a civilized sense of humour: they haven't all been dumbed down yet, so that's where we made our way. It was soon evident that, at my age, I'd find difficulty in obtaining a permanent position, so locums it would be: three in quick succession at the Royal East Sussex Hospital, in general surgery as it happened.

About one half of the work there turned out to be in urology. One busy afternoon's operating list in that specialty was a serious disappointment: when I did my sums, the average age of the patients proved to be only eighty nine and a half. Why couldn't it have been ninety?

Here I had two disappointments. The first was a man with a ruptured aortic aneurysm, a rapidly fatal problem, the aorta being the greatest of all the blood vessels. He'd been resuscitated a little and tests indicated that the rupture was in a location where repair was possible,

Access to the area was simple, as was excision of the rupture. In these cases a woven dacron prosthesis takes the place of the excised artery. All went well here, too and the normal slight ooze through the material soon stopped. On the point of closing up, firstly from the suture line, then from every imaginable and unimaginable place poured a thin red liquid:

'red ink syndrome', disseminated intravascular coagulation, resulting from excessive stresses which had exhausted all of the clotting mechanism in the patient's body. He bled to death.

The other episode was less dramatic. A naughty old boy had been fiddling with his posterior and a foreign body had impacted there. An abscess resulted and he developed a very nasty fistula, faeces now passing through a new opening in his buttocks as well as the normal route. There are a number of different types of *fistula-in-ano* and this was one of the most difficult to treat. I was confident, having George's teaching in mind, but, after the procedure had been carried out I left a day or two later as my contract had expired. When I returned for the next locum, the consultant drew me aside and indicated in no uncertain terms that I'd done the wrong thing and that he had performed a colostomy to give the fistula the opportunity to heal.

George used to rant and rave about fistula treatment and he was definitely the expert. I knew I was right, but said nothing. What point would that serve? I could feel animosity oozing out of the man from every pore.

Soon afterwards, in my role of urologist, I had to deal with a problem I've referred to earlier: urethral stricture. This man had had sounds galore passed, often right through the urethra into the outside tissues. It was a horrible mess and the only approach was to use a urethroscope and visually pass very fine bougees made of gum elastic up to the stricture. These would lodge in all or most of the false passages and around the stricture until, finally, one bougee would find the proper passage, a procedure known as fagotting because the bunch of bougees supposedly resemble a bundle of faggots. The successful bougee, with its near end threaded, passed. One with progressively larger diameters is screwed on to it and pushed in, thus dilating the stricture. The highly flexible bougees curl up in the bladder until withdrawn.

All very well, excepting that the bougee finding the correct passage was old and broke off. Through the urethroscope I could just dimly make out the broken end, right in the stricture itself. Luckily there was a very fine pair of alligator forceps available, (toothed forceps whose jaws vaguely resemble those of that repulsive beast) or all would have been disaster. All's well that ends well and, amazingly, the fellow said that his stream was the best he'd experienced for years.

The consultant whose locum I was made a point of visiting me in my clinic. He greatly praised my work, probably because he was aware of the other consultant's animus.

I noticed an ad. for a locum consultant orthopod in Tabuk, Saudi Arabia. This appealed to the nomad in me, I applied and got the job. It was with the Saudi Ministry of Defence and Aviation, managed by an American firm, Whittaker, pronounced Wutka by the Arabs.

As the plane glided in to the Jiddah airstrip, I was struck by a series of attractive buildings, constructed to resemble Bedou tents, to house pilgrims about to make their Hajj. Imaginative, even a little poetic!

There was less poetry in the customs hall. Several planes must have arrived at the same time: rows and rows –and rows—of benches were densely strewn with the contents of suitcases, every one of which had to be opened and emptied. Earnest soldiers went through everything in minute detail. Some idiot had tried to bring in some bacon. The look of savage disapproval on the face of the discovering askeri was unforgettable. The offender was marched away no doubt to be put on the next plane home. Elsewhere a wooden image of Ganesh was being sawn up, possibly in case naughties were hidden inside, its Indian owner duly anguished.

Nor was there any poetry in the chairborne division of Wutka in Jiddah, all American expats who'd obviously never been to Tabuk and who spent that night imparting useless, inaccurate information: with one exception: teaching us our first few words of Arabic: bukra mumkin insh'allah, which gave insight into the mentality of Arab bureaucrats. The translation is, literally, tomorrow perhaps, God willing: in other words, never.

They also instructed me in the art of wringing out a teabag using one's spoon, of limited use, as I hate teabags

Driving through Jiddah on returning to the airport, one was struck by the amount of new building going on. A number of the old dwellings had delightful latticed balconies reminiscent of ones I'd seen in Kashmir. Roundabouts were all adorned with sculptures, usually in steel; rather pedestrian excepting for one exceptional impressionistic representation of a flight of seagulls. The current marque of Muslim isn't supposed to represent any of God's creation.

We took off for Tabuk through a dense pall of sandy dust. Wear and tear on engines in that murk must be considerable. Any misgivings as to the standards of the pilots were soon dispelled. No problem in any of the many flights taken within Saudi were ever experienced.

From take-off to landing we were plied with coffee made from unroasted beans, a different, pleasant beverage served from traditional waisted pots with a sprig of date palm stuck in the spout as a filter.

A minibus conveyed us to the military cantonment where the hospital was located. As we left the airport we were given a taste of Saudi driving and the reason why there'd be any amount of trauma surgery ahead. The exit is served by a dual carriageway and as we bowled along admiring the unbelievable multitudes of plastic bags stuck to the perimeter fence, a car, driving the wrong way in our lane hurtled straight towards us. The driver did miss us—by inches.

At the cantonment, there was an interminable wait under a raging sun as our documents were checked, re-checked and then rechecked again. We were eventually dispatched to the recreation building, where blue-coated bureaucrats welcomed us perfunctorily and allocated accommodation.

Next day was a treat: an orientation excursion in a minibus. The driver was a Yemeni Arab of course. No Saudi would accept such a menial posting. These drivers know only two speeds: stationery or the maximum that can be coaxed out of his vehicle. We roared out of the cantonment, off the tarmac on to a road of mixed dust and sand. The microfine dust concealed bars of rock and periodically, with a resounding CRASH! We'd become temporarily airborne. We toured virtually featureless desert, occasionally passing pick-up trucks in whose tray a camel often sat, body concealed from view. The appearance of a disembodied camel's head looking around at us as we passed was hilarious. How these animals existed in the absence of any visible vegetation was and is a mystery.

We halted at a tree whose long, steely-hard, viciously sharp thorns gave us pause. One of our number assured us that these were the thorns which made up Jesus' Crown. We hit the tarmac once more, en route to Wutka's resort on the Red Sea, Haql, journeying past a series of most amazing hills, bare of vegetation, but brilliantly coloured in reds, blues, purples, even greens: volcanic dykes forced up through other rocks in ancient days.

Next came an absolutely unforgettable view. Essaying a long, steep hill which proved just too much for the overloaded vehicle, the driver, taking this as a matter of personal shame, bad temperedly told us to get out and walk to the top. There, we looked over desert sparsely studded with crooked trees, the stern, forbidding, mountainous Sinai facing us and fading into the distance. Separating the two was a ribbon of the most incredibly brilliant sapphire blue: the Red Sea, in brilliantly sparkling contrast with drab land on either side: an entirely inadequate description. The view must be seen to be appreciated.

The Haql resort was pleasantly situated overlooking the water. It was intriguing to see many female figures clad entirely in black down to ankles supervising their gambolling infants, retreating as each wavelet advanced.

There was another intake on the following weekend, the new arrivals being treated to a similar excursion with this difference: I was called to the E.R. to treat half a minibus full of accident victims lying groaning on every available perch. The idiot driver, speeding excessively, had turned his vehicle over. Nobody died, but a busy evening and night lay ahead.

One victim was a Pakistani Ophthalmologist. He and I were invited, sometime later, to a goat grab by hospitable Saudis, very pleasant people. The trauma is still etched in the mind. The host addressed my companion:

'You are an Ophthalmologist, so it's only appropriate that I offer you this sheep's eye': to eat, of course.
Yuk! But relief was short lived:

'As an Orthopaedic surgeon I can hardly offer you a bone. Please accept this instead.'
This was a large: very large piece of liver. I loathe all offal, liver in particular. It was a case of shut down mind, open mouth, chew twice and swallow; repeat for as long as necessary.

A couple of days later, a general surgeon, Leighton Bell, who'd befriended me, took me on another trip, out into the howling, featureless wilderness to a great jumble of rocks. How he managed to find it remains a mystery. Clambering over the great, confused pile, one's attention was firstly attracted to the innumerable feathery footprints of the myriad scorpions who made this their abode. These were soon forgotten as it gradually registered in my surprised consciousness that these rocks were covered in the most amazing petroglyphs: many animals including oryx; even crocodiles—a much wetter climate at that distant time?—and stylised men, uniform in scanty garments, genitals very evident. These, probably of religious significance, must surely be the only relics of some long-forgotten civilization.

Toward the end of our sojourn in Tabuk, many of these petroglyphs adorned the entrance to the cantonment. They'd been obtained by the delicate Saudi archaeological approach to conservation: blasted apart by high explosive.

Kindly colleagues continually helped orient me in my new desert home. One took me on another very notable journey along the foundations of the old Hejaz railway, built about one hundred years ago by the Turks to convey pilgrims to Mecca whilst simultaneously installing a military presence. There's actually a railway station—without the rails—in good condition in the middle of Tabuk, but, as we drove along the surprisingly well-preserved, well-constructed permanent way also minus rails, we passed several more stations, all of meticulously constructed slate grey stone masonry, their defensive nature most apparent. Think of the thrill as we suddenly came upon a skein of twisted rails. My host led me down an embankment. There, sorely battered and upside down were an engine tender and flat cars, the work of Lawrence of Arabia. One could imagine him and his group of tribesmen waiting inconspicuously in the loose tangle of scanty scrub until a lookout gave the signal to detonate the charges laid along the line. Amazingly, there was no rust on any of these relics, a sign of that region's desiccation.

Approval for wives to be admitted to the Kingdom takes time so, in the meantime, I was given a comfortable, motel type room with most mod. cons, including more than adequate cooking facilities, extremely welcome as the execrable food in the canteen was soaked in fat.

Sam's, an optimistically designated supermarket on the cantonment was preferable to shopping in the town a couple of miles away when one was finding one's way, though Wutka provided an adequate bus service. There was also a washing machine in the unit. No dryer was necessary: hang the clothes out and they're dry in minutes.

I think I've said before that in some, perhaps many, ways I'm slow on the uptake. I was intrigued by the volume of grape juice on sale in Sam's and puzzled when the customer before me at the checkout presented his purchases, mainly grape juice.

'So: you want no yeast?'

Asked the counter jumper, a question surely unique to that shop. Mystifying! Only to me! Though alcohol is banned in the Kingdom—theoretically—very many indeed of the expats made their own more or less drinkable wine. There were lots of jokes:

'Ummm, an insouciant little vintage. The year? Let me see...I'd say about three thirty last Thursday afternoon.'

Later, ensconced in our villa, there was a very occasional raid by the police, somehow broadcast by them well in advance, giving everybody time to bury their Chateau Tabuk in the sand in their back 'gardens', amongst the gnarled, struggling acacias.

Being under the influence outside one's home, however, was an entirely different matter and could mean gaol, though deportation was the rule.

Traffic breaches were very likely to lead to gaol too, apparently a far from pleasant experience. Offenders were incarcerated with very questionable types, eating presenting a particular problem, food consisting of a large tray of kepsa, aka goat grab: politeness played no part in the rush to grab what one could. We ate this quite often ourselves and the version we were served could be delicious: roasted goat on a bed of variously flavoured,spiced rice, usually liberally sprinkled with pine nuts, always eaten with the fingers of one's right hand. In prison, the food was flung into the cell and a wild melee resulted in which the slow, weak or meek missed out. Nobody was notified when someone was gaoled. When the miscreant was eventually missed, a search always included the gaol. There were traffic cops in cars at many intersections, watching for infractions, all too many of which led to the prison gates.

After not a little struggle I managed to obtain a driver's licence, absolutely necessary as otherwise one had to depend upon the moods and vagaries of the Yemeni who drove minibuses between the cantonment and a newly constructed hospital outside it, a few miles away. From the cantonment, one turned right and then, a couple of miles further on, just before the hospital entrance, were traffic lights which always seemed to be on red. Looking behind when stopped there, not only lone and level sands, but also an excellent, completely straight road, stretched far away, all too often with a lethal projectile: a car doing the ton, hurtling along its path to one's certain immolation. At least, that was the fear. Saudis, at least in the Tabuk of that time, have an intense dislike of red traffic lights. On Many occasions, faced with one, we saw drivers swerve across the road, engine roaring, through one of the omnipresent building sites, on to the desired road. What's wear and tear on the car when one can save twenty five seconds? For this good reason the journey between hospitals was decidedly hazardous. One victim, almost killed there is mentioned later.

Apart from that risk, the stroppy bus drivers ignored official timetables, literally driving when they felt like it. Crisis came when a little boy was admitted not long before lunch with a fractured femur. I ordered X-rays and, as a couple of minor procedures awaited in the new hospital, it should have been possible to do them, return and treat the child soon after lunch, at about the time that his X-rays came to hand.. Thanks to those lazy temperamental thugs, they didn't get me back until evening, the poor child suffering unnecessary pain for all of that time. Next day, fuming, I complained to the Chief of Professional Services. His reply, in effect, was: if you don't like it, you know what you can do. In all things, Wutka was totally spineless where Arabs were concerned. They couldn't even ensure a proper bus service.

My own transport being the only answer, I promptly bought a car, new and incredibly cheap, in the souk. But there was an ever-present risk of gaol because I didn't have a driver's licence. One was eventually obtained as follows: It was, firstly, necessary to present oneself at an office in town, hoping that someone with the necessary authority was there. There usually wasn't. One day, to my joy, a lieutenant whom I'd been treating was there who readily gave me a piece of paper to present with myself at the Civilian Hospital, give blood, have the paper signed to that effect, then report to him again.

The only snag was that that hospital was, to say the least, a house of horrors. Horrors? The understatement of the decade. It regarded our hospital as a refuge of last resort and when we heard that a patient was arriving thence, we shuddered and turned pale. Some of the worst, most horrifying examples of bad treatment were shunted off to us, a couple of examples being mentioned later.

I was confident that any needle they thrust into my arm would be contaminated with hepatitis B at the very least: there was much of that disease in the area. I grumbled about this to one of my physio orderlies, Mahomet Iraq—I was in charge of that department:

'Iss no prrroblem! I come with you to hospital!'

And indeed he did. When a registrar appeared, a conversation in Arabic ensued, soon after which I left the hospital with a signed certificate stating that I'd given blood but still with all of it intact, without Hepatitis B and minus twenty Saudi Riyals.

Next came the ordeal of proving myself capable of driving. On that dread day a number of fellow applicants assembled at the Chief Mechanic's (Mahondas) office. Eventually he appeared and we were driven to a remote spot. He looked us over, pointing to one:

'You take car, drive to post there, then back.'

That post was perhaps a hundred yards away. The chosen one complied.

'Ver good.'

So we all received our licences.

The library was well supplied with English papers. Every picture featuring a female was lovingly manually blacked out. There must have been intense competition for that job! There was also a good English language Egyptian newspaper, *Al Ahram*, which gave valuable insights into what was going on in this unstable part of the world.

Expats celebrated Christmas in appropriate style, but cards sent to near and dear at home were another matter. The best one could do was to send pictures of various parts of the Kingdom inscribed: Happy Auspicious Occasion.

Bureaucracy reigned supreme at Wutka, so we were inevitably inundated with bumf, but there was a Brit in the office with a great sense of humour. We always looked forward to his politically very incorrect efforts. I lovingly saved some of these, but now that they're needed to share with you, I can't find the jolly things. Sorry!

It's not what you know it's who you know is true at all times and in all places. In command of all of the consultants was a Chief of Professional Services, a Canadian who impressed none of us and who, according to the Canadians, had a dubious record at home. The point of the old saw is that he was living on the cantonment in sin with a moderately attractive female, a felony punishable by death in the Kingdom. How did he get away with it? If we knew the situation, the authorities certainly did.

At the top of our surgical, heap was a Palestinian, Farouk, a Urologist, a kindly soul who didn't interfere with us at all. I was top of the Orthopaedic contingent—hardly a heap; there were only three of us. The really useful member of our team was a Norwegian, Arvid. The practice was firstly to engage a locum and if he was any good, keep him on. This had happened to me.

There were about four rates of pay. The locals, paid peanuts; Europeans a reasonable living wage; Australians more still and Yanks quite a lot. When due for reappointment, though I'd joined in England, I flew to Oz to sign on in earnest. Why not?

When Arvid was put through his paces, I at first viewed his operating skills with alarm: he set to with drills and the like with almost manic enthusiasm. Nothing nasty ever happened, however, and it was soon apparent that his operating fury was very well controlled.

A locum from Belgium turned up: a total disaster. I had no alternative but to report adversely upon him, though an additional hand on deck was needed. Perhaps that's why this rule about locums was relaxed for the appointment of a third team member, sadly, a fat, greasy Canadian whose name I'd prefer to forget. His ignorance of the art was encyclopaedic and I doubt the authenticity of his qualifications.

There was a high proportion of children with congenital dislocation of the hip there and G (for greasy) encountering one in his clinic not long after arriving, asked me to assist. He hadn't the foggiest notion of the anatomy, much less what he was supposed to do and he began sticking his great thumbs and fingers into tissue planes where they had no business to be. I was upset at the way he was dealing with the child but she wasn't my patient. All I could do was keep him out of trouble. As it happened, this was a particularly severe case, the hip socket having no concavity at all, represented instead by three little nubbins where the bones of the pelvis came together I couldn't bear to think of what he might do, so I told G to close up. The options were limited in any case if one were not to create serious problems in later life.

Our already pleasant existence brightened considerably when Ed, an Australian radiologist, blew into Tabuk. A new broom was badly needed in Radiology, the principal practitioner there being an incompetent Swede of nasty nature. In a hospital where one had only to ask to receive, his equipment was marginal and part, the Bucky diaphragm—it fortunately didn't affect me– was held together with adhesive—because, he was toadying to Wutka. Despite claims to eminence in his specialty, his diagnoses were often awry.

I've always diagnosed my own films. Whilst one must never ignore a radiologist's report, diagnosing films oneself, always important in my view, was very necessary here. I had, for instance, a young woman with early tuberculosis of the spine, whose reports always came back nothing abnormal detected. I would, from time to time, submit another request, always with the annotation Progress: early Tb spine. The report would always comeback NAD.

Yes, a very nasty little man, whose offsider was an Austrian who, for some unknown reason, he'd cowed into utter submission. I could see trouble ahead, so collected a series of his mistakes, both films and erroneous reports. Enter Ed, who stood no nonsense, had a new Bucky in no time and brought new life—and order—to his department. He also loved to teach the Arab assistants, not always tactfully. If they made a mistake he'd say:

'But you're only a siddy dittle Arab.'

They seemed to take it in good part. He also reformed the filing system and was generally a breath of fresh air: just what S the horrible Swede couldn't stand.

The Nordic tribe stuck together like glue. One afternoon, during the conference subsequent to one of our regular joint rounds of all of the surgical subspecialties, a Swedish surgeon put up the films of a Barium series. It was a good record of a Barium meal X ray investigation and the deformed, clover leaf duodenal cap, diagnostic of duodenal ulcer, was well demonstrated. Imagine the frisson of mixed dismay and surprise when this creep began to denounce the films as a disgrace. Ed, of course had performed the series. There were more fulminations and then, to my sorrowful surprise, Arvid came out with a nasty porky: he held up a film of somebody's lumbosacral region and Ed's report: possible disc lesion.

Arvid said that the film's quality was so poor that no diagnosis should have been made. Possibly true, but I'd been with him when Ed came up with the film and showed it to us:

'The quality of this film's terrible. Do you want me to have another one done? If you look here and here you could imagine that there's a disc lesion. What do you want me to do?'

Arvid agreed that there could be a disc lesion and asked Ed to report on the film—which he hadn't wanted to do—and indicate his impressions in that report.

As soon as the meeting was over I hurtled around to Ed's office and told him the reasons why he should brace himself for an attack by the Scandinavians. Next, the slimy S exhibited a whole series of X rays which he said demonstrated Ed's incompetence, because all of his diagnoses were astray. These were presented by C, the Chief of Professional Services, to a bumbling band of GPs who conveniently constituted a committee whose task it was to decide upon professional competence. Not knowing their arses from their elbows where X ray diagnosis is concerned, they sagely nodded: oh, yes; terrible: how could a radiologist be so incompetent?

Ed was relieved of his duties and I grabbed the films. Providentially, Robbie Robinson arrived from Addenbrooke's Hospital in Cambridge, first class to say the least, to do a locum. He is/was a highly respected and capable consultant. We had him to dinner and I showed him the films. He completely vindicated Ed, who was grudgingly given some kind of provisional licence to practice under supervision—and no apology. This wasn't good enough for him—not good enough from any point of view so Ed took the next plane to Riyadh where all of Wutka's top brass—and the Saudi medical generals—held sway. Ed was never one to mince words, one might add. He arrived back in Tabuk, closely followed by a general who told him he had twenty four hours to get out of the Kingdom. Now, what wheels were within all of the wheels at Tabuk? I still wonder about that.

What pull did this execrable and incompetent Swede have over, apparently everyone? I ask this because, a little later, a rather charming Nephrologist resigned and returned to his native snows, BUT his wife stayed behind, shacked up with? You've guessed it. Under Saudi/Sharia Law, she should have been stoned—as should C's girl friend—and S (and C) decapitated. Sadly, this never happened. The unanswered question is: why not them when other notables of infinitely higher status did suffer this fate.

> The race is not always to the swift nor the battle to the strong, remember. It's whom you know.

There was some comeuppance for one of the Nordic gang, the surgeon who'd ordered the Barium meal aforesaid. He'd allowed his assistant, a Saudi, to perform a thyroidectomy under his supervision upon a moderately senior officer who woke up and—oh oh—was unable to speak. Had the lad cut a recurrent laryngeal nerve, essential for speech— it lurks close to the thyroid gland, ready to trap the unwary: rather the careless, into cutting it? An immediate enquiry ensued and our Swede immediately blamed the Saudi registrar: big mistake, especially since he was responsible for the operation in any case. He was immediately deprived of his clinical privileges and, minus a passport, became a ghostly figure wandering disconsolately about the cantonment, effectively a prisoner. The ending was happy for him because the officer regained his voice: the nerve in question had merely been stretched. He'd gained no Brownie points, however and what happened now was rather sad. He brought his wife along one day to see me. She complained of various skeletal aches and pains. It was immediately obvious that she was in the terminal stages of breast cancer, with widespread secondary deposits in her bones. I could do nothing. I sometimes undertook cancer chemotherapy, because of unacceptable delays in appointments to see a too laid back character in Riyadh who seemed to be the only oncologist in the Kingdom available to us at that time. Sadly this unfortunate woman was beyond all help. I did, to offer a straw of hope, send the two down to Jiddah to the other, better of two oncologists in the Kingdom—the ban on seeing him was waived in this case- but she died a week or two later. I think, principally because he'd been a naughty boy, the lady in question was denied a Christian burial: the practice of that faith is a criminal offence in Saudi—but, after some delay, he was permitted to fly his wife to Sweden for the burial he wished.

My experience of Saudi officialdom is that their bark is worse than their bite, especially where foreign relations—and expats—are concerned. Under no circumstances, however, will behaviour contrary to the tenets of Wahabist Islam be condoned. It is, after all, their country. All of which reminds me of what, at least at its denouement, was a hilarious episode. We were very friendly with Bill C, an American Gynaecologist and Linda, his wife, a highly trained nursing sister who worked in Tabuk as a nurse practitioner. They were in Saudi to escape the militant tendencies of his first wife and I'll relate this episode later on. There were, incidentally, quite a few Yank Obs/Gynae refugees in Saudi, mostly for a different reason: the crippling indemnity insurance that had to be paid if one were to render oneself relatively immune from bankruptcy if/when sued. The yanks seem to have an almost pathological penchant for suing one another. Like bad practices always and everywhere, this evil is appearing all over the Western world, substituting litigiousness for whatever decency there was in the doctor/patient relationship heretofore. Greedy people everywhere, egged on by worse lawyers, sue doctors on the slightest pretext. This, inevitably, has inflated the cost of indemnity insurance to an incredible degree. Bill told me that some of his colleagues were now driving taxis, so high were the fees for this insurance. The legal profession comes out of this very badly. The human body is extremely complex and its reactions to treatment tremendously variable and imperfectly understood.. Every year countless doctors the world over are being found guilty of negligence without any true justification. Some doctors are indeed negligent to an appallingly dangerous degree, but many, if not most convicted today, suffer what they feel to be a disgrace because of cases trumped up by shyster lawyers. Judges are lay people, as are the rapacious villains who urge people also to become greedy and sue.

This disgusting behaviour has added enormously to the cost of treatment. This added cost also includes the considerable cost of diagnostic procedures, too many of which are performed as a prophylactic against litigation. It's certainly an ill wind so far as certain sections of the profession: most notably radiologists and pathologists are concerned, many of whom are now rich beyond the dreams of avarice. The odd needle prick is merely an inconvenience, but every X ray, however small the dose, subjects the body to cumulative, harmful ionising radiation. Even the tiny dose needed for a simple chest X Ray has been proved to be harmful. My own Thyroid cancer was undoubtedly due to exposure to irradiation during my work.

Years ago the Queensland Government made it compulsory for everybody to have a chest X ray. I wrote to the then Health Minister, a former student of mine, pointing out the dangers. He replied with a polite but dismissive letter. This dangerous intrusion of government was only rectified some years later.

In Australia at least, general practitioners no longer deliver babies. In the good old days it went without saying that one of the general practitioner's privileges—and pleasures—was bringing new members into the family under his care. Many things can—and do—go wrong during pregnancy and delivery, a fact gleefully seized upon by execrable legal wordmongers. In this way an invaluable relationship has been lost.

But this is the age of greed. It surrounds us, clouding every aspect of our lives. It is now an endemic disease and though bankers and fund managers might be the worst offenders it hasn't escaped any one of our daily activities. That includes doctors. I'm not being holier than thou: I'm simply going to describe the normal situation say, fifty years ago. Then it was common for doctors to pay home visits quite happily—well, perhaps sometimes resignedly—to people whom he—or she—knew were unable to pay the fee. There are still a few of a dwindling breed who accept the Australian Government's ungenerous fees for various services in full payment, I'm happy to say. Not many!

One reads in the *Economist* that high-powered bankers and fund managers shouldn't have their obscene emoluments brought nearer to earth because these people would seek employment elsewhere. Apart from the question as to where they might seek it—and what additional financial horrors less qualified people could inflict, who were responsible for the financial mess in the first place?

This highlights the death of professionalism. Whereas nowadays, it seems, lawyers, doctors or members of other occupations once known as professions always have their eyes focussed firmly on the bottom line—and little else—in the good old days the occupation itself was a prime consideration, due regard being had to the necessity of earning a living. The work itself gave great pleasure and satisfaction. Doctors—always with unworthy exceptions- never charged colleagues or their families; nurses or their families or the clergy—and families if any. Hastened by the intrusion of government, i.e. politics, into the equation, the landscape is now utterly changed and darkened. Motivation is now too much focussed upon money.

Pause

After that last diatribe, let's breathe a little fresher air. I've described elsewhere the Majlis, where one could come face to face with the local Prince to make requests. A few of us got together and decided that we'd like to visit Madain Saleh, Saleh's city. Saleh is a character in the Qur'an. God wasn't at all pleased with the inhabitants of this erstwhile city and threatened dire proceedings. Saleh, in constant communication with God, appealed to His finer feelings, so, to give these naughty people another chance, He tested their moral fibre, giving them a she camel, instructing them to look after the animal well. Instead they ate the poor thing.

Oh, dear! Mistake!! God really got off his bike and flattened the place overnight by means of an earthquake.

In point of fact, this was a prosperous city of Nabataean Arabs located in an area where a narrow pass made it ideal for the extraction of tolls from passing camel trains. It was on the old spice route from Asia, so there were more than enough of these caravans to keep the coffers full, the same kind of arrangement as at Petra, similar in many ways.

It's a long way from Tabuk and the Prince, in giving his permission, insisted on our taking—and paying for—an askeri, a private soldier.

The latter proved to be pleasant enough and didn't in any way emphasise the fact that he'd brought his shooter along.

We took the long way round, probably to miss Medina, where no infidels are allowed. I'm highly chuffed that we did. The road took us close to the town of Al Jawf.

To digress once more, I had a patient, a general of that name, a jolly fellow, the local tribal chief, who'd fractured his rib, whilst, he told me, he was drunk: quite an admission in the strictest Muslim country in the world. I strapped his chest, a procedure frowned upon by some silly people—after injecting long acting local anaesthetic into the relevant intercostal nerves, actually a gaoling offence there, as I was informed by a notice glaring down at me. The Saudis normally didn't interfere in our practice at all, but there had probably been a death from using it improperly in a Bier's block: already described. This long acting anaesthetic isn't the best agent to use in these circumstances, but with most, if the tourniquet is removed too soon, dire consequences may result.

The same general returned shortly after his first visit, complaining that the pain killers I'd prescribed didn't work when he was drunk. He was delightful and the most uninhibited Saudi I've ever met.

We next travelled through the An-Nafud desert and desert it most surely was: slightly undulating pale brownish sand with a low series of featureless hills well over to our right. At one point we paused to watch vultures dancing obscenely over the corpse of some animal who'd foolishly strayed too far into this wilderness. Revolting wasn't the word.

For much of our journey we were preceded by a mirage: a most attractive body of water that didn't exist. Eventually, gradually enlarging points of black in the mirage pushed their way clear and slowly became a date orchard. This was Ta'ima and we lunched in the shade of the palms. The gentle breeze filtering through the plantation was a great relief. The heat was from Hell. Our Land Cruiser had no air conditioning and we were all wringing wet from sweat!

Ta'ima is a place of extraordinary interest. The Bible has the story of Nebuchadnezzar all mixed up. It was not he but Nabonidus who was Belshazzar's father and, the cares of office proving too onerous, he left Babylon to live in this remote place. One can be sure that he made certain that he lived, not on the Biblical grass, but in luxury and, indeed, local rumour has it that the hanging gardens of Babylon were located here.

We were resting on the outskirts of the town itself and the surroundings were dotted with most interesting mounds simply crying out for excavation. The present Saudi regime doesn't appear to favour archaeology and there could be a number of reasons for this: perhaps in some part because of their religion. I also had the feeling that it would like its people to feel that history began with Abdul Aziz, but most of all in my humble view, because the more one delves into the past the closer the Arabs are seen to be to the Jewish race until, ultimately... Dare one say it? Such a view, of course, would enrage stroppy Semites on either side of the equation.

But further to Nabonidus who is interesting though he has nothing to do with this book. The time honoured god of Babylon, evolved from a nature god as so many had, was Marduk and his worship had created amongst his priests a strong vested interest, i.e. power and wealth, par for the course throughout our race's entire history. But Nabonidus was awkward, because his principal object of worship was Sin, the moon god and he promoted his worship. No prizes for guessing what happened. Looking around for ways to rid themselves of this threat, those naughty priests enlisted the aid of Darius, ruler of the Medes and Persians. Belshazzar got wind of this, writing on the wall indeed, but only in the metaphorical sense. Nabonidus hurried back to no avail. Exit

Babylon from history's page. I'd like to think that Marduk's priests got a comeuppance, but Darius was tolerant in some matters.

Not far from where we were eating our sandwiches was an enormous well, at least forty feet across and more than that deep. All kinds of interesting-looking objects were embedded in its walls. As we watched, some men scrambled down its sides and started up a motor. The plantation was flood irrigated by this means.

Reluctantly, at least in my case, we drove on through the mirages until signs of great activity gradually emerged through their silvery glitter: trucks and other mobile military materiel. We were soon stopped at a cross roads where there was a military post. To turn left was absolutely out, because thence led the road to Mecca where infidels are decidedly unwelcome, so we turned right! After a time, we turned right again, on to the bed of the old Hejaz railway, again in excellent condition. As we travelled along in a region blessed with more rain than most of the Kingdom, we saw what had happened to the rails: they were used as fencing and though this region was less arid than Tabuk, there was little rust on them after almost seventy years of exposure to the elements.

Across to our right ran a low range of mountains. These were riddled with caves and we were told that they were still inhabited by troglodytes.

As dusk was gloomily closing in we arrived at our destination with time only to register with the officer at the tiny military post, the only habitation, eat a quick meal and deploy our sleeping bags. The night was crisp, to say the least, but the glory of the sparkling stars remains fixed in the memory. What we began to see on the following day was even more memorable. We were camped beside a part of the mountain range already mentioned, close to a narrow defile that severed it. We climbed the steepish gradient to the right of the gap to an old Turkish observation post where a few signs of a machine gun emplacement still survived.

Descending, we entered the canyon, the obvious reason for the toll collectors of antiquity stationing themselves there. On the other side was an orange grove but also, to our surprise, a large shed in a fairly advanced state of decrepitude, cascades of stylish Parisian tiles littering the ground round about it. Inside was something we'd never dreamt of ever seeing: a steam locomotive with brass plate: Glasgow, 1913. This had been a workshop, but all useful machinery for locomotive repair had been looted, leaving only the *raison d'etre*. Outside was a string of decaying carriages and goods vans, early Twentieth Century.

However this might have been, an even greater fascination awaited us: the plain beyond was dominated by a huge monolith, carved in Graeco-Roman style. Great satellite boulders, all richly decorated in Classical style and formed into mausolea for the wealthy or places of worship skirted the huge sandy amphitheatre-like expanse. It was all reminiscent of Petra—after all it had been established by the same people—but not claustrophobic, being spread out as described. Eileen, sifting through the sand, found numerous shards of clay pottery of the most exquisite thinness.

We took it in turn to drive. When it was the turn of Larry, a charming born again Christian, we happened upon a military post. When we were challenged and signalled to stop, the howling idiot accelerated. I expected to feel bullets whistling around my ears but perhaps the guard's gun wasn't loaded or perhaps he just didn't care. We did!

TABUK AGAIN

Bill and Linda C had been members of our excursion. But now Bill, normally a sunny soul, suddenly became dejected, the more so as time went on. He was diffident as to the reason, but eventually it came out, accompanied by dejected sighs. An important factor in our presence in Tabuk was the salary we received every Thursday. On one fateful occasion he'd turned up to receive his emolument but there was none. His first wife had gone to the headquarters of Wutka in the US and told them that she was entitled to Bill's salary. Typically faithful and true to their employees and without making further enquiries, they had immediately garnisheed his entire salary. Bill was contracted to work for the Saudi Ministry of Defence and Aviation, so had to toil: for nothing! Knowing our employers, we weren't entirely surprised, but felt deeply sorry for the pair, who had to subsist on Linda's exiguous remuneration. So it went on for some time, until one of Bill's interpreters plucked up the courage to ask him why he was always so down in the mouth. On hearing the tragic tale his face brightened and he used the same words as I'd heard when wanting my certificate of blood donation:

'Iss no prrroblem! This Sharia Law here. I fix it and we see judge.'

He was true to his word and accompanied Bill to the seat of Justice. Its personification was reading a paper, inhaling a fag, feet on desk. The interpreter explained the problem. The judge looked Bill up and down:

'You divorce this woman?'

'Yes.'

'You want pay this money?'

No, no a thousand times no.

'Then you don't have pay.'

Great was the rejoicing and the gathering at his house that night was a deal more than jolly, Bill repeating—and repeating 'you don't have pay!' Hilarious was the roistering, but ours was a fearful joy because the patrolling police might very well hear the noise and wait for us as we returned to our respective abodes. Indeed, it was so clamorous that Sinbad their little cockatiel parrot, who'd steadfastly refused to speak, came out, to our hysteria, with keerf halak, an informal Arab form of greeting (how's the body?) Bill had been trying to teach him/her for ages. We walked home with very studied steadiness.

Bill's end there was less than happy. I've already mentioned the Civilian Hospital as the source of some of the worst possible cases of mismanagement. One evening Bill was notified of a case emanating thence. The patient, having trouble with giving birth to her child was given a dose of Pitocin to hurry matters along. There was one miniscule problem: the cause of the trouble was the tiny size of her pelvis. The uterus, its contraction against a virtually immovable object greatly strengthened inevitably began to rupture. Bill did what was necessary and, in accordance with accepted procedure removed the torn uterus. The child, too large to be delivered, was already dead. All very well, excepting that removing a source of reproduction is deeply frowned upon in more than one Muslim country. A horde of Saudi medical generals once more descended upon Tabuk. The specimen was in a jar, formalinised. With it was the report of the Columbian Senior Pathologist, a very pleasant and capable man:

'Large tear in uterine body.'

But there always seems to be a serpent in Eden. The ghastly little offsider to this man had appended a contradictory report: the rent is small. The specimen had shrunk and thus appeared to support the junior's report. In any case Bill had carried out the orthodox treatment. A uterus so damaged is extremely liable to rupture again with the next pregnancy. He'd been about to be appointed Senior Gynaecologist, but now was deprived of his clinical privileges and now, like the Swede, had to wander, passportless, within the Cantonment walls, a virtual prisoner. The matter was eventually, grudgingly, resolved in his favour, but he'd had enough and resigned soon afterwards. After this episode, all of the new Obs/Gynae people were Pakistani women.

Work was, by and large, very congenial especially since Orthopaedics didn't involve any—or many—dangers of tripping over Islamic dogma. Each of us had an interpreter, but soon after arriving it was obvious that a working knowledge of the language was vital if one were ever to finish a clinic. Each question asked of the interpreter was followed by a lengthy conversation in which the weather, world affairs and latest sporting results must have been discussed. Learning enough of the language was the only possible remedy if matters were to be expedited.

Three interpreters—not including my man—were of enormous help and were delighted that I wanted to learn Arabic. They had made friendly overtures and would sometimes visit us on Fridays, armed with delicious herb-laced flat bread. Eileen made an excellent hummus to use as a dip. One of the three in particular was very cultured. I've studied a bit of pre-Socratic Greek philosophy, but he left me in the shade. The only technical word they couldn't help me with was paraesthesia. Farouk came to my aid there with a choice of two synonyms.

Two conditions, spasticity and congenital dislocation of the hip were surprisingly common. I had also to treat the aftermath of poliomyelitis. There has been a slight reluctance on the part of devout Muslims to have their children immunised, now largely overcome. The reason? God's central, indeed omnipresent, part in their lives. If He decides that a child must contract polio, then tough, but so be it.

This belief is taken to the extreme in that incredibly ghastly country, Pakistan, where good, brave people on immunising missions are routinely murdered. Hideous mullahs spread the lie that the vaccine is a Western plot to cause infertility.

Both spasticity and polio paralysis very often require tendon transfers: a muscle which is acting too powerfully in the former case can be either cut, lengthened or have its tendon transferred to take the place of another which is not acting. In the case of polio, a muscle which is still acting can be transferred to take up a lost function or to counter the activity of an antagonistic muscle. Muscle tendon lengthening in the former case seems presently to be a treatment less in favour, in the Western World at least. This seems especially to apply to younger children. I personally don't agree with this, as I believe that the young, developing bones can be distorted by the abnormal forces of imperfectly functioning muscles and also by the abnormal postures imposed by those forces.

Nothing had been done for the spastics round and about Tabuk before I arrived and, in the case of the Bedou, they had been kept out of sight in their tents. When the word went around that something was being done, these poor kids began to appear in quite large numbers. I can't claim anything really dramatic, especially because for most of my time there the 'physios' were NCOs in the Saudi army and though extremely willing, hadn't sufficient training. When, towards the end, proper physios did appear, they were lazy and, in the case of the senior witch—with a capital B—an Australian, harboured resentment at my position as head of the Department and were obstructive, to say the least. Despite this, little round balls of people were straightened, some managed to walk and—to their particular joy—use their hands to play with toys and perform little tasks. Problems, serious, of course, were less complicated with those who had suffered from Polio. The parents with whom I had contact understood their children's problems very well and encouraged them to do their exercises quite enthusiastically.

Young adults who'd had no treatment for congenitally dislocated hips had to have the normal hip replacement procedure performed. Sometimes this wasn't easy because the thigh bone hadn't developed fully and was thin. There were only a few of these, or at least only a few presented.

Young children were a different matter. Some operations involve forming a new hip cup—these tended to be underdeveloped in such patients—by turning bone above the cup over to form a shelf. I never did this myself, believing that any actual interference with the cup itself and its cartilage especially, was asking for future trouble: arthritis in particular. The eventual results of that approach are, indeed, seldom satisfactory. I favoured the Salter osteotomy, in which the lower part of the pelvis is more or less severed and swung inward so that the cup (acetabulum) faces rather more downward and the head of the thigh bone has a greater chance of sitting in its normal place. The cup then develops normally— very satisfying! The op. sounds a bit horrendous, but if proper care is had to tissue planes there's little blood loss and the kids stand it very well.

Another common complaint was club foot. The operation I used was a lovely exercise in anatomy and didn't involve cutting or removing any bone, the end result being kept in place by means of a single pin and plaster of Paris. It must be said that these did very well, with a normal foot as the end result. Lesser cases were treated conservatively by manipulation and plaster. I understand that this method is now being used for even severe cases. Whilst I'm unable to comment on this, if it really works, that has to be a great advance. One should always avoid surgery if this is possible.

Mention of plaster of Paris reminds me that when my predecessor took me on a round of his wards, he introduced me to the patients. It amazed me that they instantly took to my name. The Arabic word for plaster is *gibs*, but with a soft 'g' and hence the word gypsum.

Mind you, plaster of Paris bandaging isn't the only way of immobilising a fracture. Metal plates, for instance, held in place across a fracture by means of screws are invaluable in the appropriate circumstances. The really great advance, however, was the introduction of external fixation. There are a number of different types of apparatus in use, but the general principle is the same: rods or wires are drilled through skin, other overlying tissues and then the bone above and below the fracture. This is then reduced and the reduced fracture is held in place by means of special frames or rods connected to the metal wires or rods previously mentioned. The great improvement with this technique is that the limb may now be used more or less normally. A fracture of the lower leg may now be walked upon, an added plus of this being that healing is encouraged. Fractures of the upper part of the tibia are sometimes reluctant to heal and, indeed, sometimes fail to heal at all. One lad came into my clinic, however, who had had his fractured leg immobilised in a completely different way. You'll come across him a little later on.

One condition probably not seen elsewhere than the Middle East is *bejel*, the 'j being pronounced as an 'h'. This is caused by an attenuated strain of the spirochaete which causes Syphilis, but is not a venereal disease. It causes a characteristic thickening of the shin bone, but, more importantly, can eat away facial features in a truly dreadful manner. It responds readily to penicillin. It's spread by people living very closely together. When one suspects it, the first question is:

Were you born in a tent?

The same question put when, at college, somebody left one's door open, especially on a cold night.

Sometimes when I was about to leave the villa for a day's work, the roar of numerous Hercules aircraft would cause me to look up, in time to see them discharging lines of dark bobbles, each of which gradually mutated into a body dangling from a parachute. At first I thought that that presaged an exceptionally busy day, limb fractures being added to my operating list. I was wrong: there was an occasional fractured leg or arm, but surprisingly few accidents.

I'm a strong believer that, with the exception of very severe cases of lumbar disc lesions where, for instance, the nervous control of the bladder has been affected, careful manipulation a la my friend John Jeffries yields vastly superior results to surgery. I've seen many, many—too many by far— lives ruined by back surgery. It was both distressing and frustrating to have one of these people presenting—sometimes as a last resort—and being unable to do anything substantial to help.

My manipulation clinics were very busy. I did have one intractable case: a fat old boy who was over sixty, the compulsory age of retirement in Saudi. I couldn't make out why, though relieved of his symptoms at the time, he came back regularly because they'd recurred. At that age he surely held some clerical position. Finally the penny dropped and I asked him if he still made jumps. He did! The ground must have trembled as he made contact with it!

I found it rather strange to see a general or colonel walk into my manipulation clinics arm in arm with a private! I don't think that there was anything funny about it. Whether or not that affected discipline is anyone's guess, but it did seem rather charming.

Perhaps the saddest episode to be experienced in Tabuk was a motor vehicle accident. Five brothers had just bought a car, so decided to put it through its paces on that very same day. When they had fairly got under way, the driver decided to test the vehicles turning ability. At a hundred miles an hour he attempted a U turn with the inevitable results. Three were killed instantly and I spent the night trying to save the other two. After having had innumerable fractures mended, the vital functions of one of the lads slowly petered out. The other, similarly injured—for some reason no organs such as spleen or liver had been damaged in either— survived for a time, but then developed the dreaded acute respiratory distress syndrome. In this, the lining of the lungs becomes progressively less permeable to oxygen. The treatment, which should be—and was in this case—under the care of an expert in the art of resuscitation, involves increasing the pressure under which oxygen is delivered into the blood stream. It was thus now out of my hands from this point of view, but the victim was a most charming man who seemed to put some value on my presence. The gas pressure needed to keep him alive increased inexorably until an impossible level was reached. The poor fellow was fully conscious virtually until the last moment and, when he knew that he was going, indicated his thanks. Very moving.

At about the same time another case of ARDS was admitted, this time from the unspeakable Civilian Hospital. All the man had was an untreated fracture of the femur, but he'd been left with little attention in a draughty corridor. Fortunately, with the appropriate treatment, he survived.

The intensivist in each case was the same person. He was also an anaesthetist and a good one at that. Not so the Senior member of that team, who hailed from Finland. I hated it when he chose to give my anaesthetics as he suffered from a severe glossolalia. From the moment he appeared until the blissful moment when I escaped, he didn't even seem to pause for breath. If anyone had ever had the good sense to fling his weighted body into the Arabian Gulf there's no doubt that he would have continued, unabated, until he hit the bottom, if not longer. On one occasion I had a man with a broken neck. I've already stressed the importance of handling these people with great care in order to prevent a

serious paralysis, or worsening it if that has occurred already. For some reason which I forget, I decided to adopt the posterior approach. The man was on a Stryker frame and, whilst he was being anaesthetised and prepared, I walked into the anteroom to escape the deluge of words. When they notified me that all was ready, I saw on my return that they'd turned the man on the Stryker so that he was face down ready for my ministrations. I also noticed that his abdomen had swelled enormously. So I immediately yelled:

'Turn him over immediately and remove that endotracheal tube. It's in his oesophagus you fool.'

That ghastly character, intent upon whatever drivel he was spouting, had passed that tube into the man's oesophagus and was inflating the stomach with gas. At the same time, the patient was deprived of oxygen. This example of negligence does occur occasionally and it can have fatal consequences due to the inevitable anoxia. I worried that the man might have suffered from brain damage until I spoke to him after he'd awakened.

Eileen and I love the desert and spent many evenings strolling across its trackless wastes. We'd drive out towards the multicoloured mountains mentioned previously and sometimes scramble down a declivity beside the road, towards them, but more often strike out across the desert on the other side of the road. Here were patches of ash, scattered there many aeons ago by now defunct volcanos whose flattened peaks silhouetted the horizon. As the sun sank lower, we'd look for 'desert diamonds', small globules in the sand made evident by their refracted light: a faintly golden glow. A number of us had them cut in Thailand and they came out well. There were discussions as to their real nature, topaz being favoured. Of course they might have been only quartz.

Many Saudis resented our presence, honking at us as they passed when we were out on these occasions. Some made a show of steering at me. I stood my ground, prepared to jump to one side if they really meant it. If they had, they'd have gone over the edge of the road and down the declivity—point of no return. None actually did. Many Muslims appear to have a thing about Europeans' presence in their country: witness the well-armed objections to our presence there that many Afghans are demonstrating at the time of writing. It's rather anomalous that many of the same people have no objection to living in Europe and at the same time collecting all of the freebees going.

On many weekends we'd go as a party to Dhuba, a couple of hundred miles more or less South Eastward along the coast of the Red Sea. It was necessary to obtain a permit from the Prince to do this but there was never any problem about that. A visit to the majlis to obtain his consent, described elsewhere in this book, was always a pleasant experience. The Prince, incidentally, is/was the youngest son of Abdul Aziz, the first King of the country who had umpteen wives and more children than one could shake a stick at.

Our journey to Dhuba took us past those magic mountains until, a few miles further on, at 'Tin City'—an aggregation of huts constructed in the main of that material and probably inhabited by Palestinian refugees who hadn't received an official nod—we'd turn left and more Eastward. Here and there we'd pass Bedou encampments: capacious tents beautifully woven of goats' hair and all topped with a TV aerial. The flocks, goats with some sheep, were tended by colourfully dressed women and the whole scene, TV aerials excepted, had a decidedly Biblical air.

Eventually we'd come to the edge of a low escarpment overlooking the coastal plain and the sea. On the left, extending so far as the eye could see was a jagged mountain range, in many different shades of yellow, cream; even white. All was shrouded in a sea mist which imparted a most romantic air to the scene. One could easily imagine Sinbad the sailor being carried by the Roc to its eerie in those crags.

The roads were wonderful and it was with no trouble that we cruised at ninety miles an hour or more. New-looking cars scattered along the way were evidence, one supposed, of their well-to-do owners having put too much strain on their engines, or, perhaps, merely run out of petrol. Having descended to the coastal plain we'd travel through gnarled scrub until a particular motor tyre hanging from one of those crooked trees indicated a right turn. Thence the unmade, sandy road presented some difficulty. One was amazed at the skill with which Saudis would drive through sand which was quite untrafficable for us. We'd finally halt at the edge of the sea, on old fossilised coral thrust up, over the ages, to some feet above sea level.

The tectonic plates are active here, widening the Red Sea by about an inch every year.

We'd camp on a level spot and then prepare to dive into the water. Here, just feet from the shore, was an aquatic wonderland in which thrived brilliantly coloured fish as inquisitive of us as we were of them. They would swim up to inspect us and there was often, literally, an eye to eye engagement. Everywhere abounded gorgeous coral and various aquatic plants, including the fire coral, which inflicts a painful sting if touched. Occasionally there were sharks but they never troubled us and, rarely, a huge, harmless whale shark: that Leviathan Thou hast made to take his pastime therein, would saunter by. I couldn't bring myself to spear those charming, lively fish but inconsistently, ate them with great pleasure when somebody else had done the deed. One of the spear fishermen was imprudent enough one morning to tangle with a scorpion fish. He refused all attention though he must have been suffering agonising pain. Another unpleasant cousin of this nasty, the butterfly cod, is there in some numbers: a beautiful but menacing presence. It was always with reluctance that we hastily packed, then hurtling back in order to return before the curfew.

After a time, Leighton Bell took off for the Yemen. Wutka had a hospital in Sana'a and he'd signed a contract to work there. I didn't envy him his transfer. As soon as they're big enough, if not before, Yemeni children arm themselves with guns and have no hesitation in firing them at what or whomever they feel might make a suitable target. They also have a great liking for chewing Khat, a plant growing in the mountains there. It has been described as a mild psychotropic drug. I beg to differ, having had to treat a number of addicts who were completely out of their minds when they met with one or another disaster. One, for instance, stepped out of a second story window. Because, despite the opinion he held at the moment of opening it, he was unable to defy the force of gravity, he was hospitalised for some considerable time.

Before Leighton left, he bequeathed to me the daughter of a charming family, the al Eids. The poor girl had suffered quite severely from Polio and I had to perform several operations upon her. She would never be able to walk without some kind of aid, but at least was able to ride her bicycle.

We became very friendly, to the extent that they honoured us by admitting us to the 'family' section of their home, where their daughters were unveiled. This, especially for Westerners, is a considerable compliment. Mahomet, the father, tried to convert me on occasions but I was stony ground.

Our daughter Tracey was at school in England at the time and came to visit us on her vacations. There was a choice of two airports: Jiddah in the Kingdom or Amman in Jordan. A taxi driver had attempted to grope me when being driven from the airport of the former, so felt it to be safer to opt for Amman, especially as the arrival time there was during daylight. It was necessary to obtain the Prince's permission to make such a trip—or any journey greater than ten miles from the cantonment. It was therefore, as usual, necessary to ask the Prince in person at a majlis. It can hardly be said that this was a chore. One sat with the other petitioners in a large rectangular room, easy chairs having been arranged around its periphery. Attendants plied one with excellent coffee whilst each petitioner made his plea in turn, clockwise around the room. It was quite an eye opener. After some had made their cases, the Prince would say a few words and then his assistant would delve into a huge box and present the applicant with a bundle—usually large—of one hundred Riyal notes. At that time, one hundred Riyals would have been worth twenty pounds. 'Shukrn' (Thank you) and a few gestures of thanks combined with respect and the lucky recipient was off. Paper work? None at all.

Permission was duly granted for us to make the trip, the only proviso being that we had to be accompanied by a Saudi. This proved to be no problem, as Mahomet al Eid readily agreed to his second eldest son, Ibrahim, coming along with us. He proved to be a pleasant and informative guide.

In Jordan the section of the Hejaz railway in that country is still in operation. It was also quite fascinating to have him point out the old crusader castles including Krak des chavillers and to hear an account of those ghastly crusades from an alternative—and probably more accurate—point of view.

At sundown, we'd pull over to the side of the road whilst our passenger 'purified' himself with the roadside dirt, water being unavailable, prior to making his obeisances to Mecca and then praying.

On our return, the border guard virtually dismantled our car in a vain search for nasties and made a feeble effort to confiscate Tracey's text books.

Wutka's abounding bureaucrats were known, because of their dress, as Blue Coats. One is unable to say that these were universally loved and more than once the chief physio at the time, Mahomet Iraq, he who helped me obtain that blood donor certificate, would growl:

'Blue coats? One day they be red coats!'

The same Mahomet Iraq was that strange, typically Middle Eastern mixture, at once a spy for the government and an active member of the PLO. He once smuggled his brother over the border to see me. He had a fractured Scaphoid bone of the wrist. He refused treatment, despite my telling him that, untreated, he would eventually develop serious problems.

Untreated, fractures of this bone won't unite, the end result being a painful, weak, arthritic wrist. Cases of established ununited fracture of this bone are sometimes, nowadays, treated by removing the bone and replacing it with a similarly shaped prosthesis. I tended to frown upon this, opting instead for a freshening of the broken surfaces and chiselling a little gutter across the fracture line and inserting a graft: a fiddling business and one to be performed very carefully. If the blood supply to the bone is interfered with, disaster will result.

One fine sunny day a deputation of Blue Coat which even included the Lord High Bureaucrat bore down upon my clinic. Their faces were so heavy with seriousness that I wondered what great catastrophe had afflicted us: had the Israelis invaded? Had the sky fallen in? No, something even more world shaking: Prince Sultan, the then number three—he later became number two but recently died—in the Kingdom wanted to consult me. I presume the reason was that I'd been treating the local Prince's deputy for a knee condition and he had recommended me.

So off I set with my retinue—a cacophony in blue—to the Prince's redoubt—and redoubt it certainly was, surrounded by thick adobe walls. Entrance was gained through an immense iron-studded pair of wooden gates. Once inside, in the courtyard, one was quite amazed to be greeted by a horde of guardsmen, carefully chosen Bedou, all dressed traditionally in greyish-dun desert robes decorated with crossed bandoliers. Their weapons, however, were not at all traditional. I'm far from being an expert, but they most certainly appeared to be highly sophisticated. To round out the defence of this particular piece of real estate, the remaining space in the enclosure was occupied by pick-up trucks, each with a formidable-looking gun mounted on the tray.

To their no doubt great disappointment, the blue brigade was halted there whilst I was ushered through a small entranceway, down a hall and into a comfortably furnished room and plied with excellent coffee. Given time to relax with my brew, I was then summoned into the presence: a relaxed and friendly but much overweight individual. After the pleasantries, he got his Swiss doctor on the phone for me. The Prince was suffering from pain and pins and needles in the inner part of his Right foot. The Swiss had been giving local injections of corticosteroids which in my view are excellent if given as a one-off or only occasionally in the same place but bad if used as a continuing treatment. I didn't like overtly to oppose the Prince's medical advisor so used a little doubletalk and suggested ultrasound instead.

A formidable force then set out for the hospital physio department, where I duly administered the treatment, accompanied, of course by the Boys in Blue—as far as the door of the treatment area. The next day I wrote a report suggesting a shoe prosthesis which would relieve the pressure upon his Posterior Tibial Nerve, the cause of the problem, but went on to suggest, strongly, that the Prince lose weight. The gold watch confidently predicted by my interpreter friends didn't materialise. I concluded that this was because of the suggested weight loss.

I never had any trouble with my Saudi patients, who were all pleasant and cooperative but one had to be excessively careful with females. One of the GPs, a very decent fellow who was undoubtedly innocent listened into a bitch's chest, the interpreter probably momentarily absent. She had a chest infection so this was appropriate. She set up a hue and cry and the GP was out of the country next morning.

Paradoxically, osteomalacia wasn't uncommon amongst womenfolk in this country where sunlight could hardly be said to be lacking. This condition is more or less adult rickets: the bones are insufficiently provided with Calcium and become soft and deformed. As you're undoubtedly aware, sunlight playing upon the skin produces the Vitamin D necessary for the healthy metabolism of that mineral so essential for bone's hardness. If one is entirely clad in black from head to toe, the sun is effectively excluded. Butter contains this vitamin but the amount it contains of course depends in part upon the level of sunshine in its country of origin. The Saudis had a predilection for Danish butter and that country is too close to the Arctic for it to contain enough of the Vitamin. I had to straighten a couple of very bent backs in consequence. Perhaps more seriously, the pelvis of these sufferers tends to become deformed—often into the so-called cloverleaf deformity—and this can cause obstructed labour in those of child bearing age.

Another cause of osteoporosis there is thalassaemia: a blood disorder fairly widespread amongst Mediterranean peoples; also the Saudi. It comes in two forms: major and minor, the latter being enervating, sometimes severely so; the former is life threatening. I saw an effect of the latter which I haven't seen reported, though I could easily have missed it: deformed hip bones, occasionally demanding replacement. This is due to a blockage of the blood vessels there.

When I first arrived in Tabuk there was only one hospital in operation on the cantonment, an old, one storied colonial-style building. My consulting room wasn't large and, because big movements were afoot, not especially well equipped. There was only one chair for the patients. Women, of course, were never unaccompanied and when a family turned up, the man invariably sat down, even if his wife was the patient. From

where I sat I could see much of the passing traffic and it amused me in a
wry sort of way to see families pass by. The husband would always stride
ahead, the little woman struggling behind with sundry children tugging
at her black accoutrements. The tragi-comedy was that hubby would push
through the slatted swinging doors separating the various regions and the
trailing family would arrive just in time for the doors to swing back and
clout them a fourpenny one: smack! A nurse once, out of politeness stood
back to let an Arab male pass. She followed: smack!! I came out to see if
she was all right. Fortunately she was.

'Cor!' she said, 'I'll never do that again!'

This wasn't necessarily the norm. There are more than enough
pigs in any collection of humankind. The number of charming, polite
and civilized Saudis we met quite counteracted in our minds the
unpleasantness of the porcine portion of the population.

Before long a hospital outside the cantonment was opened and, for
a time, was the main hospital. It had been built by the Italians and was
quite good, excepting for the facts that it was outside the cantonment and
perhaps a mile or three down a road which led, as I've already mentioned,
in one direction, straight as a die, out into the howling desert. The car
I bought to make travel there practicable was a Honda Accord with all
of the trimmings, including the necessary air conditioning. Brand new,
it cost 17,500 Saudi Riyals, less than 3,000 Great British Pounds at that
time. Makes one think, doesn't it? Another reason for buying a car was
the manner in which the Yemeni Arab drivers in general drove. Hair
raising isn't the word. There was also the added danger of that traffic
light just before the hospital and, even when I was driving myself, I'd look
back, not in anger but in acute apprehension. As often as not, a car would
materialise on the horizon, usually travelling at about a hundred—in miles
per hour. I didn't exactly savour the idea of being killed, but the thought of
being made paraplegic positively terrified me and was an added reason for

my not renewing my contract when it ended. A number of innocents were in fact killed there.

Early one morning I received an urgent call to this hospital. A man whose car was halted at those lights had been hit from behind at some colossal speed which had killed the offending driver and reduced both vehicles to a virtually unrecognisable tangle. The stationary driver was lucky—he'd merely had his Right leg virtually torn off. The badly fractured leg was actually attached to his body by the Sciatic nerve and nothing else. The femoral artery had been torn but must have contracted afterward as he hadn't lost excessive amounts of blood. That man, in late middle age, must have been careful with his diet. Normally one would have expected his arteries to have been made rigid by atheroma. Medics, too, must, one imagines, rapidly have been on hand to staunch any subsequent flow of blood. However it had happened, he arrived in the theatre alive and resuscitated.

A general surgeon and I cobbled the mess together. The patient was lucky that his Sciatic Nerve was intact as this obviated some intractable subsequent sequelae in the foot and lower leg. Sometime later I was standing in the local souk when I was struck hard on the back by a stick. Whirling around angrily, I was confronted by this former patient, smiling and walking well—I put him through his paces—with only the slight aid of that stick. When his thigh muscles became re-innervated I'm sure he'd easily be able to dispense even with this.

About half way through my term, the new King Abdul Aziz hospital was opened. Located within the cantonment, it was/is a magnificent affair, huge, faced with travertine and fantastically well appointed. The only problem was that one had to walk vast distances on terrazzo floors: hence my Morton's neuroma! This hospital, being within the cantonment, was much more convenient, though it was still necessary to visit the one outside on a regular basis.

There was a curfew and when called out after that time, one wouldn't have moved far from home before a police car stopped and asked what was afoot. I must say that they were always most polite, doing their job as pleasantly as possible. Sometimes one had to visit the outside hospital in an ambulance. On our way home it was usual for the driver to sound his siren to facilitate our return, a practice which I'm sure police, firemen and ambulance drivers the world over use to get themselves more expeditiously to their luncheons.

Perhaps the international situation was becoming more fraught, but, whatever the reason, a Pakistani armoured division turned up and set itself down not far away. I met several of the officers in a professional capacity; nothing serious, but they were charming, civilized people, at least on the surface and they kindly invited me to dine with them in their mess. This was a most pleasant occasion and I had the pleasure of meeting there one Ginghis Khan. He may well have been no descendant of his notorious namesake, but he was cocky and aggressive and no doubt disapproved of my non-Muslim status. There are sadly too many of his type in the Pakistani armed services, especially in their ISI and this is far from being a positive factor in present day world security. The Saudis wouldn't have been at all pleased with my hosts' assessment of the capabilities of the army of the country they were helping to defend.

From my point of view there was an interesting spin-off of this new military presence. One of its humbler members, a sepoy, private soldier, presented with a nasty black lesion on his Left foot: Madura Foot. This is a decidedly unpleasant condition which, untreated, leads eventually to a rather grim, prolonged death. It's quite well known in tropical countries where the people usually go about bare foot. It's caused by a fungus, often inoculated via a prickle.

One of the surgical team had been a Professor in the Sudan. That condition is relatively common there, so with whom better to discuss treatment? I was rather shocked when he said, without hesitation: amputate the leg—it's the only way to save his life. A picture immediately formed and grew in my mind of a haggard, one-legged man, no doubt with starving family, forlornly shaking a begging bowl on some street corner in Islamabad.

As a private soldier and not a Saudi at that, he wasn't really entitled to treatment here but, as usual, the Saudi authorities winked at such matters. The ultimate line, however, was that he couldn't be admitted for in-patient treatment but nobody seemed to mind if even that rule was bent a little. It's more than likely that he'd either seen or heard of others who suffered from this affliction and was well aware of the consequences. However this may be, he accepted my regimen of treatment and its accompanying no doubt severe pain unflinchingly and without the slightest murmur. Using local anaesthetic in one of the wards: a general anaesthetic would certainly not have been permitted, I firstly excised the main lesion. Because this curse spreads firstly up the lymphatics and only in its late stage through the blood stream, I gradually excised his affected lymph vessels one by one and then injected an antifungal drug into the tissue planes I'd been attacking. I couldn't give the poor fellow an epidural anaesthetic. That, ideally, should have been carried out in the theatre. In any case, these procedures were, with bureaucratic concurrence, jealously guarded by the anaesthetists. The poor fellow wasn't officially in the hospital in any case. On one occasion whilst I was injecting. Some of the fluid hit me in the eye. I hoped that it was free of Madura fungus!

As an aside, I did manage to reduce wrist fractures in the Casualty Department under regional blocks to save everybody trouble: the staff, who didn't have to set up for a general anaesthetic; the patient who was spared one and last and least the anaesthetist who didn't have to be called out. The difference here was that these fractures usually occurred after normal working hours and many of the anaesthetists, their chief in particular, tended to come out in a rash if late night anaesthetics were mentioned.

The Yankee theatre nurses were terrible bitches too and had our best anaesthetist sacked for no good reason—he was soon ensconced in a better job in another part of the Kingdom. I had no desire to do anything which might result in my own sudden departure. I therefore had to delve in the depths of the sepoy's leg under local anaesthetic in the ward and had to respect the maximum dose of this agent. Were I to administer too much at the one time, the patient could be in mortal danger. He must have felt a good deal of pain in consequence. The affected parts are easy to identify because they're pitch black. After many no doubt agonising sessions I was satisfied that I'd got the lot, but who could be sure? I therefore got him into a hospital bed and administered a course of intravenous anti-fungal treatment. This couldn't have been much fun either as he developed rigors. Despite this, I very carefully persevered, slowing the drip to a minimum. This meant that he had to spend a whole day in the hospital. Nobody raised even a peep, mainly, one suspects, because of the decency of the sister in charge. I made a point of seeing him just before I left and the problem hadn't recurred. I can't say that his foot and lower leg were things of beauty though. The main consideration, however, was that he could still walk, even march, on that foot and leg.

Talking about lower legs, a serious-looking bunch of elders once turned up with a lad of about nineteen. They rather embarrassedly raised the boy's thobe (flowing garment). The left lower leg proved to be encased in a splint made up of bamboo slivers attached to canvas. I'm sure that this has a name. Gamgee springs to mind but may well be the wrong word. Whatever its name, it was held together by a series of adjustable clips of the kind used to secure the hose which connects the radiator to the engine in a car. When I took this paraphernalia off, the leg was literally as skinny as a rake. The amount of surviving muscle must have been minuscule.

Desert treatment! There probably had been nobody in yonks who was qualified to treat him. The x ray showed healing in good position and to my great surprise there were no obvious nerve lesions or contractures. Despite my suggestion that the lad receive physio in an attempt to build up his leg muscles, he and his companions disappeared into the dust. I have no idea as to the end result.

I mentioned a decent sister a few paragraphs ago so now seems to be as good a time as any to launch into yet one more Jeremiad. I thank the Lord regularly that I never have been and never will be muzzled by the politically correct mind police. You'll just have to take my word for it, too, that I always try to tell the truth. The title of this Jeremiad is: Nursing sisters, past and present. Nursing standards everywhere have deteriorated to an alarming degree. Because of my experiences, I discussed this problem with a couple of English nursing sisters whose work I admired. No, they were young, so there was none of the lament for the good old days about it. To my remark that nursing standards were considerably better amongst British trainees, both said immediately: Perhaps so, but they're steadily worsening. Before long they'll be as bad as all the rest.

Saudi Arabia afforded one a good opportunity of judging relative nursing standards. I've already mentioned the Yankee gaggle in one ward who hadn't the energy to raise themselves off their steatopygeous posteriors. In other wards Americans were more concerned with their patients but equally nescient. On one occasion a drainage tube had ceased doing its work—one used suction drainage a great deal to prevent blood from collecting in the wound.

'OK, sister' I said 'remove the drainage tube please.'

'Oh, doctor, I shouldn't like to do that.'

I reeled back in dismay. There can be fewer simpler procedures.

There were a couple of Australian sisters there, too and they were only marginally better. Another ward was under the care of an Irish sister, the others were English. When I visited those wards, the sister would greet me at the door and immediately, without any prompting, tell me of any problem patients. When we did a round, they knew all about their patients. This is how it should be, but seldom is any more. Why? Because nine hundred and ninety nine of every thousand of them have lost it. And what is it? Well, it is actually them: love and dedication.

In the good old days (there he goes: what else would one expect of a nonogenarian?) nurses began their training in the ward and ended it there. They attended lectures which were often held outside of working hours. First year trainees in particular had to empty bed pans and scrub the wards under the highly critical eye of the sister. There were, of course, full time cleaners too, but they also worked under the sister's eagle eye. Sloppiness wasn't tolerated and adventitious infections were few and far between; no! fewer than that! If the probationer felt that the going was too tough—and it wasn't so very bad, strict discipline being at the core—they were free to seek other employment. Everything revolved round the patient's welfare. Of course at all times and in all places there are the good and bad, the conscientious and the lazy nursing sisters, but there were matrons in the equation, too, who kept the nursing staff under constant surveillance. Things, in short, were better. And there were no Christian names to inject an entirely spurious note of mateyness.

Nowadays nursing is a university course, the early training being almost entirely in the classroom. Why? Modern medicine is indeed becoming more and more technical, but the best way of helping nurses master these technical problems as they concern them is surely—after relevant briefing in the lecture room—in the ward itself. Nursing's no longer a calling. It's just a job. Why? Apart from the prevailing ethos of selfishness I blame a pushy, bolshie sensitivity about a nurse's *amour propre*. A senior ward sister is now, in many parts of the world, a clinical nurse consultant, God wot! Nurses now are bachelors of nursing. I look forward to the happy day when doctors of nursing inhabit the wards. The medico appears to do his round:

Medico: 'Good morning doctor.'

Nurse: 'Good morning doctor.'

Or perhaps some pejorative word will be found for the medico. At least there'll be less confusion then and the exchange will then be:

Medico to nurse: 'Good morning doctor.

Nurse: 'Good morning, drug prescriber.'

With a bit of luck surgeons will still be just plain mister. All of this stupid nonsense has been counter-productive of course. A once noble calling is now just a job for many. An occasional gem may still be found. You might disagree with those observations, but, if you're honest and not too abominably politically correct you'd have to agree that nursing standards have taken a steep, steep dive. Here endeth the Jeremiad.

Now evil things in robes of sorrow assailed poor Wutka's high estate. Whether their system of bribery had gone wrong or they'd committed a faux pas somewhere along the line I'm unable to tell you, but, to say the least, Wutka was out of favour in a big way. On one singularly dread occasion, we weren't paid. Our humourist in the bumf department made the most of it with some absolutely hilarious essays and predictions.

One equally tangible sign of disfavour was the sacking of our Liaison Officer, a very pleasant fellow, cousin of the late King Idriss of Libya, done in by that country's late reigning maniac. That functionary's job appeared to be to smile at us when he wasn't driving round in the Jag kindly given to him by Wutka. His replacement, pharmacist, was an entirely different kettle of fish. We were all called to assemble before him and the general tenor of his speech was that we'd have to do better and he'd jolly well see to it that we did. I thought we'd been doing rather well as it was and as my contract was coming to an end it seemed, all things considered, to be a good idea not to renew. The CPS called me in and more or less asked me to stay, but didn't press the point. Wutka was on the way out and so was I!

Homeward Bound

Our car was so good and such a bargain that it seemed a pity to leave it behind. Moreover, we'd accumulated quite a number of oriental carpets. Tabuk was directly on the land route to Mecca and people making the Hajj would stop off and flog off carpets they'd brought with them to help defray the costs. Some of those we'd bought had obviously been well used, to say the least and were odoriferously full of dust and one shudders to think of what else. We'd take them home, beat them—with bated breath: who knows what pathogens they harboured—and then Eileen would wash them in our bath. They came out of it well and lost no colour, to our surprise. I'd also bought a huge and magnificent Afghan carpet in Riyadh. The chief medical officer of Wutka had taken to me kindly and on one occasion took me to what was apparently the best place for such a purchase. It was close to the fortress successfully stormed by Abdul Aziz when he was conquering the city. Over the way was the main mosque outside which, on Fridays, Sharia punishments were carried out. I was particularly taken by the cruciform engine, wires attached, which was used during the removal of the hands of convicted thieves. I must say that, once again, though executions are carried out for murder and some hands are removed, the latter punishment is only inflicted for very serious, repeat offences.

It also has a salutary effect as is evidenced by the gold souks which in Saudi are remarkable. Vast numbers of gold ornaments in great variety and usually twenty two carat—none of this nine carat stuff!—are festooned upon and around numerous stalls. One is at liberty to saunter around, picking up and examining any and all items that catch one's fancy, all in a relaxed friendly atmosphere. Guess why!!

When I'd made my carpet purchase, there arose the question of bringing it back to Tabuk. No problem! It was already wrapped up in cylindrical shape twelve feet long. All I had to do was struggle with it on to the plane and lay it in the corridor to one side, so that people could pass by. The cost? Why, nothing, of course!

For those reasons and also out of a sense of adventure, we decided to drive back to England. There was one problem: the number plates. They were property of the Saudi Government and had to be handed in before one left. The prospect of driving through numerous countries without number plates was too daunting to allow of any contemplation. There was a German who specialised in producing substitute plates and I was certain that he'd oblige for two reasons: we'd been customers for a good, poison-free Saddiki—some varieties on sale were decidedly lethal—which, suitably mixed with coffee etc, made a very reasonable post prandial Tia Maria. Moreover, the son of this man, when frolicking amongst the sand dunes on his motor cycle, had sustained a rather nasty fracture of the femur. This had done well and his family had made overtures of friendship. When they knew that we were leaving, all interest ceased: no false number plate from there. There was only one thing for it: we'd make our own. Fortunately these number plates are made from embossed metal. It was easy to make papier mache out of egg cartons, press it firmly into the plate and cook the result in the oven. The colour of Saudi plates vary from year to year. Fortunately, the colour scheme this year was black numbers on a white ground and Eileen made a very creditable paint job. I'd hoped to obviate this task by asking permission to keep the plates as far as London and then hand them to the Saudi Embassy. I went to the Majlis and the Prince gave me a most courteous hearing. He then rang someone—surely not King Fahd!—to see if this would be all right. Sadly it wasn't;

'But Mr. Gibbs, I shall personally contact Captain Asseiri at the frontier and see that you are hospitably treated whilst the plates are removed.'

That was no token gesture. At this exit point, cars are literally taken to bits looking for nasties and people are searched. Searched? Where do you suppose those forged plates were? Wrapped fore and aft on Eileen's torso. Gaol if they were discovered! The Prince was as good as his word and, though the car was disassembled, I had coffee with the captain whilst the procedure went on. Poor Eileen had to sweat it out in the car as it came down around her ears. But more importantly, neither she nor I were searched!

I was a little worried that continued exposure to rain might be too much for the false plates, so I photocopied them as well—the paper went into my wallet—and pieces of Perspex into the car to enclose them in case of need.

Next stop was the Jordanian border post. As is the custom in these parts, the officer wanted bakshish. After a brief negotiation I handed it over. The official then suddenly realised who I was. He had a bad knee. What did I think? I went through my usual kerbside consultation and made some suggestions. A model of honesty, the patient spontaneously refunded some, but by no means all of the bakshish.

It's not really the place here to describe our travels but it seems a pity not to say a few words about some Middle Eastern highlights. We'd been to Jordan before, to pick up Tracey, but the sight of the Hejaz railway in full operation in this country was a fascination, as was the Roman amphitheatre behind the hotel in which we stayed in Amman. We also bought a few well-made glass objects from a roadside artisan: Coke bottles into his little furnace; delightfully fabricated blue glass out. We also followed the River Jordan down to the oily, unattractive Dead Sea.

We separately feared for our lives on the next stage of our journey, but each didn't want to cause the other undue worry. We had all of the necessary papers to travel through Syria and hoped to visit Palmyra, but Hafez Assad's brother was playing up, trying to stir up a coup. That interesting journey wasn't to be. In the office of the border post I counted one hundred and twenty pictures of Assad, on bunting and in various poses: the beneficent ruler; suave man about town; eagle-eyed general and so on ad nauseam. The baksheesh was stiff and my protests brought a promise that some would be refunded as we exited the country. To make matters worse, we were then instructed to wait to join a convoy which would take us directly to the Turkish border with no deviation. The convoy would leave at 3am. It was freezingly cold to say the least, with a bitter penetrating wind and we scoured the cantonment for somewhere which would afford some escape from the worst of it. Eventually we came upon a ruined building in which we shivered until the appointed time.

The convoy consisted of ourselves and a German couple. As we waited to leave an evil-looking thug in leather coat stuck his AK47 through my window. The heating in his Land Cruiser had packed it in. We must now pay for a taxi to take him and his cronies a couple of hundred miles to the border and back. I pretended not to understand his Arabic and, after a time, he reluctantly moved forward to our companion in distress.

The scene was acted in silhouette, thanks to the placing of the powerful cantonment lights: Leather-coated yob pokes his shooter through the German's window; driver turns and listens. Brief pause whilst he takes in the message, then driver almost hits the roof of his car, waving his arms wildly. No pussy footing for him.

We were told that we had to keep up with the convoy—or else. Then we moved off out of the cantonment and down a dark, unlit corridor. This, I thought, is where they cut our throats. Eileen thought the same, but we came through unscathed.

Some time after dawn we were ushered into a roadhouse where we refuelled and breakfasted, but, after travelling two or three miles further, we were directed well off the road to a hut. I can't say whether this was some clever play-acting or not, but we'd been there for only a short time when somebody, allegedly a Turk, was escorted, yelling and screaming, into the wide blue yonder. We were told that he'd been there for a week and didn't have the correct papers. Incidentally, the Yobs had our passports.

We four travellers stubbornly failed to react, so, after more time, we were on the road again: for a few more miles. We were then directed off the road once more and told that we'd now have to wait there for the next convoy: a further twenty four hours if, yes, if there happened to be one. Have you guessed it? They wanted more baksheesh. From their point of view there was just one snag: we weren't prepared to play. Eileen got out some knitting and the German lass did much the same. Both males reclined their seats and pretended to sleep. The yobs continually conferred, the tone of the discussion progressively deteriorating until, finally there was a blazing row, after which our passports were literally flung through our windows and the one continuing dissentient in the discussions took us to the border. He was the smartest: he did collect a handsome swag of money.

It wasn't quite over. When we arrived, after the usual haggling, we were told that we'd have to visit the Turkish post first, then return to collect our refund. The Germans were angry and impatient and hurtled off with a few words as impolite as they judged to be safe. Whilst I presented myself in the office, I felt suddenly sad for the staff; I could only count ninety six pictures of Assad, considerably fewer than noted at the post where we'd entered. These people won't get on. I thought. All was eventually well: I'd overlooked two strands of bunting with a total of forty eight more.

We'd done nothing about our number plates up until then as we carried with us a multi-paged manifest in Arabic which could, so far as we knew, mention that they'd been removed. The Turks don't speak or read Arabic—as a general rule, so now was the time. More than a mile separated the two actual frontier posts, so, after our initial visit to have our passports stamped by the Turks, we stopped midway, beside a charming Graeco-Roman ruin. I hurried back to claim my cash. On my way back a man providentially—perhaps—suddenly materialised to change the money into Turkish currency—but Eileen was in trouble.

When I came within sight of the car I saw a nasty looking, bearded, leather coated, AK47 bearing thug advancing down an adjacent hill towards her and the car. Eileen was skilfully screwing on the false plates behind her back, ostensibly drinking in the ambient beauty. But the unbathed one continued his advance. I hurried into the car and Eileen joined me, all but one screw successfully driven home to secure the plates.

We wondered what we'd done wrong when we returned to the Turkish side: they actually smiled at us—did they have us where they wanted us? How had we erred? No: they were just being friendly.

There's no point in describing the remainder of our trip: it was most pleasant and, despite the confident forebodings of our friends in Tabuk, our throats weren't cut in some remote Turkish valley.

But I must tell you one more thing: there is a fish restaurant in Iskenderun second to none in the world. We finally drove to a hotel in that town, which was at a very pleasant, palm-lined esplanade. One of the guests there kindly showed us the way to a superb repast in pleasant surroundings with first-rate service.

Iskenderun, formerly Alexandretta, was founded by Alexander of Macedon. After his death he lay in state there. It's also the alleged place where Jonah came ashore after exiting the whale. The Apostle Paul was born a little further West of here. Throughout our journey through Turkey we came across very many sites of ancient civilisation, both Greek and Roman, not forgetting Side, the place where Antony and Cleopatra together admired the rosy fingered dawn. All of these antiquities were in a much better state of preservation than those in Greece itself.

England Khamis Mushayt England

I was too old to hope for a permanent appointment, so contented myself with locum appointments of which there were always plenty. Almost immediately I found myself at Stevenage Hospital, where I performed my last stint at general surgery. It was pleasant enough, with an enormous amount of bowel surgery, mainly for cancer. In my generalist days I'd always enjoyed this, especially because of the delicately obliging tissue planes: *Sauerbruch's richtiger Schicht*. Little else was memorable and, before I'd left there I'd had a request to return to Saudi, but this time as a locum at its easternmost part, Khamis Mushayt, Thursday market.

The country here is very highly elevated and the onshore winds bring with them a good deal of precipitation, so the country is greener. Many of the houses are Biblical in appearance, with flat roofs and, one day, to my delight, a Hoopoe bird actually flew past.

The nursing staff were a more uniformly pleasant crew, the Americans less adipose and there was a lighter workload. One embarrassment was the fact that my predecessor had had a penchant for injecting corticosteroids into people's joints. This is all very well on a once or twice basis: it certainly greatly relieves the symptoms of arthritis. Continued on a more or less regular basis, however, it leads all too often to a dissolution of the joint. When I refused to be a party to this, I caused a deal of anguish, though eventually those concerned accepted both my reasoning and my alternative treatment. One such patient, who took some convincing, was a female member of the Royal family, though how she got to Khamis I can't say.

My work was routine: no remarkable cases that I remember. The surroundings were another matter. I still had my Saudi driving licence and had no trouble persuading the manager of the car fleet to let me have a vehicle as and when required. Khamis is adjacent to an escarpment and some of the most spectacular scenery to be had anywhere in the world. At the edge of it, the land, richly clad in trees, tumbles away into the most fantastic gorges and declivities down to the coastal plain. I'd often drive there after work and gaze at this magnificent view.

As at Tabuk, there was a swimming pool: no mixed bathing of course. When I didn't feel like driving to my favourite view, I'd swim there, after work, at dusk. From the pool there was also a pleasant outlook. An unusual looking hill in particular captured my interest and I determined to climb it. Next Sabbath I set out with my sandwiches, undeterred by the disapproving honks of motorists who hated to see horrible unbelievers treading their precious soil. From the pinnacle I enjoyed lovely views, but imagine my surprise on looking down. There were unmistakeable signs of circumvallations all the way up to the top. This was an early Iron Age fort. One couldn't help wondering if the Queen of Sheba rested here on her way to see King Solomon. The scope for archaeology within the Kingdom is virtually boundless.

I shared a villa with two other consultants. One was an Australian radiologist whom I later caught up with on the Isle of Wight, the other a cardiologist from Denmark. The former had been informed by the Chief of Radiology Services that he, the chief, was a personal friend of the local Prince and that he could arrange for him to be entertained at his premises.

Of course he lied, but it set up a yearning in both of my companions. This almost metamorphosed into nagging, so, to keep them quiet and, not least so that I could haggle for Bedou jewellery on the Yemeni border, we set out early one Sabbath (Friday) morning.

So that I could actually take in its atmosphere, I detoured and drove some distance into the Rub al Khali, the Empty Quarter. It certainly lived up to its name, being nothing but glaringly white, bare sand hills rolling away into the distance on every side. At the Yemeni border I acquired some very interesting baubles. It's principally of silver and though it's of a lesser standard than sterling, some of the work was very fine. The Bedou also do some interesting niello work.

Then I had to face the embarrassing ordeal of knocking on the Prince's palace door. Oh, dear! My fractured Arabic made me the spokesman and I hope that I explained the position, including a mention of the lying radiologist. (I didn't tell my hosts that that was my opinion). The Prince, of course, wasn't at home—to us, at least, though the minions were too polite to say so. However that may be, Arabian hospitality demanded that they turn on a meal for us. It was probably a goat grab, though I can't remember. What I do recall is one of my hosts insisting upon my drinking a glass of camel's milk. It's laden with the germs of Tuberculosis, so I must have been mad to give in, though, being actually curious to learn what it tasted like, probably lowered my resistance. It wasn't unpleasant; rather salty. Having made our pleasantries, we now faced a drive of perhaps a couple of hundred miles home in the dark. As I drove along I became more and more ill at ease, with uncomfortable feelings in my hands and increasing difficulty in keeping my eyes open. To my great relief we finally made it to the villa and I hurried inside to a mirror in the hope of making a diagnosis. It wasn't difficult: I was unrecognisable, with a face swollen to incredible proportions. I was most fortunate that my breathing wasn't affected at the same time. I'm not very keen on corticosteroids, though they are, of course a great boon when used properly. There wasn't a great deal in the pharmacy otherwise, so I settled for ephedrine and calamine lotion. Now, when asked about my allergies I'm proud to include: camel's milk.

Once more back in England, I was surprised to learn that Bedford Hospital had rung, asking if I'd do a locum there. Someone, I've no idea who, must have given them my name. From that time onward until I left for Oz, I'd be spending most of my time in that hospital. I had to have a room in the place to sleep on those occasions when I was on duty. The grasping NHS always charged exorbitantly for inferior lodgings. These in particular were execrable and Eileen and a friend, Heather, the wife of Haydn, with whom we'd maintained friendship since Fiji, took about a day to remove the ordure and make the tiny hole in a wall habitable. The salary was also derisory but has improved a good deal since those times. There and then I was exploited, but despite everything, this was a happy workplace, at least so far as I was concerned.

There were three orthopods at the hospital, two dear old boys and a more recent appointee who though deaf as a board, was very competent. I was shocked at the archaic nature of much of the treatment. They even—proudly—treated some leg fractures in Tobruk plasters, despite other, much better approaches than this relic of second World War expediency. Some of their treatments had been in use for more than thirty years: not that this in itself is necessarily a criticism.

Most types of leg fractures may be treated using external fixation, but the necessary equipment wasn't available in the hospital. I wrote a report at the surgeons' request in which I discussed the pros and cons of the different marques. Needless to say, the hospital opted for an el cheapo Italian version which wasn't nearly as good as the one I recommended but which, I suppose, more or less did the job. External fixation was a tremendous advance on older methods. It has been described elsewhere in this book.

Thigh fractures have for a long time—more than half a century—been treated by means of an intramedullary nail. A late Nineteenth century surgeon called Hey Groves, ahead of his time in other ways, too, first used an intramedullary nail, but the steel he used wasn't stainless, the main reason for this being that it hadn't been invented. It was probably for that reason that many of his cases became infected. Don't take the word nail literally in this case. Some people call them rods. There are many variations on the theme but the one I always used was the Kuentscher nail. This is hollow and clover-leafed on cross section and comes in various sizes and lengths.

The idea is to reduce the fracture and then through an incision over the prominence of the bone at the hip, drill a hole in the top end of the femur of a diameter just sufficient to accommodate the nail and then hammer it as far down the middle of the bone as is judged to be necessary. Some 'refinements' of this added a nail—much finer, of course—driven across the bone well below the fracture, through a hole across the lower end of the nail. This can be quite tricky, needing additional equipment and I never used it, believing it to be quite unnecessary. The idea of that approach was to prevent the lower part of the fracture from rotating. Though that's hardly desirable, the knack in my view was to judge the width of the hole down the middle of the bone and use a nail of a diameter which fitted very snugly: without bursting it. The shape of the fragments in many—if not most—fractures of the femoral shaft are such that rotation is unlikely in any case. Some, like Arvid of Saudi Arabia, routinely reamed out the hole down almost the entire shaft. When this is done, it's probably advisable to use a nail which requires a transverse pin at its lower end. There are any number of these, but the good old K-nail for me!

For other fractures, most notably of the Humerus, a different nail, the Rush nail may be quite useful. This is solid (the K nail isn't) and thinner, has a sharpish lower end, a gently curved shaft and a fairly acute curve at its top. This latter curve enables it to fit snugly outside the bone, thus adding to the stability of the bone fragments and making the nail relatively easy to extract.

One day a thirtyish woman was brought in. She'd been walking over to her telephone when she suddenly crashed to the floor. X Ray showed an ominous gap in her thigh bone. Cancers of the bone, especially those which are secondary deposits from lesions elsewhere, notoriously cause pathological fractures—and this was one such, so cancer of some kind had strongly to be suspected. The picture wasn't typical, however, so I decided to operate and, as I assumed that it would be a soft lesion, free of bone, I asked the Pathology Department to make provision for a frozen section. For this, a biopsy is performed and the technician hastens away, freezes the specimen and, after suitable treatment, the Pathologist examines it under the microscope. This is not infrequently done in cases of suspected breast cancer where the surgeon isn't completely sure of the diagnosis. This procedure means that, if the lesion is benign, more radical surgery is avoided at the slight cost of a somewhat prolonged anaesthetic. Bone samples, being hard, of course, can't be treated in that way. I asked them to be doubly certain—this test is more liable to false positives than the normal approach which involves fixing the tissue in formalin or some such, embedding it in paraffin wax and then staining a very thin slice.

This takes several days. On those rare occasions where there were any doubts at all, I'd close the wound and wait for the result of the more prolonged procedure. This lesion was benign, so I excised it thoroughly. This left quite a gap in the bone. I rapidly considered the alternatives. Anything radical would take ages: a number of further operations before the patient was mobile and free of pain again. Accordingly, I took a punt and drove a tightly fitting example of my friendly old K nail through both fragments and then filled the gap with cement.

The cement in question isn't, of course, the kind that is made into concrete. It's actually a substance called methyl methacrylate, a powder which, immediately before use is mixed with a hardener and when it is, the clock begins to run. One only has a limited number of minutes in which to finish the job before it hardens. It becomes extremely hot whilst that's going on, so in this case I did my best to have the adjacent soft tissues kept well away whilst it set. I hope the end result was satisfactory: it certainly was for as long as I was there. If it wasn't, then the other, much less pleasant options, bone grafts with or without metal plates, were still open.

Bones can actually be lengthened, though probably not to the extent needed in that case, by using a contraption known as Wegener's apparatus. The shortened bone is cut across after its outside layer, the periosteum, has been raised from the bone for a little distance above and below the proposed cut. The periosteum is kept as intact as possible and an apparatus similar to those used in external fixation then applied above and below the cut. The difference in this case is that there's a small wheel attached to the apparatus which, when turned, gradually distracts the bone fragments. The patient is sent home and turns the wheel regularly so that, very gradually, the bone is lengthened. With luck, the periosteum continues to lay down bone until, eventually, the desired result is obtained. In this case the gap was too large. In any case, no Wegener was in the hospital armamentarium.

The few hiatuses in my work at Bedford were readily filled in. In particular I worked on several occasions on the lovely Isle of Wight, in the Royal Isle of Wight Hospital, a gift of Queen Victoria to the people of that Island, but at that time it was an Orthopaedic hospital: a very nice old building. It has since been largely demolished and unsightly trash substituted. How this could happen to a gift of a monarch, specifically for the people? The answer is that governments in power can do whatever they like. Whether or not they bothered with an excuse on this occasion I'm unable to say.

There were three consultants in my discipline there, all very pleasant people. One, Robin Boyd, was the son of the author of my favourite Pathology textbook. He had a new method of performing a hip replacement which he urged me to try. It appeared to work very well but I only used it at that hospital, because the traditional Charnley operation has always served me well.

There are any number of ways of replacing a hip. The favoured older approach to that part of the body, as used by St.John Buxton—remember? Was the anterior: one operated from the front. Certainly the joint appears to be closer, but tiger country in the shape of the great femoral blood vessels and the Femoral Nerve stand awkwardly in the way. Another approach is the lateral, which I'll mention soon. By far the best, in my view, is the Southern Exposure as its great protagonist, Austin Moore, described it. An angled incision is made over the relevant buttock and the large Gluteus Maximus muscle split, to reveal the Sciatic Nerve and several muscles and tendons, only one of which, with its two small associated muscles needs to be cut. The joint capsule is next incised and the leg grasped and rotated until the joint is dislocated—and inspected. The head and more or less of the neck of the thigh bone are then cut off by means of an oscillating saw. The rapidly moving blade can spray blood and finely divided bone for quite a distance at this stage! The remainder of the neck, if any, and the interior of the upper part of the bone (femur) is then reamed out enough to accommodate the new prosthesis. The next step is, in my view, most important: a plug is inserted at the lower limit of the reaming process. The new head of the femur is now readied. It's considerably smaller in diameter than the original design. When Charnley was developing his wonderful new method, he at first used a prosthesis with the same diameter as the natural femoral head. This worked very well with one exception: like Sir Thomas Tom's armour, it squeaked. He consulted an engineer, who studied the problem, finally deciding that by reducing the diameter one would reduce the friction and, hopefully, the squeak. That suggestion was absolutely on target.

The surgical sister, meanwhile, has mixed the cement and the clock is very much ticking. A catheter is then passed down to the bottom of the bone cavity, suction applied and the cement pushed into place using a plastic syringe-like instrument. The suction, if the whole thing's carried out properly, should ensure an even distribution of the rather viscous cement right throughout the cavity. The prosthesis is then rapidly inserted (there's lots of trouble if the cement hardens before the manoeuvre is completed). Great care must be taken to maintain the bone's original length, with the head inclined slightly forward. All too often sloppy surgeons leave the patient with one leg longer than the other. The acetabulum, the socket, is now reamed out with a hemispherical bit whose head is about the same diameter and spiralled with cutting blades. There are a number of different choices for the new socket. I never had any trouble with high density polyethylene. More cement is now used to anchor the socket into its place. The new head is then popped into its socket—the whole procedure helps keep one fit: legs can be heavy!—and the wound closed with suction drainage. Care must be taken for some time postoperatively not to flex the leg too much, as in sitting on a low chair, or to rotate the leg inwardly. Dislocation can result. It doesn't take long for the joint to stabilise. The length of time needed for rehabilitation varies enormously, to say the least. Positive, fit people need practically none at all. I had one man upon whom I operated on a Tuesday. He made such a song and dance about leaving the hospital: business needing his attention; family needing him; sky about to fall in, that I allowed him out on the Friday, with multiple cautions. I attended a fair on the following day and there he was, striding across the rough open ground as if nothing had happened. He brushed aside my remonstrances.

Lots of other methods, using differing materials, are in use, the most important probably being the employment of high density ceramics. I'm sure they're very good, but I never saw a need to change my ways. Of course nothing, not excepting prosthetic hips, last forever and this is especially a problem where young people are concerned, but the more care taken with the operation, the longer it will last.

Just a note on knees whilst we're at it. Many knee replacements do extremely well, but knee movements are very complex and, to date, no prosthesis has managed fully to reproduce them. If the problem in the knee is predominantly in one compartment (one side) there's a lamentable tendency to use a hemi-prosthesis for that side only. This seldom works satisfactorily. The answer to this, in my view, is to operate upon the leg bones in such a way as to alter the direction of the upward thrust from the foot, through the Tibia to the knee, when, in walking, one puts the foot to the ground. Achieving this involves a Tibial osteotomy: a wedge is cut from that bone in such a way that the following objective is attained: if the inner compartment of the knee is affected, the base of the wedge is on the outer or lateral aspect. (In this case, the fibula's length usually must also be adjusted). The forces are thus directed more to the outer compartment of the knee—draw yourself a diagram! Of course, this is a much lesser (less expensive) operation. Why bother with that when one can have such fun—and remuneration—excising the knee along the dotted lines indicated with the prosthesis—and inserting a lovely shiny prosthesis?

The same applies to hip fractures. Too often nowadays these are treated by replacement rather than by reducing the fracture and then fixing it with pins or a nail plus or minus a plate, the latter necessary in order to add stability in certain types of fracture. I always issued strict instructions to my registrars on this count. If they were eager beavers especially they were likely to perform a replacement rather than the lesser method. The interests of the patient are no longer completely paramount. Perhaps they never were, but I do see a change for the worse in this regard.

Current teaching, too, could be responsible. A few years ago my late brother who, because of some medical treatment had developed osteoporosis, suffered a pathological hip fracture. His surgeon, no doubt in good faith, performed a total replacement. It proved too much for his frail system and he died a few weeks later. He may have lived longer if the lesser procedure had been performed.

I don't think I'm hypercritical, but here I must also mention yet one more example of substandard treatment of my near and dear. Some twenty years before my brother's fatal experience, my father-in-law became troubled by diverticulitis of his descending colon to the extent that he felt that only surgery would offer him relief. I agreed. I was in Oz at the time, but, having been away for years and knowing no surgeons to whom he might be referred, asked a GP of my acquaintance whom, up to that time, I held in some regard. He gave me a name and the incompetent socialite cutter agreed to operate. After some hours he gave up, unable to remove the affected part. Worse, much worse, was to come. Quite early postoperatively, a chest infection developed and the causative organism was an MRSA. It did respond in some degree to only one antibiotic, one well known for its devastating effects upon the kidneys. It should only be given for a few days: five at the very outside. It was given for several weeks with the inevitable result. This infection must have been caused by poor sterilization of the endotracheal tube used during the anaesthetic. In other words, the hospital, a large and I think still well regarded private one in Brisbane was responsible. The attitude of staff changed remarkably as the poor man's condition deteriorated. They obviously thought that we were about to create a fuss. We didn't: a) We're not litigious; b) It wouldn't bring him back; c) even if we took the case to law they'd lie like pigs in mud and the only people to profit would have been the lawyers.

Eileen flew out to Oz and was fortunate enough to arrive before he died.

Oz Again-With Some Clearing up in Britain

Eileen now became worried about her ageing mother, so we decided that we should return to Oz in order to keep an eye on her. As it transpired, it was entirely unnecessary. The lady in question was sturdily self-reliant and needed no help, thank you very much. She was living in the seaside town of Caloundra and, whilst organising something permanent, we lived with her.

She had a very bad bunion, so I took the opportunity of correcting this. There are a number of different approaches to this problem. The one I've always used is as follows: the metatarso-phalangeal joint, the one at the base of the big toe, is excised in such a way that the toe regains its original alignment. Then the distal half or so of the proximal phalanx: the bone nearest the foot, is cut off. What's left of this bone is then screwed on to the adjacent metatarsal bone so that it's inclined ever so slightly upward. This leaves the toe a little wobbly for a time, but this stabilises. The result is a shapely, pain-free foot. In this particular case the second toe was also well out of alignment and had to be straightened.

One must eat, so I scanned the ads in the press. Eileen is an accomplished potter and she was hard at that when I popped in to the large shed at the back of the house where she was working.

'How would you like to live in Port Augusta?'

'Where on earth's that?'

'Somewhere in South Australia. They're advertising for an Orthopaedic surgeon. Shouldn't be too much doing there: should be a nice quiet place in which to spend my declining professional years!'

How wrong I was!

Just then our neighbour over the back fence engaged me in yet one more kerbside consultation. Her brother had been on a ship and had foolishly fallen a considerable distance from a mast on to the deck. Since that time he'd suffered from severe pain and headaches, always made worse by the physio his Orthopod had ordered him. Just by chance she had his X rays with her and showed them to me. I didn't need a viewing box to see that the poor fellow had broken his neck. That physio, albeit acting upon an Orthopod's instructions, had placed him in serious jeopardy. Certainly the radiologist had missed the diagnosis, a serious error. If the Orthopod had merely relied upon the radiologist's printed report without looking at the films then I'd say that he was negligent. If he had looked and missed it, too, then what can one say? I invariably studied all of the films of the X Rays I ordered. All specialist doctors have, I believe, a moral obligation to do the same. Even Homer nods and radiologists most certainly do, too. We're all frail creatures of accident and error. In medicine, as little as possible should be left to chance.

I'd promised to do a number of locums in Britain and advised my prospective employers accordingly before the job interviews in Adelaide and flew into that town on my way back when my application had proved to be successful. There were three or four other interviewees. After my success, the Hospital's CEO and the local State MP drove me to the town, allegedly to allow me to inspect Port Augusta and the hospital itself.

There was an ulterior motive which amused me no end. On the way into town we paused and the CEO suggested that I might care to view the place from the elevation of the local water tower. I agreed and as it was obvious to me that they were, in fact, testing an ageing doctor's stamina before finally appointing somebody who couldn't cut the mustard, I hurtled up the ladder to the top. It was the CEO who was out of breath. The view? Remarkable.

The hospital was well set out and modern enough, though the appalling government of that state has since squandered money on another, admittedly excellent but unnecessary building. A Lord High Medical Bureaucrat was there, probably to look me over. I told him that, to do my best work, I'd need an image intensifier: an X ray machine which enables one to see one's work in real time. As one would expect, he lied. Pointing to a large crate which had just been delivered.

'There it is!' He exclaimed.

Oh, yes: it was an image intensifier but not a mobile one for use in the operating theatre. It was a static one for the diagnosis of medical, especially cardiac, conditions. It's equally likely that he was stupid and didn't know the difference between the two. After huffing and puffing I did finally receive a proper one.

Back in Britain there were locums in Bedford, the Isle of Wight and Brechin in Scotland awaiting me. There was nothing out of the way in the former two hospitals but a few words about the latter might be of interest. It was an orthopaedic hospital pure but not entirely simple. It had, in better days, been a Great House, owned by a noble former Prime Minister who was by no means ignoble: H relinquished his coronet so that he could sit in the House of Commons; unwillingly, but did so because he thought that his duty. A *rara avis* indeed.

The house itself, pleasant to the eye—on the outside—had been turned into a warren to house the medical staff. A delightful orangery was still more or less intact. Faint vestiges of aristocratic pursuits remained: there was an adjacent trout stream where one or other of the staff could often be seen Attending of his trembling quill. It wasn't near to any town and was an oasis of calm: until one of the staff let loose with his gun at a rabbit or wood pigeon in the hospital grounds.

The consultant whom I replaced was on leave, waiting for his wife to give birth. A pleasant Irishman, he took me in the evenings to sundry atmospheric hostelries. One nearby town boasted a distillery. Though perhaps not up to the best Speyside malts, Fettercairn was a very acceptable medicament.

The only surgical matter of interest was the approach to the hip in vogue here when performing replacements: the lateral one. The senior registrar, probably in imitation of his chief, though I'm not sure, was a rabid advocate who nagged until I adopted it. Why not? One must always keep an open mind. It might be an improvement on the Southern Exposure. As it transpired, it was needlessly fiddley, also demanding the severing of the Greater Trochanter: the uppermost part of the femur, then reattaching it afterwards. No doubt subsequent healing is usually complete, but unnecessary interference of any kind never appealed to me.

Back in Oz, it was first necessary to visit Adelaide to register as a practitioner in that state: a delightful experience! Not even hello or kiss my foot.

'Sign here. You can't do this and you can't do that.'

As you can guess, it was a well bolshevised state always open season for doctors. The emoluments were on a fee for service basis, based upon the Commonwealth Government's rates: not princely but very fair. Someone in the bureaucracy asleep? Not on your life. When my pay cheques began to arrive, the swine were remunerating me as a GP. Fuming, I decided to have a knock-em-down-drag-em-out with the creeps, but on the way in to Adelaide for the contest, Eileen saw a notice on a building informing all and sundry that the offices of the Commonwealth Department of Health were located therein.

'Stop the car' she cried, speeding into the building and returning soon afterward, a satisfied smile on her face: 'Thank you for letting us know. We've been trying to catch those blighters for some time. Leave it to us. That's what they said and they were very pleasant!'

In due course the matter was rectified. It's nice to feel wanted!

In line with that general welcome, the accommodation offered was a wretched little rubbidy dub. When we complained, a reasonably habitable house came to light.

Often when I take on a new posting a case turns up which helps the locals trust me. This happened once again here only a day or so after we'd arrived. A butcher had missed his mark when cutting up a carcase, driving his knife into his femoral artery: very likely to prove rapidly fatal. Fortunately for him he was blessed with both fortitude and presence of mind: he stuck his thumb firmly into the breach whilst colleagues phoned for help. Two of the local GPs, both endowed with plenty of nous (one now a highly regarded Dermatologist) hurtled forth, bringing him back alive.

The sister-in-charge of the operating theatre at this time was first class and all was in readiness in no time. Whilst one of the two rescuers continued to press on the artery the other gave the anaesthetic.

The wound being high in the groin, I had to make an incision a couple of inches above it, across the lower abdomen. I exposed the artery just above where it disappeared into the leg, having first carefully moved the peritoneum out of the way. I then applied a vascular clamp—it stops the blood flow without damaging the vessel's lining. With a sigh of relief, Iain was able to remove his thumb at last!

Fortunately, the wound being along the length of the artery, sewing it together was a simple matter. When about to remove the clamp in such cases, there's always an expectancy: will the sutures hold? Has the bleeding been stopped? Fortunately all was well. The handling of the bleeding by my helpers had been so skilful that there was no postoperative infection.

To say that I was busy is to understate matters to the nth degree. We lived in a house more or less overlooked by the hospital and, if we went out, to dinner or for any other reason, as soon as we returned, the phone would inevitably ring the moment the front door had been opened—that's the truth! I always remarked that a cockatoo was permanently stationed on the roof over the way to observe me and alert the hospital whenever I returned.

There was much trauma work for a number of reasons: the flying doctor service base there served a great deal of the state; the town was at that time host to a busy railway workshops and a large coal-fired power station; it's on a busy highway and people, especially children, had a propensity to sticky beak over galvanised iron fences, of which there were many, a problem because, to pull themselves up to look on the other side, they did so with their hands; worse, sometimes their wrists. Their body weight caused the cruel iron to cut into their wrists, cutting the tendons and often the nerves as well. When suturing nerves, it's vitally important to connect them up as they were before the injury. Nerves consist of bundles of fibres, all of differing diameters and shapes. If the repair is done carelessly, a nerve fibre with one function, bound for ending X, is often connected to a fibre leading to Y: most unlikely to result in either sensation or return of muscular function. When operating under magnification, it's not difficult to match up the bundles. It does take time, though, and when there are tendons to be sutured as well, the toll on one's back is heavy. Aching isn't the word!

The finest of fine thread is essential, with tiny atraumatic needles: i.e. the end of the suture is incorporated into the needle itself. The suture material in a normally threaded needle bulges out on either side, creating unnecessary tissue damage. Atraumatic sutures don't have that bulge

A very special needle holder is also essential. Left handed ones are rare. I went to Leeds to buy mine from the manufacturer. It was a lovely little instrument.

I must say something now about hand tendons because this is important in connection with a later story. The chief tendons to the fingers pass through a tunnel in the wrist, already described. Apart from intrinsic muscles, those in the hand itself, also acting upon the fingers, there are two tendons to each finger, the deep and the superficial. The deep one, inserted into the terminal phalanx, can bend the whole finger. The superficial tendon can't bend the terminal phalanx. For this reason, orthodoxy says that, when both tendons are cut, the superficial tendon should be excised and the deep tendon sutured, because, after trauma, there's always swelling, with exudate that might stick the tendons together, direly affecting the hand's functions. It's vital that the hand should always be kept elevated postoperatively to lessen this malign swelling.

As a matter of fact I always sutured both sets of tendons, with extreme care, then encouraging early movement. It worked for me.

For some time my income enjoyed a modest increment thanks to the fact that a major film, the *Light Horseman*, was being shot close by. When a horseman fell off his mount, fracturing one or another bone, I was naturally consulted. These injuries were all quite minor until the last day of the shoot. Vast quantities of alcohol sloshed around at the celebration. At their conclusion, the male lead, decidedly tired and emotional, took off in his car for home, fame and fortune. It was night and, sadly for him, an elderly gent had halted his pickup on the highway, obeying a call of nature. The movie star, insufficiently alert crashed at full speed into the stationary vehicle. He was brought back to Port Augusta. Iain and I did what we could for the poor fellow: little more than resuscitation and the flying doctors took him to Adelaide, then Sydney, his home. He lingered unconscious, for ages.

Some indigenous Australians were a fruitful source of trauma cases. They become extremely violent when drunk and, sadly, that's all too often with a significant proportion. There was obviously a deep seated dislike of Europeans amongst many of them, as evidenced by the fact that one was routinely sworn at and spat at by drunks whilst trying to help. I can readily understand it. From their point of view the white man is an interloper who has interfered not only with their traditions but also acted sacrilegiously towards much that's sacred to them. They're animists and almost everything: every rock; every stream, is sacred. Their leaders are very smart, never missing any opportunity of capitalising on our differing cultures and belief systems. Not so long ago poor Nicole Kidman was roundly castigated for blowing a didgeridoo: women aren't supposed to blow them. But this episode happened in Germany, if you please, when she was suddenly presented with a commercially produced, well varnished instrument during a television programme to ballyhoo her latest film with the portentous title *Australia*. One can hardly blame her being upset. Instead of apologising, she should have said to the part-aborigine activist who kicked up the fuss:

'Grow up. Sexism and superstition have no place in the Twenty first Century.'

And as for the ridiculous myth that females who blow that instrument will, ipso facto become barren! Words fail!

One day a highly intelligent girl was admitted with a leg so badly fractured that it had almost been wrenched off by her violent, drunken partner. She was an inpatient for so long that it was hoped that she might be persuaded to take a job in Port Augusta when she'd been discharged. To this end Vin, one of the two who'd kept the man with the knife wound alive, found an excellent position for her. Eventually she decided to return to her violent boyfriend. Next time they got drunk, or the time after, her wounds would probably be fatal. Sad.

Another poor lass—a nice aboriginal girl—periodically presented with a fractured ulna, courtesy her husband. That's the forearm bone that presents to an aggressor about to hit one's head with a cudgel.

Australia's corporate sense of guilt and the skill of the indigenous—too often very partly indigenous—negotiators has led to many stupid responses to the problem. One pleasant, upright family was in receipt of all kinds of concessions including a very nice van because of their indigenous origin, courtesy the Australian taxpayer. The husband had a broad Welsh accent, his wife, ever so slightly coffee coloured. Technically they were/are aborigines. By one definition I'm an indigenous Australian too. That Welshman wasn't even that. Nice work if you can get it.

I had an unofficial job: keeping an eye on the hospital in Coober Peedy, the opal mining town to the North. It was an occasional source of people, dead and nearly so, who'd fallen down one of the innumerable mine shafts littering the landscape, there and which in places caused a positively lunar landscape. Surprisingly, some survived, albeit with spinal injuries and assorted fractures.

Many inhabitants of this town are troglodytes, often in more senses than one. The local doctor was one, without the pejorative sense. Chinese, he was capable and lived in a cave dug by one of those machines possessed of gaping, rotating circular jaws, like the ones used in digging out the Chunnel but on a smaller scale. His house was fascinating: extremely well appointed cylinders running in several different directions. Here and there opal glittered from the walls. Why live underground? Because it's cool within, whilst outside it's furnace-hot.

There's little finesse about the mining of this precious silicate. A shaft's dug and, if the miner's lucky, he drills a number of holes, fills them with gelignite, absents himself, explodes the charge and then collects the opal from the debris: all shattered, of course, large specimens having been blown to pieces. The rubble is removed by means of air blasts blown up through a cyclone: a cylinder in which it's hoped that opal has been separated from the dross by centrifugal force. Sharp-eyed Eileen climbed one of the heaps of extruded rock and found a lovely, sizeable piece.

Andamooka, further East, closer to Lake Eyre, looked even more like a lunar landscape. The proximity of one of the largest Uranium mining ventures in the world may have resulted in a tidy-up since then. Specimens from here are quite different, being more translucent, though often beautifully coloured.

I had patients from here, most with bad backs from working in cramped conditions. One was very different. Betty was: still is, I'm happy to say, a GI bride from Bishop's Stortford. After the war, the two settled on the husband's farm in Dakota. One day, Hank was backing his tractor when their infant son ran under its cruel wheels and was killed. The distraught couple, couldn't stand the constant reminder of their tragedy, so emigrated to Australia. With two new additions to the family they bought an old banger and proceeded to explore the country. Thanks to the vehicle's imperfections, they came to rest—yes, in Andamooka, camping there. Rain there is as rare as gems, so Betty was lucky that some fell. She washed her infants' nappies in a stream that began to run.

Hank was active and entrepreneurial, persistingly searching until he finally found opal. He bought a few acres, built a home and literally made the desert blossom like the rose. His sweet corn and potatoes are amongst the most delicious one could ever taste.

He managed this by building a dam and, buying a water tanker. He'd drive to all of the worked-out mine shafts, pump water that was in them into his tank and thence into his dam. He even made irrigated hay and raised a few head of cattle.

Betty was hurrying one day and fell down a flight of stairs, badly shattering her knee: that's how we got to know them. Though fragmented, the lower end of her femur—thigh bone—could be repaired quite well without causing irregularities in the joint surface that would lead eventually to arthritis. Joint surfaces after injury must meticulously be aligned. Loose bits were screwed together, but the badly displaced lower end of the bone had to be immobilised at the correct angle by means of specially designed apparatus: part of it a plate, to be attached to the femoral shaft; part a nail, at an angle to the plate, rather tricky to apply. For a good result: the nail must be driven through the bone at such an angle that the fragment is held in the right position when the plate is fixed to the bone's shaft.

At about this time a completely different knee problem presented itself. Soon after Eric M set out from Adelaide, bound for Alice Springs, his Right knee became painful, progressively more and more severely so as he travelled, until, at Port Augusta he couldn't stand it any longer. On inspection the knee was painful to move, hot, red and markedly swollen: the hallmarks of inflammation. The question was: what had caused it? If due to infection, Eric was in for a bundle of trouble. I inserted a wide bore needle and aspirated. Fluid shimmered in the light as I drew it out, confirming my suspicions: this was a case of acute gout. The fluid's appearance was due to innumerable urate crystals. He settled quickly with treatment and was on his way in a few days.

We became friends with the good people from Andamooka. Sadly, Hank had a bad heart and, towards the end of our stay in Port Augusta, clearly wasn't much longer for this world. Theirs is a very devout family who'd built a church to facilitate their worship. When Hank died, they naturally wanted him to be buried in the grounds of their much-loved church.

People, schmeeple! A nasty local resident objected and their request for Hank's interment was refused. The family wrote to England asking us to support their plea to have that heartless diktat overturned. Fortunately it was.

Talking of knees, let's consider for a moment ruptured cruciate ligaments, most commonly sports injuries, but also sustained because of other trauma, car injuries included. There are two of these: anterior and posterior. As their name suggests, they cross one another and, if either or both are torn an unstable knee results. It's sometimes possible to repair them, seldom with good results. A favoured treatment uses carbon fibre, attached firmly; tautly to both bones. I looked a little askance at this. Admittedly tough, it's nevertheless inert. The fibres must ultimately suffer fatigue from the continuous movement, sometimes eventually snapping.

Perhaps my views are coloured by Eileen's contribution to the construction of a state-of-the-art racing yacht. Her name, inscribed on the hull, along with many others now lie at the bottom of the sea. The hull, of *avant garde* carbon fibre design, quickly came apart when subjected to the severe stresses of an ocean voyage.

To repair an anterior cruciate, I'd split off a suitable thickness of patellar tendon, retaining its attachment to the Tibia, drill a hole through the lateral condyle of the femur, draw the tendon through, tighten it and attach it firmly to the outer part of that bone. The two femoral condyles move over the upper surface of the Tibia with a sizeable gap between the two.

There was an Orthopaedic Surgeon in the adjacent, not very close town of Whyalla. Very capable, he was Chinese, as was his wife. Unfortunately for me, she very definitely decided against gracing salubrious Whyalla with her presence, remaining in Adelaide. Felix, the surgeon, consequently spent weekends with his wife, leaving the hiatus, the vast majority of the State of South Australia to be filled by yours truly for emergencies. Admittedly this was sparsely populated, but it meat a deal of extra work. I didn't mind. He couldn't do much else and was a very nice man, but, rather longish in the tooth, I already had a fearsome burden of work in my own bailiwick. When patients had been badly hurt, I had to travel the miles to the hospital at Whyalla.

One case from the distant West, however, was flown directly to me. He'd fallen off a ladder on to his Left foot, badly fracturing both bones of his lower leg, necessitating open reduction with much pinning and plating. Whilst examining him I noticed that the soft tissues of his Right foot were deformed, with a good deal missing. When questioned, he told me that he'd been a soldier in the German army and lost the tissues of his foot because of very severe frostbite. To my surprise he added that he'd sustained it a couple of hundred miles, east of Moscow, rather going against the orthodoxy that Hitler's army got no further than Stalingrad.

Exacting, the work was nevertheless most congenial, not least because all of the doctors were friendly and cooperative. The same couldn't be said of the nursing staff, who were increasingly bolshevised, though I must emphasise the fact that there were many who were both delightful people and good nurses. One of the problems was the innumerable stupid meetings which kept them out of the wards: a modern sickness afflicting the entire Western world. Proper study sessions, yes, especially if they're after hours or in the form of leave, i.e. don't take the nurse out of the ward. Already mentioned were many cases of wrist injury requiring suture of the tendons, often nerves as well. One absolute essential of postoperative care is that the hand must be kept elevated. Towards the end of my time the situation became well-nigh hopeless. The sisters—they call them nurses now: clinical nurse consultant, for instance, which sounds most impressive—knew less and less about the patients under their alleged care:

Sorry, it's been my day off; sorry I've been to this that and the other meeting and so on.

I gave marks at the end of my rounds:

Only one out of ten today, sister; absolutely none out of ten today!

Not only were they habitually in ignorance of what was going on, but, to my extreme disgust the hands of tendon suture cases were invariably, yes, invariably, hanging down whenever I made my rounds. I had to revisit the wards repeatedly at all hours to keep them raised as much as possible.

Before concluding this Jeremiad, I must mention two points. Firstly, new edition nurses call their patients clients. I'm not sure what the bolshie rationale for that is, but consider the Latin roots of the words: patient is from *patere*, to suffer; client is from *cliere*, to listen. Have I made my point? The other is that, unlike my old chief George and despite severe temptation on occasions, I never called a trained nurse any other name than sister.

Bolshies of a feather don't always stick together but they certainly did here! A new marque of theatre sister arrived and she and her subordinates smoked incessantly in the office within the theatre complex. Patients awaiting operation were inevitably exposed to this carcinogenic irritant. The concentration of the fumes was high and would do patients inhaling them a whole lot of no good. I also failed to see why I should have to spend my days smoking passively. I asked them to stop—No way, Jose! I asked the CEO to intervene and was on the receiving end of a long, meaningless diatribe. I sought out the—I shudder to name the position: it's become such a farce—the local Health and Safety officer. He was polite: yes, he understood the problem and the practice would assuredly cease, not now; sometime in the sweet bye and bye. In other words, in case I'd reap some satisfaction in gaining a point, it would happen after I'd left.

There's a sting in this tale: A number of consultants used to fly in to the hospital, do their stuff and fly out again. One day I walked into this office, thick with smoke. One of the smokers was the visiting Gynaecologist who owned his own plane, flown around by his wife.

'That'll kill you.' I said.

He was dead next day. During his flight back to Adelaide he sustained a coronary occlusion, dying next morning whilst undergoing an angiogram.

Nurses' bolshevism assumed a sinister character in my late months. Whilst I was in Britain attending a hand surgery refresher, a general surgeon had been appointed. There were two finalists, one, an Australian, with an alleged Fellowship of the Royal College of Surgeons, Edinburgh, the other, not only a Fellow of the English College, but also a former Hunterian Professor of that institution; also senior assistant to a number of distinguished surgeons, including Christian Barnard of heart transplant fame. I'm a Fellow of both Colleges; though proud of both, my pride is greater for the English Fellowship. John Hunter who died in 1793 and after whom this professorship is named, is the father of modern surgery.

A no brainer, isn't it? On the one hand a Hunterian Professor of an illustrious college and on the other a possible Fellow of, yes, another illustrious college. Enter the Royal Australasian College of Surgeons: the learned colleges are involved when consultant appointments are made. Their decision, crucial to the selection process, was that X, the Hunterian Professor lacked the necessary experience, i.e. he hadn't been a junior doctor in Bullabakanka District Hospital. Even worse, he was, shudder—dare I pronounce it? A Pom. I'm sorry, but it must be said that many Australians are not merely nationalistic, which is fair enough, but hypernationalistic. Australia is a lovely country and its citizens can hold their heads up with the best, but everything in due measure. They appointed W, a pleasant enough person with a charming wife for whom, as the saga unfolded, one felt sorry.

On his first weekend he asked if I would look after his patients so that he could familiarise himself with his new surroundings. I readily agreed. My rounds of his patients revealed a surprisingly high proportion of sick people but I put this down to their condition before they'd entered the hospital. He made the same request on the following weekend and I readily agreed to that.

Just before making night rounds, I received a call:

'Would you please come up and take a look at Mr. Christensen? I think he's going to die.'

This, in a matter of fact tone. I assumed he would be an elderly cancer patient or some such: certainly nothing urgent. Arrived in the ward, the man was as white as a sheet and very poorly indeed. Scrawled across the front of W's clinical notes was: PD (provisional diagnosis) adhesions. That was all. No history; no record of any examination or treatment. Whilst I was busy looking through the notes in an unsuccessful effort to find something substantial, the sister arrived carrying a large—and I do mean LARGE bowl containing at least two inches of blood: between two and three litres. The poor fellow had passed this *per rectum*. Still conscious: just, I took as concise a history as I could. He'd been taking NSAIDS (non-steroidal anti-inflammatory drugs) for aches and pains. An important, fairly frequent side effect of these is bleeding from the gastrointestinal tract. The man was over seventy years of age, now clinically flat as a tack. People of this age are susceptible to kidney failure and if they go flat more than twice it's usually curtains, the kidneys failing to resume their functions.

I was on the spot and suitable blood arrived most expeditiously. Whilst waiting for it I ordered intravenous anti-ulcer treatment. Waiting until the transfusion took effect; pleased to see him revive well, I sought my bed—in the wee small hours. Three or four hours later I phoned the ward:

'How's Mr. Christensen, sister?'

'Oh, he's come around very well.' She recited the vital signs, all satisfactory.

'Thank you sister. Now please note: I'm not a resuscitologist but Dr. Raj is. Should he go flat again it is him whom you should ring, letting me know too, of course.'

Happy, I resumed my slumbers. After a late breakfast I phoned again:

'Oh, I think he's going to die.'

I donned my running shoes. To save money, this hospital used local GPs as the medical foot soldiers instead of employing resident doctors and this worked well. The town was fortunate in the overall quality of its medicos. A roster system was supposed to be operating, with a specific doctor on duty at any given time. Not on this occasion, so far as the nursing staff was concerned. Soon after I'd phoned in the very early morning, the patient had gone flat again. Did they ring Raj? Did they ring me? Oh, dear no. They rang the GP on duty:

'Give him more blood.'

He perked up, but soon went flat again. Did they phone Raj? Me? The original GP? No! For some inscrutable reason the sister—or perhaps it was a nurse—phoned another GP who gave the same order. Unbelievably, this happened yet once again.

By now he'd been flat so many times; sure that he'd die of renal failure, I thought I was dealing with a dead man. I had forty fits. Whilst thus expressing myself I had them phone Raj, an exceedingly accomplished anaesthetist.

'Do you think you can get him up to speed for a gastrectomy?'

'I can try.'

It was years since I'd performed this operation and of course it had to be a Billroth 1. Paddy, the first GP they'd phoned in the morning assisted. The thing about the operation that impressed him most was some of my language when the going got tough. Tough it certainly got. I rapidly resected the requisite amount of stomach, then inspected the duodenum for bleeding. There, far down, almost as far as—and dangerously close to—

the *Ampulla of Vater*, the common bile duct's entrance into the duodenum a small fountain of blood, pulsating from an artery steadily sapped vital resources. It was now essential, as quickly as possible, to dissect, with the utmost care, a little of the duodenum from the adjacent pancreas, in order to excise the ulcer, at whose base the artery was pumping away and thus the offending artery as well.

Now was the problem of bringing the cut end of stomach into tension-free contact with the duodenal end: a long way indeed, necessitating much mobilisation of the organs. To this end I incised around the outer side of the duodenum where it meets the abdominal wall posteriorly. Some people have found this a barrier, but that's psychological, The tissue planes here are very obliging and, due care being taken, the duodenum and its attached pancreas may be mobilised without any blood loss or damage to the organs. In those circumstances I deemed that safer than greatly mobilising the stomach, a more lengthy procedure necessitating the cutting of many of the stomach's blood vessels. Tthe two cut ends were thus brought together entirely without tension, but they had to be sutured together. I was unable to visualise the needle as it passed through the duodenum in the neighbourhood of the common bile duct. Puncturing that would cause leakage of bile into the peritoneal cavity.

His condition was so fragile that, if renal failure didn't carry him off, biliary peritonitis certainly would. A long time was taken over this stage, the needle inserted with utmost care, using touch to guide it away from the duct. To my amazement renal failure didn't supervene—nor biliary peritonitis!—and the hardy old boy was home within the week.

The personal cost, however, was high; the stress of operating upon so sick, elderly a man immense, added to the circumstances under which it had occurred. I was no longer a youngster and the life of constant stress now caught up.

Things weren't made better when I began to tear out my hair over

the episode with the woman whom, fore sake of argument we'll call
the matron: she had some other designation. Was she angry? Contrite,
perhaps, on behalf of those negligent nurses who almost caused a death?
Not on your life! In true bolshie style she effectively told me to shut up
or she'd sool the Health Minister—another red—on to me. I didn't have
any wish to end my career with a disciplinary black mark so—I shut up,
with a very nasty taste in my mouth.

When that incompetent idiot of a so-called surgeon returned, I
told him what had occurred, just exactly as it was and suggested he took
more extensive histories and make more thorough examinations in the
future. I endeavoured to make allowance for the fact that he was in a
new environment. Moreover, I didn't want to demoralise him and didn't
rant or rage for that reason, ending the session by assuring him that, if
ever he was in doubt, I would do my best to help. I most certainly didn't
allow him anywhere near Mr. Christensen again!

Would that it all ended there! Here was certainly a man who knew
not that he knew not. The extraordinary numbers of cases of severed
tendons at the wrist has already been mentioned. W, obviously with no
experience of the meticulous treatment that's so essential, began to poach
these cases. In itself that didn't bother me—my strongly held view is
that, whilst a patient might not be master of his soul and is certainly not
captain of his fate, he/she is most certainly master of his/her body. The
law-abiding patient's body is the entire property of that individual; all
decisions concerning it must finally be theirs. When discussing options
for treatment, I always said:

'It's your body: you decide.'

Everybody is entitled to all of the facts as currently known and
accepted, of course, so that their decision is as informed as
possible.

So it wasn't the poaching that angered me when I was told about it:

it was the fact that that idiot had no idea of what he was doing. This first came to my notice when the Head Wardsman phoned me:

'Can yer please come ter th' theatre? That silly bugger hasn't any idea as ter what he's doin.'

Yes, the Head Wardsman. I went and did my best to extricate him. After this I heard rumours of some of his other cock-ups.

Please understand my position; my reaction to that maltreatment. The idea is passé, but, without trying to sound priggish, I've always believed with a passion that a doctor's professional life is first and foremost the alleviation of human pain and suffering. That's inherent in the task and money and status should be entirely secondary. That's why I operated upon so many patients in Ipswich for nothing with no hope of furthering my career thereby, before I became a salaried consultant. The reason is the example of my father, as I've previously mentioned.

To resume: I was greatly distressed by what I was hearing of W's mistakes when a patient presented upon whom he'd operated for severed tendons at the wrist. He'd done precisely the opposite of what he should have done: excised the deep tendons and sutured the superficial ones. This greatly interfered with the patient's grip as there was now nothing to bend the finger tips forward: they bent backwards when a grip was attempted. All one could do without the deep tendons was stiffen the end joint of each finger, setting each finger-tip in a slightly flexed position. Another, identical patient presented after, thank God, W had gone.

Even the manner of his going was distressful. Iain, then Medical Superintendent, had for some time been suggesting to him that he seek fresh woods and pastures new. At first he failed to see the point, but, as Iain became more insistent, he received the message. Incredibly obtuse, he felt badly done by and, when I was called to an emergency, he'd accompany me in the lift, into the changing room, complaining bitterly and seeking my assistance in staving off the gross wrong being perpetrated upon him.

It had all proved too much. The work had been incessant, day and night and I knew that if I continued there I'd soon be handing in my dinner pail. I resigned. The local doctors, most kindly, expressed concern and all signed a letter asking me to reconsider, promising that they'd make my load easier. When I expressed polite scepticism, they suggested I retire to Adelaide and visit, say, three days a week. I was most gratified, of course, but knew that things would gradually creep back to the old situation. With great regret I said farewell to Port Augusta—as a surgeon.

I've returned as a visitor many times.

THE DYING FIRE

I hadn't given up completely. There was still a little life in the old dog, so we returned to England, buying a house in Kempston, a village on the outskirts of Bedford. I looked forward to doing locums for the Orthopods there whenever they went on leave.

A small development was being constructed up a slight rise to the rear of our house and every evening a little, crooked old man would issue from his house across the way, burdensomely making his way up the hill to inspect the day's progress. I diagnosed scoliosis of the spine at that distance but couldn't make out why he walked in the way he did. Perhaps a couple of weeks later he failed to appear, so Eileen suggested I knock on his door to make sure that he wasn't in any trouble.

'The door's open.' He called.

Jim Rust, for that was his name, lay on his bed, resting he said because he was in pain in his stomach region. Fearing that he might have an abdominal emergency, the more I questioned him the less sense it made. Eventually he agreed quite readily to an examination. I wasn't in any way prepared for what I saw. Undoing his pants and lifting his shirt he undid a homemade contrivance holding a diaper in place. I was confronted by a large, red raw patch on his lower abdomen which oozed urine. He had exstrophy of the bladder, described earlier. Exquisitely tender, for his entire life, he must have endured continuous pain. With his permission, I rigged up a padded plastic dome which protected the bladder from the constant rubbing which occurred every time he moved. Eileen gave him lunch for a few days until he settled down and then I learnt his history of bravery and determination.

His father, a drunkard, kicked his wife hard in the tummy when pregnant with Jim. Rightly or wrongly he blamed this on his misfortune. Not long afterwards, with Jim still *in utero*, the reprobate died of the influenza which raged worldwide after the Great War, leaving the mother to try to support a large young family by taking in washing.

It wasn't practicable for Jim to go to school: he was more or less written off to spend his life vegetating at home. He had other ideas. He helped his mother as much as he could until adolescence when, one day, a friend asked if he'd like a doubler on his motorbike. Being on an errand to a place some miles north of Kempston, he thought the outing would do Jim good. The place in question was a canvas fabricating factory where heavy goods such as marquees were made. Jim took one look:

'Any chance of a job?'

He worked there for more than twenty years, no doubt in agony each time he lifted the heavy canvas fabric. Soon on familiar terms with his boss, he was trusted in many ways in his absence, more or less deputising there. One day a customer paid a substantial bill. Jim accepted the money and gave a receipt. On his return the boss castigated him for taking the money. Jim gathered up his things.

'If that's the way you feel then, goodbye.'

'You'll be back.'

'No I won't'

And he wasn't, soon at an even more strenuous job in a leather factory where he worked until well over retirement age. During that time, his hand catching in some machinery, he was hospitalised, spending some time postoperatively in a rehabilitation centre. All very well, excepting that he became an object of curiosity, doctors and nurses goggling at his deformity. A sensitive man, for that reason when I detected an early cancer developing there, he flatly refused to go anywhere near the hospital.

I tried to do something, so applied 5 fluarouracil ointment daily. It's quite good used locally for removing small squamous celled skin cancers. Used intravenously I dislike it as a shotgun anticancer treatment, highly toxic, which certainly hastened my dear daughter's departure. It made no difference to Jim's problem, so I made use of the sensitivity cancer cells have to heat, applying heat every night.

It was always a pleasure to have anything to do with this charming man.

'Allo, guvnor!'

When I put my nose through the door and he'd usually insist I share a whiskey mac with him. One evening, his radio was playing.

'Nice piece of music' I said patronisingly.

'Oh, yes. That's Tchaikowsky's Third Symphony.'

He'd not only worked but also cultivated his mind.

I feel badly at this point: the growth progressively shrank, but I'd arranged to go to Australia. I got his brother in, instructing him repeatedly upon the treatment—but he didn't do it. By the time I'd returned the lesion had grown again.

Whilst I was away Eileen kept an eye on him and one day, bringing him lunch she found him collapsed at his doorway. He'd been bleeding from the cancer so much that he needed a transfusion. This bucked him up but, not so long afterward he needed another and the hospital instructed domiciliary nurses to attend him. The government, rightly, supplied him with dressings.

Jim showed me the letter of approval: it said that he had but six months to live and this certainly preyed on his mind. I checked him. He had no evident metastases, so I tried to reassure him. Next, he suddenly became excessively drowsy. The nurses were giving him pills. I checked: they were haloperidol, a major tranquilliser, in high dosage which incurs a significant mortality rate. Jim was obviously slipping. Eileen insisted that he only pretend to take the tablets—the nurses stood over him whilst he took them—and spit them out when they'd gone. Finally, those nurses suggested he be admitted to a hospice:

'If you don't like it you can always go home.'

We pleaded with him, but he agreed with that suggestion. We visited him that night. He didn't recognise us. He was on a machine delivering doses of morphine so high that he was deeply unconscious. Of course he only lasted a couple of days; dying six months almost to the day since he'd received his death sentence. It was irksome to see those nurses laughing and joking as they cleaned up the house of that wonderfully brave man.

Why his crooked back and strange walk? He indeed had scoliosis. His pelvic bones hadn't joined, causing an instability which affected his gait.

Jim was an outstanding hero and it was a privilege to have known him.

I'd been accustomed to a long, uninterruptedly pleasant stint at Bedford Hospital whilst one or the other of the old boys went on leave and retired and before a new one actually took up his post. A very different new boy was appointed who demonstrated an unusual degree of unpleasant arrogance. On the day he took some leave I must say that I was flabbergasted, then shocked.

He'd just operated upon a patient with anterior compartment syndrome: most commonly after injury, a haemorrhage occurs into the muscles of the front of the lower leg. Pressure increases until the blood flow, especially to the muscles and nerves, is jeopardised. The same kind of thing can occur in other places as well and from time to time I've had to treat cases in which the whole leg had been affected in a football injury, colloquially known as corking.

The condition can be very serious; very occasionally fatal from kidney failure due to an accumulation of muscle breakdown products. Other outcomes can be loss of muscle function and/or nerve palsies. It's perhaps commonest in the lower leg because of the inelastic fascia enclosing the muscles, nerves, arteries and so forth. Excessive exertion and some fractures of the Tibia are also causes; there are others. Injury is the commonest. The treatment's simple enough: merely cut the constricting fascia, but for there not to be serious sequelae this must be done in time, six hours is the maximum time after injury.

This surgeon was going on as though the operation was a very big deal. It's not. It's simplicity itself and the only requirements are ensuring that the pressure has been completely eliminated and that the operation is performed within the time limit.

One of the last cases I'd dealt with before leaving Port Augusta had been a boy who, when riding his bike in the town of Woomera had been knocked to the ground by a car. A doctor who'd been called phoned me. Most anxious that be brought in before that deadline had arrived because of the distance one was relieved when the efficient flying ambulance brought him in before, but not long before it had expired.

Postoperative treatment in the absence of the rare kidney complications is simplicity itself, yet this man—who'd obviously only dealt with one such case, questioned my ability to look after this man who presented no other problems. In short, we got off on the wrong foot.

Matters worsened. To avoid unused time in the operating theatre, when one consultant leaves he arranges the operating list for the next day. It's good practice to visit the patients concerned and examine them before they come to theatre. On this occasion I could barely believe it. There were three patients listed and I totally disagreed with the suggested procedure in every one. One had a scintilla of merit, so I shan't trouble you with it. The others!!...

The first was listed for total hip replacement. When I looked at the X Rays, It was immediately obvious that the man had sustained a pathological fracture of the neck of his Right femur the result of extensive infiltration of the bone by secondary cancer. His pelvis was heavily involved: softened and if I'd replaced his hip the entire joint would soon have collapsed into the pelvic cavity, causing extreme agony and shortening still further an already limited life. Hip replacement, too, in a terminally ill patient is too big an operation.

Using the image intensifier to visualise the operation in real time, I reduced the fracture and inserted several special screws across the fracture, thus holding it together, a much milder, shorter procedure. The man was up and out of bed, walking on crutches next day, virtually pain free.

The next case was even worse and made one wonder just what went on in that surgeon's brain. It was Elaine, a young child of three who, three weeks previously had suffered a supracondylar fracture of the elbow. (This injury occasionally also causes compartment syndrome). The growing point of the Humerus just above the elbow had been disrupted and displaced more or less backward. It's as simple as ABC to reduce if one knows what one's doing: one rotates the arm of the anaesthetised patient so that the forearm dangles downward, pulls gently until the muscle tone is overcome, pulls a little more and then, whilst an assistant holds the upper arm, pushes the fragment firmly into place. Many doctors have great trouble reducing these fractures properly because they can't interpret the X rays. The carrying angle of the elbow causes the appearance in the X ray film of the fracture to be odd; the lower fragment strangely displaced when in fact it isn't. This aspect of the pictures must be ignored. One must rely upon a knowledge of this pitfall as well as clinical findings: by a careful, continuing examination—and assessment of the elbow itself as the reduction proceeds.

This man had had no success at all and stupidly held his mess in place with wires inserted through the fracture and the bones on either side, bringing the poor child back, three weeks later, for 're-manipulation'.

In a child of three, the fracture would inevitably heal solidly by that time in a horrible position to boot. I did nothing. Later in life she'd probably need corrective surgery. Good grief!! A consultant? Words fail me!

Operating session concluded, I hurtled around to the office:

'Don't ask me to do any more locums for Mr. X. I'll work for the other two; never again for him.'

That more or less put paid to my surgical career. It had still been a pleasure, more muted, one must admit, than in the good old days. The problem was that, in doing my rounds I'd encounter this incompetent and, quite frankly, found it distressing. After two more locums I told them that I wouldn't do any more.

Swan song

It was my last day, conducting an outpatient session. Little Joyce with a mallet fourth finger of her Right hand arrived with an anxious mother, It had been treated in the usual, sloppy manner—by horrid X though it was now the general custom there for mallet fingers to be treated unacceptably. A collodion splint had been applied to the affected finger, bent at the middle joint with the finger-tip hyperextended.

A mallet finger occurs when, hand extended, the tip of the finger's hit with some force. This causes an avulsion of the extensor tendon at its insertion into the terminal phalanx, with or without a portion of bone. The characteristic appearance: finger-tip bent permanently forward, occurs because the flexor tendon's pull hasn't been countered by the avulsed extensor.

At that hospital, at least at that time, the splint was kept on for some weeks—up to six. When removed, all usually appears to be well, but, almost always, the improvement is temporary and the mallet finger deformity recurs: totally unacceptable.

So it was with Joyce. I looked at her bent finger and wryly said to her mother:

'I'm sorry about that. The deformity's permanent I'm afraid, but it won't really interfere with her activities significantly—unless she's a violinist.'

'But that's just what she is!' exclaimed her mother, 'Her teacher says that she's extraordinarily talented!'

She was my last patient and it was lunchtime. I phoned the theatre frantically and they came up trumps, finding an afternoon slot,

I drilled two tiny holes in the terminal phalanx and attached the tendon with its minute fragment of bone to the terminal phalanx, using steel wire, bringing it out through the skin on the back of the finger, knotting it firmly over a button padded to avoid necrosis of the skin from pressure. When the tissues healed, the wire could easily be pulled free. Bidding farewell to the hospital, one thought little more about it until some time later.

Eileen had previously owned an art gallery in Australia, so it seemed a good idea to set one up in Kempston, an occasion duly recorded, with our photographs, in the local paper. One afternoon a couple came into the gallery:

'Is Mr. Gibbs in? Yes? Do you think he'd mind if we spoke to him?'

'Of course not.'

When I appeared, I immediately said:

'Wiggle your fingers, Joyce! Now bend and straighten the injured one!'

I'd recognised Joyce and her mother, who told me that they hadn't had the opportunity of thanking me before I'd left the hospital as I'd left for the last time immediately after her op. Noticing my picture in the paper, they'd taken the trouble now to do so.

All was well and she was still making good progress with her violin.

Though my last case, was a relatively simple one, it was very moving to have these people go out of their way to show their gratitude: a happy ending indeed.

But I still do pull a few legs; literally!

That is now only occasionally: completely aghast at the relentless exploitation of ordinary people by big business and the blatant criminality of banks and other financial institutions, unpunished by their political puppets, like *Candide*, I've retired to cultivate my garden.